MUMPRENEUR

ANNABEL KARMEL
MUMPRENEUR

THE COMPLETE GUIDE TO STARTING
AND RUNNING A SUCCESSFUL BUSINESS

Vermilion
LONDON

1 3 5 7 9 10 8 6 4 2

Vermilion, an imprint of Ebury Publishing,
20 Vauxhall Bridge Road,
London SW1V 2SA

Vermilion is part of the Penguin Random House group of
companies whose addresses can be found at
global.penguinrandomhouse.com

 Penguin
Random House
UK

First published by Vermilion in 2015

www.eburypublishing.co.uk

A CIP catalogue record for this book is available
from the British Library

Hardback ISBN 9780091954789
Trade paperback ISBN 9781785040221

Printed and bound in Great Britain by Clays Ltd, St Ives PLC

Penguin Random House is committed to a sustainable future for
our business, our readers and our planet. This book is made from
Forest Stewardship Council® certified paper.

For my children Nicholas, Lara and Scarlett,
who have inspired and supported me
in reaching for the stars

CONTENTS

INTROD

A RECIPE FOR SUCCESS

❝❞

**YOU'VE GOT TO FOLLOW
YOUR PASSION. YOU'VE
GOT TO FIGURE OUT
WHAT YOU LOVE, WHO
YOU REALLY ARE. AND
HAVE THE COURAGE
TO DO THAT. I BELIEVE
THE ONLY COURAGE
ANYBODY EVER NEEDS
IS THE COURAGE TO
FOLLOW YOUR DREAMS.**

Oprah Winfrey

UCTION

When you have a child, your life changes beyond recognition. Before children you may well have carved out a successful career. You may hear mums on the school run sharing stories of what they 'used to be' before they started a family. Many mums leave those successful careers behind to have children and then struggle to return to the workplace – due to high childcare costs and the incompatibility between their new life as a mum and the inflexible long hours often expected as an employee.

Some mums choose to stay at home and be full-time mums; others, like me, know that they wouldn't be as good a mother as they'd want to be without an independent life outside of the children. It's a personal choice; there is no right or wrong. But this I know for sure: an increasing wave of mums are desperately seeking alternatives to provide them with an income that they can fit flexibly around their family commitments.

If you are someone who wants to maintain some independence and keep active while still being a good mother, the chances are you are unlikely to want to return to a job with long hours and that barely covers your childcare costs. Subsequently, many women turn to the part-time job market, yet are left frustrated by the poor pay and lack of opportunities to use their frankly impressive set of skills. The result is an army of highly talented, intelligent women who have had their confidence knocked by the lack of options that maximise their true talents.

Starting your own business gives you a way forward which embraces your need for independence and to contribute to the family finances. It makes good use of your hard-earned skillset and means you can still be a 'mum' without incurring astronomical childcare costs. Indeed, the more mums I've spoken to, the more I've realised how attractive an alternative self-employment is to being employed. A reported 74 per cent of women starting their own businesses do so when their child is under two years old (according to Empoweringmums.co.uk).

I have written this practical book to help those mums who are considering starting or who have recently started their own business. It provides a blend of inspiration and information to equip and empower mums to start their own enterprises with confidence. I aim to help mums become 'more than mummy' as they realise (through the advice, anecdotes and tools provided) that anyone can do it, including them.

NOBODY CAN GO BACK AND START A NEW BEGINNING, BUT ANYONE CAN START TODAY AND MAKE A NEW ENDING.

Maria Robinson

A REWARDING ROLE

More women than ever before are, like you, reaching for their dream careers. This is hardly surprising, there are plenty of wonderful reasons why starting your own business is an appealing and exciting choice for mums.

When you run your own business, you are the mistress of your future. You are in control of pursuing your own dreams rather than financing someone else's; you are creating something for yourself. Working from home, you regain control and the freedom to be yourself and make things happen on your own terms. You can make decisions that suit you, work at your own pace, wave goodbye to the earnings glass ceiling and say so long to the office politics, the unsociable inflexible hours and the lengthy commute.

Being your own boss gives you an amazing opportunity to define your destiny, to define your purpose in life. And you get to enjoy a flexible lifestyle, which enables you to do the school run and partake in your children's plays and sports days.

There is a whole other life out there of mums who get the best of both worlds – dropping their kids off at school then devoting their days to working on their business. They can be 100 per cent mum between school- and bedtime, and then return to work on their business once the kids are safely snuggled up in bed. Or, for those with younger ones, work while they are sleeping and enjoy their children's every move in between.

The possibilities for what you can achieve are endless too. You could end up winning the buy-in of some of the UK's biggest and most powerful retailers, expanding overseas and franchising your brand across the nation. And there are lots of other rewards: networking and getting to meet interesting like-minded people, entering for top industry awards and being able to engage with your growing customer base. It's a rewarding role, being an entrepreneur.

Starting your own business gives you the chance to be creative outside of making salt-dough models or robots out of toilet rolls. It gives you the chance to tap into your own talents and play to your own strengths so that you can provide an amazing product or service which you know is better than what's already out there. What's more, you'll notice a renewed ability to command respect when you tell others what you do for a living. Nurturing an entrepreneurial streak while simultaneously juggling home and family life is invigorating. What's more, it could change the way your family functions for the better.

❝❞

SHATTERING THE GLASS CEILING WITH A CHANGING BAG OVER YOUR SHOULDER IS NO LONGER LIMITED TO THE REALMS OF FANTASY.

Annabel Karmel

And you need not be an entrepreneurial whizz with business studies qualifications. The inspirational leading ladies I've interviewed for this book did not have any formal business training whatsoever. All they had was a dream, a vision and an idea which stemmed from a gap they spotted in the marketplace. They harnessed their raw passion and existing talents to bring those dreams to fruition. Take Liz Earle, for instance. She turned her lifelong passion for plants and the natural world into one of the biggest and most successful independent beauty brands, selling unique products using botanical extracts. Liz grew her business from humble beginnings as a small mail-order company into a multi-million-pound global brand. She and her business partners sold the Liz Earle Beauty Co. to Avon in 2010, although she remained a consultant to the brand she helped to build. Like so many other mums across the country, she and her co-founder Kim Buckland started with nothing but an idea and a strong belief that their idea could work, so they made it happen. And so can you.

As a musician, I had never considered starting my own business. My own journey as a business owner was driven by the pain of a very personal tragedy – the death of my first daughter, Natasha – as I wanted to create a legacy in her memory. That, and my determination to give my second-born 'fussy-eater', Nicholas, the best start in life, led me to develop recipes for tasty, healthy meals that my son wouldn't be able to resist. Those recipes, which were completely different to any baby or toddler food available at the time, formed the basis for my bestselling book *The Complete Baby and Toddler Meal Planner*, which regularly remains, after more than 24 years, in the top five in the bestselling cookery book charts. It has been translated into 25 different languages and has even become the second bestselling non-fiction hardback of all time in the UK since records began. It brings me great joy and pride to know that millions of mums all over the world are cooking my recipes to give their growing families the very best start in life.

Since then I've also turned the recipes from my books into successful supermarket food ranges and have developed menus for some of the world's biggest hotels, leisure resorts, retailers and nurseries. Like the entrepreneurial mums interviewed for this book, I did not have a traditional business background but learnt along the way, by doing, asking, listening and applying a blend of common sense, instinct and intuition.

WARNING: NO CHANCE TO PUT YOUR FEET UP

While commuting to the kitchen table is preferable to commuting to the city via a crack-of-dawn train journey, there are important considerations to bear in mind before taking the plunge to start up in business. You really must be made aware that the romantic notion of kitchen-table start-ups where traffic-jam-sitting is replaced with home-made-jam-making and trundling off to the beach to work on your laptop at every occasion is not a realistic one. The reality is a lot, LOT harder, but can be much more rewarding (and both the jam-making and beach-frequenting are way more achievable than when you are working for someone else).

So here's the truth. You may have thought multi-tasking with three children demanding your undivided attention was difficult, but running your own business throws another (rather large) ball into the air to juggle. You will probably end up working longer hours than you would have done as a full-time employee. You may miss the buzz of catching up round the office water cooler or photocopier. You may have to play off more time with the kids during the school holidays with extra work in the evenings while they sleep to stay on top of your growing enterprise. Yes, there is a chance you may forget to eat lunch until 3pm, or dash out to do the school run clutching a piece of cold toast, and you may have less quality time with your partner.

Many of the women interviewed in this book have confessed that the lack of sleep they had while their children were tiny prepared them for the late nights and early starts that they've needed to put in to cope with the workload. 'I work very late,' confessed uber-hard-working Myleene Klass, who runs multiple businesses across a multitude of time zones and replies to emails from her bed. 'I don't think anything of going to bed at 2 or 3am and then getting up again and doing the school run, trying to grab a nap in the day, sleeping in cars.'

Setting up your own business is never going to be a walk in the park. You are in the driving seat but, in order to gain all these worthwhile benefits, there are sacrifices:

- There is no sick pay or holiday pay. If you're ill or you go away, unless you have a team to take up the slack or have established some passive automated revenue streams, you won't get paid.

- The buck stops entirely with you so you'll feel the brunt of your own mistakes (but those mistakes are fantastic learning tools so will come in handy anyway).

- There is no such thing as easy money from the outset. You'll work harder than ever before – every hour possible around the kids (but you will be able to be there for them).

- You'll no longer have the safety net that a regular salary provides and you'll probably earn less income initially as you build your business (although there is no limitation to your earning potential and no glass ceiling).

- You won't be 100 per cent in control as you will occasionally be at the mercy of other people, such as suppliers, manufacturers, distributors and partners.

- It can get lonely as a sole trader working from home (although social media and online networks for women in business, such as WiBBLE.us, Mumsclub.co.uk and Everywoman.com, can provide you with a forum for conversation and support).

- If something can go wrong it generally does, so be prepared to go round brick walls.

If you're still with me and aren't jogging back to the security of a desk job, being your own boss can be incredibly rewarding and completely worth all of these sacrifices and more.

The best (and only) way to sustain yourself over all the obstacles is to feel passionate and fanatical about what you are doing. Passion sustains you during tough times, and we'll explore the need for that vital passion and purpose in Chapter 1. So please don't launch your own business purely for the money and earning potential; rather, do it for the passion, fulfilment and flexibility.

Sometimes it feels like leaping out of a plane minus the parachute but, if you follow my recipe for success and have the right ingredients to start with, you'll be able to land safely and be energised to take on each challenge and celebrate each victory, just like you already do as a mum.

**ENTREPRENEURSHIP IS NOT
A PART-TIME JOB, AND IT'S
NOT EVEN A FULL-TIME JOB.
IT'S A LIFESTYLE.**

Carrie Layne, founder of BestBuzz

Building a business and a brand is a journey. Your business and action plan will be your routemap, and this book will help you to take the right steps at the right time in the right direction, and prepare you for obstacles en route. This is your toolkit to help you on your personal journey, so that you can take your light-bulb moment and/or hard-earned skillset and make your business happen.

This book will help you to get on track and stay on track by addressing your worries, concerns and questions with practical guidance, tools, advice, examples and inspiration. From your initial idea and research phase to raising finance, hiring talent, collaborating with others and building a brand which attracts and retains a tribe of loyal customers – I'm here with my trusty female entrepreneurs to help.

I absolutely love running my own business. So much so that whenever I go away I miss my work, and in order for me to relax my iPhone has to be forcibly removed and locked in the safe. I love the fact that through my books and food products I am there at every stage of a child's life, helping to look after them and mummy too – from eating while pregnant to feeding babies, toddlers and, most recently, families as well. I wanted to be somebody who held a mum's hand through the difficult time of feeding her child, and I think I've achieved that. Now I'm equally thrilled to be in a position to do the same to help mums through the journey of starting a business.

WHAT YOU'LL LEARN

In this book, I'll reveal all that I've learnt over the past two decades. From chilled-aisle challenges to persisting despite publishing setbacks (my first book was rejected 15 times by publishers before going on to become a global bestseller); from transferring my invaluable pitching skills gained as a jobbing harpist to pitching successfully to supermarkets; from testing recipes on the playgroup I started striking deals with Disney to create a range of award-winning snacks.

Ultimately, this guide brings together all of my 25-plus years of business experience, with a blend of practical lessons hard learnt through both success and failure. The advice within it reflects my own journey.

I have grown my business and Annabel Karmel brand organically and completely on my own terms. Over more than two decades I have learnt the recipe for success in business – precisely which ingredients should be added to the mix to confidently create a thriving enterprise while still being a good mum. And now I want to share that with you.

Each chapter is based around one of my ingredients for success in juggling business with motherhood. From the importance of passionate belief and making the most of connections to embracing failure, building a valuable brand and persisting during challenging times.

Throughout the pages of this book, you'll learn how to:

- Test the viability of your idea in the marketplace, gather feedback and build your tribe.

- Harness your frontline experience and transfer your invaluable skills (from your previous jobs and from motherhood) to push forward and stand out from the crowd.

- Build a strong and valuable come-to brand with loyal customers.

- Harness the power of existing networks and relationships to gain custom and develop collaborative strategic alliances to fast-track success.

- Know when to diversify, innovate and scale up, and when to hire talent, delegate and move out of the home office.

- Create the right environment in which to flourish (as a businesswoman and mum) and juggle the demands of both roles.

- Persist against all odds and learn from mistakes.

- Use your passion and belief as the fuel to drive the business forward.

- Achieve goals and focus during your toddler's nap time or your child's school/sleep time.

- Build a business and be a great mum without the guilt.

- Take on talented staff and investment without diluting your brand values.

- Choose the business model and revenue streams best suited to the idea.

- Gain clarity around your marketing messages and have confidence in your sales pitches.

- Engage with all stakeholders, from customers and partners to investors and your own family.

- Plan and delegate effectively, manage the business and grow in the right direction.

Within these pages, I also share the insight and stories of some of the UK's most successful business-owning mums. From Thea Green, the founder of Nails Inc., to Jacqueline Gold, CEO of Ann Summers, among many others, these mums form my 'Kitchen Cabinet' – a resourceful and truly inspirational team brimming with fresh ideas, vital lessons and practical advice. They reveal the secrets of their success, the mistakes they've made and what they'd do differently with the benefit of hindsight.

Their combined wisdom and incredible stories are peppered throughout these pages, and you'll find a few key feature pieces about these women in each chapter to illustrate my ingredients in the recipe for success.

The Kitchen Cabinet has come together to help and inspire you to pursue *your* dreams in whatever venture you are embarking on – whatever your age, whatever your level of ambition; whether you want to create a lifestyle business from home or an entire empire with an ambitious exit strategy. Because anyone can do this.

This book provides a fusion of stories, experience, tips and tools, revealing all the ingredients for you to run a successful business while keeping everyone happy at home too. It crucially shows you how to honour both parts of your life – mum and business owner – without cheating either and without feeling guilty.

After all, running your very own business sets a great example for your children: bringing in income by being your own boss while still being flexible enough to be there for them. And that's what really counts more than cash flow or profit margins: your children's happiness and future. So are you ready to carve out that new and rewarding life as a mum in business? Let's begin.

THE SECRET OF GETTING AHEAD IS GETTING STARTED.

Mark Twain

01

BELIEV
YOUR I

GET PASSIONATE
AND PURPOSEFUL

E IN

DEA

WHAT'S YOUR WHY? DEFINE YOUR STORY

Smart businesses have a compelling story behind them.

When you start a business of any kind, your main objective is to move people (prospective customers, investors or partners) to take action (invest in your business, buy your product, sign up to your service, return to your store, sign up to your newsletter or spread the word about you). PowerPoint slides, spreadsheets, website copy, products, prototypes and all the persuasive tools at your disposal simply won't move people enough to take action unless there is an emotive reason to do so, something that connects with them. The best way to connect to people is to tell a story – your story, your product and business idea's story, your 'why this business/product/service exists' story.

'People are moved by emotion,' says Peter Guber in his book *Tell To Win*. 'The best way to emotionally connect other people to our agenda begins with "Once upon a time …"' Science backs up the notion that storytelling is the most powerful means of communicating a message. More powerful than dry factual arguments, stories are relatable and engaging; they enable people to identify with you and your product or service. Stories stick in the mind far better than bullet points or clever arguments. In fact some scientific estimations suggest that stories are 22 times more memorable than facts alone.

However, there's no point crafting a story simply to lure people in. Your story needs to be genuine and real. There are two reasons for this. First, today's savvy consumers will see through anything that isn't sincere. Second, you can only be truly passionate about your story if it evokes a fire in your belly and means something to you. It is that passion which will see you through the tough times, of which there will be many, and it is the story behind that passion that will enable you to connect with all stakeholders: your customers, investors, staff, suppliers and partners.

Stories are the precursor for everything else. They inspire action, they share values, they connect people to you and your brand and they reveal the 'why'. The place you get your hair done, the shop you love to buy your children's clothes from – there's a story behind each and every one of those businesses.

The good news is, if you're already thinking about starting a business, you'll already have thought about what drives you, and this is the story behind your enterprise. So what is your 'once upon a time'? Perhaps you are passionate about fitness, and understand how hard it is for new mums to get their confidence and figure back, so you're setting up exercise classes for mums with a crèche? Or maybe you enjoy sewing and are keen to give something back to a charity that has helped you, so you've decided to set up a boutique toy-making business with a percentage of profits going to that charity?

Or perhaps you've noticed that there are limited options for busy women wishing to pamper themselves? That's what Thea Green, ex-fashion editor of *Tatler* magazine, did when she spotted a gap in the UK market for a professional yet quick manicure service, and decided to bring the US nail bar concept to the UK. We'll hear more about Thea's story and about finding a niche or gap in the market in chapters 3 and 5.

MY WHY: THE ANNABEL KARMEL STORY

My entire business grew out of one event that was so personal and painful that the only way I could come to terms with it was to put all my energy into helping my children, and others, enjoy healthy, tasty diets – something that grew into my ultimate passion.

It had taken me almost two years before I became pregnant, and when our daughter Natasha was born I was overjoyed. She was everything I had dreamt of. However, one early evening, three months later, some sixth sense told me there was something wrong with her. I called the doctor, who agreed to see her, but after the initial examination they explained how all first-time mothers can panic and worry unnecessarily. But the following morning things had got worse and I knew then something was terribly wrong: Natasha's eyes were rolling back in her head and her little hands were twitching.

I went to another doctor and was standing on his doorstep at 9am that morning. After examining her he rushed me straight to St Mary's in Paddington – he believed Natasha was very ill indeed. They ran a number of tests and towards the end of the day did a CAT scan of her brain. That evening the consultant put the scans up on a screen and told my husband and I that our daughter had suffered encephalitis inflammation of the brain caused by a viral infection, and that her brain was very seriously damaged. He said she might die and that, should she survive, she would never be normal again.

I felt numb. It was as if this was happening to somebody else. We went to Great Ormond Street Hospital and I stayed with Natasha for five days and five nights. One afternoon we were given a stark choice and had to make the decision to turn off her ventilator. I held Natasha for several hours until the moment she took her final breath and died in my arms. She looked so perfect, as though she was sleeping. I was heartbroken.

I was almost suicidal when I lost her. I'd wake up in the morning and think it was a nightmare and then realise it was real. I didn't know what to do with myself except cry. All I could think about was that I wanted to have another child. From that lowest of low points, I set my mind to rebuilding my life. I took a fertility drug and fell pregnant within three months.

My second child, Nicholas, was born only a year later in rather dramatic circumstances, delivered by my husband on the staircase after I was assured on the phone that I was only in the early stages of labour. And Nicholas was determined to continue making an impact. As soon as I started weaning him he was very fussy with his food, and just wasn't eating. The baby foods I was buying seemed bland and tasteless; he just spat them out.

When Nicholas was about nine months, we went on holiday to the south of France. While out there, we visited a doctor as Nicholas had been ill. I told the doctor that my child refused to eat and he shared a range of recipes using foods like aubergine, basil, quince and all kinds of weird and wonderful ingredients. All the recipes in the books I'd seen for children were really bland and uninspiring and yet, just across the Channel, babies were being exposed to all kinds of tasty foods.

And there it was: my first light-bulb moment. Maybe, by using tasty combinations of interesting ingredients I could get my child to eat – and enjoy – food. I had long had a passion for cooking and so I started experimenting with a vast array of different ingredients – fruits, vegetables, herbs, spices and meat, turning them into delicious purees. Soon Nicholas was eating my home-made food. It was a revelation!

I had been feeling lonely as I didn't know many mothers who had babies the same age as Nicholas, so I decided to start a playgroup in St John's Wood with a few friends of mine. I found a hall and set up the playgroup, which we called Babes In The Wood. On the first day 80 mums turned up, and it soon became 100 mums coming each week with their babies and toddlers. Much to my surprise I found that most of them also had children who were fussy eaters, so I handed out the recipes I had made for Nicholas. Each week the mums would tell me how much their children loved them and would ask for more. After a while, they encouraged me to write a book of recipes. At first I thought they were crazy, but soon I realised that writing a book to a) help babies and toddlers have a healthy diet and b) give mums the confidence to use fresh food and a variety of ingredients would be a wonderful tribute to Natasha – a legacy to make something of her life, so that she still lived on and was able to help other children.

Writing a recipe book was my second light-bulb moment. I didn't care whether it made money or not, I just thought, 'I am going to write this book with all my favourite tried-and-tested recipes.' I was going to put my heart and soul into it. And so I did.

It took two years to research and write the book. I tested all the recipes on lots of babies and toddlers from the playgroup and soon discovered that, despite the long-held belief that babies only liked bland food, it was the tasty recipes they preferred. I introduced new combinations: avocado with banana, goujons of fish coated with crushed Rice Krispies and Parmesan, and chicken and apple balls. I went up and down the country interviewing experts on child nutrition, and worked with Professor Margaret Lawson at Great Ormond Street Hospital and the Institute of Child Health so that the advice in my book was based on scientific fact and research. I had my third child, Lara, in the meantime (another child to test my food on), but it was worth all the hard work – working late so I could be with my children during the day, scheduling calls and frantically writing emails around dinner and bath time.

I dedicated that first book to Natasha. I found it hard to come to terms with her death and yet the thought that I would never have written the book if I had not had Natasha gave her life some meaning.

My story has been about taking something unbelievably tragic and turning it into something positive that helps others. The best decision in my life was writing that first book. It was groundbreaking – changing the way thousands of parents fed their babies. I didn't realise what I was doing at the time, I just knew that I absolutely must do it. It was that deep-seated passion coupled with my circumstances that fuelled my desire to write. Doing so provided me with a way to create the right working life for me.

You don't have to go through adversity or face hardship to find your passion, but it helps if you can find something you love and mix that with a purposeful desire to provide a solution to a certain set of people. All of that is what creates your story and will propel you forward, especially when times get tough.

USE YOUR PASSION TO DRIVE YOUR BUSINESS FORWARD

Whatever background you come from, however little money you start off with, there is no getting away from the value of talent, hard work and vision. If you have passion for something and plenty of entrepreneurial spirit, you can do it. To paraphrase Napoleon Hill: What woman can conceive and believe, she can achieve.

You need to believe in your business idea. You need to have genuine passion for it. Don't pluck an idea off the shelf because you think it could make money, otherwise you will fall at the first hurdle. Ultimately, if you don't believe in it, how can you expect anyone else to?

Passion is what drives you in your journey towards your business and life goals.

Here's why having the courage of your convictions is a primary ingredient for success in business.

- **Passion and belief are persuasive and infectious.** Passion bolsters belief in your business and it makes you authentic. In being passionate about your business idea you will persuade others to believe in it too. Says Liz Earle, 'You'll need to convince plenty of other people, be it customers, suppliers or stakeholders, as to why your product is unique and something they should believe in, and that's so much easier to do if you are genuinely passionate about it yourself.'

- **Passion and belief give you energy to overcome obstacles.** It's far easier to ride the roller coaster of business ownership if you love what you do. Optimism and resilience are great partners. One fuels the other. Passion for what I am doing has definitely helped me to leap over obstacles in my path.

🙶🙷
WITHOUT PASSION YOU DON'T HAVE ENERGY, WITHOUT ENERGY, YOU HAVE NOTHING.
Donald Trump

ANNABEL'S KITCHEN CABINET

PERSUASIVE PASSION: JACQUELINE GOLD

Sheer passion for your ideas and belief in your vision can get you far. It's what helped Ann Summers CEO Jacqueline Gold persuade a risk-averse all-male board to take a punt on her pioneering party-plan idea. Up until then the two Ann Summers shops and mail-order catalogues were aimed at male customers.

After attending a Tupperware party in south London, she'd discovered that the women would like to buy sexy underwear and spice up their sex lives but wanted to do so on their own terms without having to go into a sex shop to buy them. And so Jacqueline came up with the idea of holding Ann Summers parties, where women could preview the products from their own living rooms.

'When I started out 33 years ago, attitudes to business were completely different. Back then it really was a man's world, and going to the board with an innovative idea was a challenge,' says Jacqueline. However, she knew she was on to something and wasn't about to let any obstacles stand in her way. 'I felt very passionate about my idea, and when one board member stood up and told me, "Well, this isn't going to work because women aren't even interested in sex," it was very difficult to keep tight-lipped when all I was thinking was, "Well, that says more about your sex life than anything else!"'

'They weren't keen at first because this was for women rather than for men, but what persuaded them to go with my idea in the end was just being very passionate,' says Jacqueline proudly. 'They agreed to invest £40,000, which wasn't enough money but it was enough to prove that I knew what I was doing and that it was a good idea after all.' The party plan part of the business then went on to make a profit and turned over £83,000 in the first year. 'We grew to 500 sales organisers in the first year and then for quite some time after we were performing with a 20 per cent growth year after year, without further advertising, it was all through word of mouth.'

That's how good an idea it was. So much so that Jacqueline says that the Ann Summers Party Plan was her best decision yet. Find out more about Jacqueline's lessons in persistence in Chapter 10.

GET ENERGISED BY LOVING WHAT YOU DO

66 99

PASSION IS ENERGY. FEEL THE POWER THAT COMES FROM FOCUSING ON WHAT EXCITES YOU.

Oprah Winfrey

Seeing as you spend most of your waking life at work, you surely want to enjoy it as much as you can and not just do it for the money. And the best way to enjoy your work is to do something that you enjoy and have a passion for.

It's true what people say: if you love it, it isn't really like work.

That's certainly been the case for Chrissie Rucker MBE, founder of The White Company. For her, passion is a vital component to fuel inspiration, even now that she is surrounded by a large creative team who develop many of the ideas for new ranges themselves. She says, 'I am always inspired by things I see; my phone is filled with photos that I have taken that inspire me, which I then send to the office. Wherever I go, I am looking around me for new ideas. I am completely taken in by my surroundings. I love what I do, and to me it does not feel like work. It is my passion and I can do it for hours without ever feeling overwhelmed.'

Running your own business gives you the opportunity to make work fun. That doesn't mean that it's not hard, with long hours and huge challenges and pitfalls along the way, but enjoying what you do and having that depth of feeling about it gives you a positive 'possibilitarian' attitude, enabling you to see the opportunities, even among obstacles.

Your raw passion is your key strength to stimulating that kind of 'can-do' attitude to make stuff happen. So harness it. It will not only persuade people to buy from you, supply you and invest in you; it will also shape your purpose, your vision and the actions you take to get you there.

CREATE YOUR VISION AND PURPOSE

❝❞

WHAT WE HAVE DONE FOR OURSELVES ALONE DIES WITH US; WHAT WE HAVE DONE FOR OTHERS AND THE WORLD REMAINS AND IS IMMORTAL.

Albert Pike

Today, more than ever before, businesses need to have an overarching purpose which drives everything they do, say and sell. This is because consumers have been over-marketed to and have consequently developed a kind of immunity to what they are fed. These days, in order to really compel people to take notice, smart businesses link to a purposeful cause which evokes an emotional response and makes them more memorable than their competitors.

Having a purpose helps businesses to capture people's hearts and minds, rather than just their data and credit-card details. Purposeful businesses provide all stakeholders – customers, staff and investors – with something to believe in and stay loyal to (and, if that purpose is evocative enough, it will provide them with the motivation to go the extra mile for your company).

Google's purpose is to organise the world's information and make it universally accessible and useful. Facebook's purpose is to make the world more open and connected. My own company's purpose, which underpins everything, is to give babies and children the very best start in life with good, tasty food. Companies with a cause, whether linked to a charity or with a purpose (that they want to make something happen), are more likely to be recommended like wildfire, as people tell their friends who tell their friends, and so on.

SO WHAT IS YOUR PURPOSE?

- **What is your point and reason for existence?** What message do you want to deliver? What contribution will you make to people's lives? What are you aiming to do? Empower women? Create a safer world for children? Create a healthier world?

- **What kind of world do you want to live in?** A happier, healthier, safer, more honest one?

- **What do you want to do better than anyone else?** (More on this in Chapter 3.)

- **Which values do you rate the most?** (The ones that you'd most like to teach your children and anyone who works for you.) Honesty? Kindness? Loyalty? Quality? Accuracy? Good ethics? Do these values match with your business idea?

Here's an exercise for you to complete to help you gain clarity about your purpose. I suggest you take your time over this and keep coming back to it to ensure it still resonates and feels right as you embark on your journey.

FILL IN THE BLANKS:

I want to live in a world where

_____

_____

_____

```
┌─────────────────────────────────────────────┐
│  So I've created                              │
│  _____  │
│                                               │
│  _____  │
│                                               │
│  _____  │
│                                               │
│  In order to                                  │
│  _____  │
│                                               │
│  _____  │
│                                               │
│  _____  │
└─────────────────────────────────────────────┘
```

There's your purpose right there. Now your purpose should inform everything: strategic decisions, your mission, your values, your growth plan, the way you communicate and behave internally and externally – everything.

What you stand for, your purpose and your values, are incredibly valuable. They inspire you and everyone around you. As such it's important to embed your purpose and values into the heart of your business. In doing so you'll be able to engage everyone (in your target market) who comes into contact with it. Your wider purpose should shine through your product or service, your branding, tone of voice and every communication you have about the business. It is this that will attract and sustain customers and staff, engage and unite your team and influence how you are perceived in the marketplace.

Your values stem from your purpose and are the human face of the business. They bind your team, define your business culture (your way of doing things, even if it's just you) and enrich your offering. For example, if your purpose is to create a safer world for children, your values must tie in with this, so they might be: honesty, transparency, trustworthiness, reliability, environmental friendliness and quality. Values associated with my brand are integrity, honesty, expertise, quality, friendliness and understanding.

Your purpose will also bolster your passion to keep the fire in your belly burning strong. And it will keep you focused on your underlying mission. What I love about my job is that it genuinely helps mothers when they need help and guidance. I wouldn't have the same satisfaction if it wasn't like that, touching people's lives for the better.

Furthermore, your purpose helps shape your decisions about where you take the business in the future. If you have clarity of purpose it is far easier to check whether a new opportunity, partnership or idea fits within that wider mission.

For example, Liz Earle's passion for botanics, ethical sourcing and the natural world (which stemmed from her first memory of picking supper from her garden) took her on a journey which stayed true to her original purpose and inherent values. After growing the Liz Earle Beauty Co. business and passing it on, she now runs a lifestyle website, LizEarleWellbeing.com, which aims to provide a wealth of information on how to feel good through better food and healthcare, how to look good with the best beauty advice and also how to do a little good along the way with links to charities and organisations. She also runs a worldwide charity, as well as an organic farm.

Says Liz, 'The best piece of advice I've ever been given is this: "Go out into the world and do well, but, more importantly, go out into the world and do good."'

Similarly, Dame Anita Roddick was one of the first, if not the first, woman in business to link purpose with business. The Body Shop turned their shops into action stations for human rights by lobbying their customers to speak out on issues which impacted on them. They used their shops to deliver a message and make a point. Having an ethical purpose as a foundation has also enabled her daughter, Sam Roddick, to build a trusted brand in Coco de Mer – an erotic boutique business with strong values and a strong identity. For more on Sam's story, see chapters 6 and 11.

CLARITY OF VISION

It is always a good deal easier to be and remain passionate about your business idea if you know where you are headed. For that reason you need to have a clear vision of what you hope to achieve – in terms of where you see the business going in the future and precisely what your finished product will look, feel or taste like. And, while I personally don't think it's worth planning too far ahead (no need to start running five-year projections just yet – better to work on your idea, test it out and take small steps as you discover its strengths and weaknesses), you should still do some blue-sky thinking to see the bigger picture and to gain absolute clarity around what you want.

The great thing about launching your own business is that it's just as easy to take steps towards a big vision as towards a small vision, so you may as well dream big.

HOW CAN YOU THINK BIG?

- Consider where you'd ultimately like to end up. What are your ambitions? Where do you see the business in three years' time?

- Would you like to sell your business to a big corporation? If so, who might be the best suitors?

- What achievements would you like to have realised? To franchise the business? To have expanded your product range by upselling and cross-selling related products to the same customers? To license your brand/products to others or provide 'white label' solutions (so you license your product/software/service to others who sell it under their own brand name)? To reach as many people with your products via word of mouth?

- What precisely do you want from the business, both professionally and personally? A long-term career? To leave a legacy behind?

- Do you want to grow the business rapidly (through external funding by giving away equity)? Or organically by reinvesting profits back into the company?

- Is yours a short-term or a long-term vision, and why so?

Having a clear vision will inform your goals and guide your actions. It will help define which tasks you need to do in order to achieve your daily, monthly and annual goals and targets en route, getting you a step closer to your ultimate destination. For example, if your vision is to reach as many people as possible within a specific niche and make your product so appealing that it generates momentous word-of-mouth marketing, your actions will be to make the product the best it can be by finding the right materials, designs, illustrations and so on.

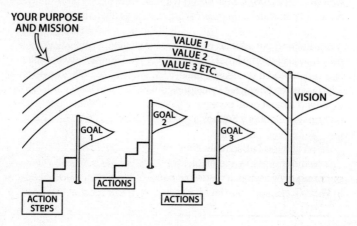

ANNABEL'S KITCHEN CABINET

THE POWER OF PASSION: THOMASINA MIERS

Thomasina Miers was the first woman to win BBC's *MasterChef*, in 2005. Two years later she opened her own restaurant in Covent Garden, Wahaca, bringing the best of Mexican street food to London. The chain now has 15 sites, as well as two mobile street kitchens. Her story is a surprising and moving tale of finding a focus in life based on your passion, no matter how long it takes you to find or rekindle that passion.

Thomasina Miers had a passion for cooking and food from an early age, but took a significant detour en route to her dream. 'In my late teens I lost my way a little,' says Thomasina.

In her gap year before university she had a scholarship with Arthur Andersen as a VAT consultant but was fired only days before the end of her time there and had to forgo the scholarship money. She then struggled with her degree in modern languages and economics at Edinburgh and decided to take a year out, working in the advertising agency J. Walter Thompson in Santiago, Chile. 'That was a good yet tough experience,' recalls Thomasina. 'It forced me to deal with situations where I was on my own and knew nobody, and it immersed me in different cultures.'

After finishing her degree Thomasina found a job in London in a digital agency, working on Internet strategy at the height of the dot-com boom. However, she found it dull and unmotivating. When she was made redundant from the agency she then dabbled in financial journalism and PR. 'I was going nowhere, in my eyes, while my friends were starting to become successful in their careers. I was wondering what was wrong with me. I felt like I was damaged goods.' Thankfully a change of direction was imminent.

'I was helping out a friend modelling for a catwalk show, and in the changing rooms I met Clarissa Dickson Wright ... I knew she had renounced a successful career in law for food. We chatted and Clarissa asked me what I was passionate about in life. I said, "I love clothes but most of all cooking." Clarissa's advice was, "Get ye to the Ballymaloe Cookery School" in County Cork. So I did.

'When I arrived I absolutely knew that finally, FINALLY, after all this searching, at the age of 26, I was on the right path and was pursuing my passion. It made me super-motivated. I made cheese in West Cork, sold sourdough bread at farmers' markets and ran a cheese stall for the Irish government at an international food fair, during which I asked every single person I met whether they needed someone to work for them. That led to a job in London at the Villandry shop on Great Portland Street, running the shop and later working on the marketing side.'

I started thinking about tapas and street food, the kind of food I had eaten when I was out in South America. Bizarrely someone offered me a job opening a cocktail bar in Mexico City, so I spent five months there touring round Mexico, eating food, cooking with local women and learning about this amazing cuisine – peasant food but so good and so nutritious. I really thought that this kind of food could work in the UK.

'I returned to London, with no money, and noticed an advert asking for contestants for *MasterChef*. I had never even seen the show, so I sauntered into the auditions thinking it was a bit of a joke … and got in. Suddenly it was all very serious. I was permanently terrified for the whole seven weeks, but in life you have to be a bit scared.'

Winning *MasterChef* gave Thomasina the confidence to go and work in a restaurant kitchen for Skye Gyngell at the Petersham Nurseries Café. 'I learnt a lot, not only about food, but also food costs and pricing,' she says. But in the back of her mind, Thomasina still had the idea of bringing Mexican food to London.

'I was re-introduced to an old university friend, Mark Selby, who had been working with Nando's on their financial side and was looking to make an investment in the restaurant business. I took him over to Mexico to show him the restaurants I had been to which I was so passionate about,' says Thomasina.

Her passion was infectious. 'He came back as enthused and convinced as I was. So we decided to open a restaurant. It took a year to make it happen, looking for a site, finding the name Wahaca, designing everything on the menu … In the end we opened in a massive 6,000-square-foot space in Covent Garden. It was terrifying. I lost three-quarters of a stone in the first week.'

Having coped with the sheer terror of *MasterChef* helped Thomasina get through the first six months. 'I also had an unshakeable belief that people would love the food we were serving: it was fun, tactile, it had a real yumminess and it was cheap … From week three there was a queue round the block, which was very exciting and, because we could see the queue from the kitchen, extremely motivating despite the long hours.'

Thomasina's dream had come true; she was now able to earn a living doing work that she loved. 'I have learnt how rewarding it is. I never thought I would feel so proud of building something, especially the people who work for Wahaca – training them, putting money into building people up through the company.'

Passion paid off.

02
BELIEV
YOURS

GET CONFIDENT AND
DRAW ON YOUR EXPERIENCE

"
BELIEVE YOU CAN AND
YOU'RE HALFWAY THERE.

Theodore Roosevelt

COMPETENTLY, CONFIDENTLY YOU

As well as believing wholeheartedly in your business, you must also believe in yourself. Yet self-belief is something that many women can struggle with. Self-doubt can easily prevail as we tell ourselves that we can't do this or that, especially if it's something new, something that requires change or something which we haven't done before.

It can be downright scary returning to the workplace after having children, whether that's into a job or into an enterprise of your own. Despite it being the most wonderful thing in the world, having children can be a complete confidence drain (as well as being exhausting). This is partly because you have taken a step away from practising the skills you learnt during your job and have endured 'pregnancy brain'. You may have even met with rejection and disdain when you have attempted to get back into the workplace, simply because you are tarnished with the 'working mum' brush and are considered by some (bad) employers as less employable than you were before. Or you may find your new life as a mum incompatible with your old job and are thus left with poor-quality part-time jobs for which you are way overqualified.

Lack of confidence is damaging. It needs to be conquered. Especially as confidence is sometimes more important than competence. Fortunately there are many methods to help overcome this obstacle of self-doubt, which we shall explore – along with recognising your competencies – throughout this chapter.

Of course, we all have doubts from time to time – especially when it comes to business. Whether it's doubting whether we can manage the financials, earn enough, keep customers satisfied, persuade a retailer to stock our goods or keep all the balls that we're juggling in the air, it's natural to feel nervous when we are doing something outside our comfort zone. The danger is if those doubts spiral out of control, creating unnecessary anxiety and negative self-limiting beliefs which prevent us from doing something that we really want to do (and, deep down, know that we *can* do).

Those self-doubts led me to make one of my biggest mistakes in business, which was not going into the food retail sector early enough. For 15 years, I stayed within my comfort zone of writing books as that was working out just fine. However, since getting my first book published in 1991, I had wanted to venture into making my own food for children. I had the recipes, they were fantastic, and I had the credibility after writing my first few books, but I just didn't have the confidence to take that step forward. Why would the supermarket giants take me seriously? How could I afford to make a success of food when I was up against some big competitors?

And therein lies one of my reasons for writing this book – to give mums the confidence to grab the bull by the horns and go for it.

There will always be concerns. From the very beginning of my career, I recall the worrying self-doubt creeping in as I wrote my first book. I wondered whether, after spending all that time on it, anybody would ever buy it. That concern lasted right up until the book was on the shelves. And right up to the present day, I still worry. My publisher arranged for me to appear on QVC to promote my new *Family Cookbook*. Weeks before going on I worried whether I might in fact be the first person on QVC never to sell a book and have really bad sales. In both instances, as is often the case, I really needn't have worried. The sales figures for both my very first book and first ever *Family Cookbook* were amazing.

However, often we need to see the proof that we can do something to really believe it; we need to witness the sales and increased customers to gain the confidence that our passion and instinct were right. But until that point, we need to find other ways to build our self-confidence levels. A little bit of worry is entirely normal. It helps us to do our utmost to generate the best possible outcome. But if you start to believe you absolutely cannot do something and don't feel confident in yourself at all, that can be problematic, because alongside belief in your product, you need a healthy dose of self-belief to propel you through the tough times.

Says Sam Roddick, 'Women need to believe in themselves but they often don't realise they have the skills. They think that the commercial world is a mystery and is beyond them. So that disenables a lot of women to actually step up, they don't realise that most of what it takes to run a business is common sense. All you need is to have a brain and to have experience in life, you can basically manage your way through it and you will learn as you grow.'

Sam is absolutely right. Believe me, you already have the skills you need to run your own business, and any gaps in your skillset can be filled. This book will help equip you with practical tips, advice and a plan of action. So take a deep breath and read on.

Sometimes people stay in jobs they don't like or opt *not* to do something they'd love to do because they are financially dependent on the money they bring in and cannot risk losing that financial security. There are ways round this. You can de-risk a move into self-employment by saving three to six months' salary to act as a buffer before launching forth, or you can start your business part-time by working in the evenings while still in employment. Sometimes, people simply lack the courage and choose instead to settle for what they have rather than take that leap. Yet the minute you settle for less than you deserve, you get less than you settled for. By the end of this chapter you should have the courage to take that first step. After all, this is your one and only life, so it's important to make the most of it.

🗨

COURAGE IS THE GREATEST OF ALL VIRTUES, BECAUSE IF YOU HAVEN'T COURAGE, YOU MAY NOT HAVE AN OPPORTUNITY TO USE ANY OF THE OTHERS.

Samuel Jackson

Here's the bottom line: the more you believe in yourself and in your chances of succeeding, the more likely you are to do just that. Conversely, thinking you cannot and that you are bound to fail could well become a self-fulfilling prophecy.

🗨

WHETHER YOU THINK YOU CAN, OR THINK YOU CAN'T – YOU'RE RIGHT.

Henry Ford

Here are two powerful ways to boost your confidence and self-belief:

01. Harness your own experience. Examine your existing competencies and achievements and you'll soon realise that you do have what it takes, even if your skills seem unrelated to your venture. There will be transferable experience, knowledge and contacts among your skills.

02. Learn or outsource. Fill in the gaps to give yourself peace of mind.

Let's explore these further.

HARNESS YOUR OWN EXPERIENCE

Just because you have never run a business before does not mean you lack the necessary skills. You'll be surprised how many aspects of business, from budgeting to time management, you are already competent in, particularly as a mum. The extra assortment of skills that you gain from being a parent are super-useful as there are a great many parallels. Take multi-tasking for example.

'As any mum will know, the art of multi-tasking seems to be something you have to master very quickly once you become a parent, and undoubtedly being able to juggle numerous projects and priorities at the same time has helped me as an entrepreneur,' says Liz Earle.

Time management and organisation are business-applicable core competencies that you polish as a diary-managing parent. Indeed, the organisational skills required when you have children are enormously important. Before I could even think about writing my book I had to make sure my children's day was fully planned, with play dates organised and mealtimes catered for, so that I could take a few hours out to work on my passion.

That inherent requirement to think ahead, to think, 'What's going to happen at 3pm after school?', and so on, makes mums terrific planners. And, as any good entrepreneur will tell you, planning is an imperative skill that self-employed people need, both in terms of the day-to-day planning of setting schedules, targets and plotting actions, and in terms of writing a comprehensive and compelling business plan which sets out strategies, objectives and assesses strengths and weaknesses. That organisational nous is paramount.

'For me being a mother has made me more organised than ever before, and time management is key to being successful in business,' says Alex Polizzi, hotelier, TV's The Fixer and The Hotel Inspector, in the programmes of the same name, and co-owner of Millers Bespoke Bakery. 'You just cannot let yourself obsess about anything – you have to move on. And you have to be very clear about what your goals are; you have to give yourself achievable time frames.'

'I think being a mum you know how to juggle and you learn that you have to delegate as well as knowing what to prioritise,' says Jennifer Irvine, mum of four and founder of The Pure Package and Balance Box. 'The other thing that has really helped me from being a mum is learning how to choose my battles,' she adds. 'You can't get your way on everything, so that's one of the things you can translate into a corporate setting. For example, there's no point fighting about little things. If it's going to cause a lot of stress and not even for a worthy cause, I try to let it go.'

When you start your own business, just like returning to employment, you add another spinning plate to the mix, but as a mum you have already developed 'needs-must' coping strategies and will find a way to schedule in what you need to do. You just will.

Sam Roddick believes that it takes the same skills to run a house and a family as it does to run a company. 'Managing a budget is like managing a household budget,' says Sam. 'Plus there is an element of managing people which is like managing children ... They need clear expectations, healthy boundaries and encouragement to grow and take responsibility … As a mum and a business owner you need the ability to be proactive and reactive, to firefight, to admit when you're wrong and change your course of action if you need to.'

Notably, too, having children can fire up your ambition to succeed, to provide for them and inspire them to work hard to achieve what they want in life. Sam started Coco de Mer when her daughter (now 16) was two years old. 'I think that I became a better businesswoman by becoming a mother. It actually gave me the ambition and the confidence,' Sam says. 'I don't actually think I had the self-belief until I had my daughter.'

Whether having children has crippled your confidence or heightened your ambition, putting your experiences to good use will certainly help you to feel more able. Ultimately, though, it's not just the skills you've gleaned from being a mum: you can draw upon whatever life and work experience you have had up until this point, all of it, to inform your decisions, to gain strength and inspiration and, crucially, to boost your confidence and belief in yourself.

MY EXPERIENCE: FROM MUSICIAN TO AUTHOR TO RETAILER

Before I was a mother, before I ever started writing, I was a musician. I started playing the harp at the age of seven and music became a huge part of my life. I studied music with a harp professor, Ed Witzenburg, who was based at the Royal Conservatoire in The Hague, and then I went to study at the Royal College of Music just opposite the Royal Albert Hall in London.

As a young harpist I had to go and find work. I'd seen people playing the harp in hotels in America and wanted to earn some money so, aged 17, I found myself a regular session at the Inn on the Park off Hyde Park Corner by pitching myself to them. The general manager asked me whether I could play every kind of music. I gaily said 'Yes', not really being able to at all. So when he asked me to start the following week and play in the lounge at teatime, I scurried off to Chappell's music shop to buy the current hits and work out how to play them on a harp. During my time at the hotel, I learnt how to focus without getting distracted by the clanking of plates, and I also met lots of interesting people.

Six months later, the InterContinental Hotel, on the other side of Hyde Park Corner, were auditioning for a musician to play in their cocktail lounge. I knew lots of professional musicians were going for it, and, although I had confidence in my abilities, I thought to myself, 'Well, I may not get it but I may as well try.' I was determined to give it a go, and I'm glad I did as I got the job playing another regular session there. I would play at the Inn on the Park from 4pm, change into a different dress and have my harp kindly moved from one hotel to another, then I'd play from 7pm until 10pm at the

InterContinental. It was hilarious when people told me I was much better than the harpist at the Inn on the Park, as that was me too. I was competing with myself!

I went on to perform many solo concerts, including harp concertos at the Royal Festival Hall, and I also played on a variety of TV shows. I gave harp and poetry recitals with Dylan Thomas's daughter Aeronwy, accompanied tea at The Savoy and performed in their Saturday-night cabarets. I also became a guest on Russell Harty's chat show (which was like *The Graham Norton Show* at the time), alongside Sir Bob Geldof. I made an album with guests like Julian Lloyd Webber, performed cabaret at the Monte-Carlo Sporting Club, played Cinderella in pantomime with Dennis Waterman and even featured in a Boy George video.

It was an exciting and varied career, and I loved it. I thought I had the best career in the world. But it didn't fit well with being a stay-at-home mum.

Losing my precious daughter also made me realise what I didn't want, and that was to be away from my children. After losing Natasha I felt that I needed to give some meaning to her life, and writing a book as a legacy to her, which would help other children, was therapeutic for me and helped me come to terms with her death.

WHAT WE HAVE DONE FOR OURSELVES ALONE DIES WITH US; WHAT WE HAVE DONE FOR OTHERS AND THE WORLD REMAINS AND IS IMMORTAL.

Albert Pike

I needed to find something that would fit my skillset, my passion and my circumstances. Playing the harp was never going to work; it would have taken me away from my home too often – practising or performing when I wanted to be with my children. I didn't want to miss out on my children's upbringing, so I was keen to find a serious profession that I could still do from home.

As well as music, I loved to cook. When I was studying at the Royal College of Music, I took a cordon bleu cookery course and would cook lunch for the quartet I had formed. Back then, cookery was a hobby, something I did for fun, and something I thoroughly enjoyed doing. I didn't realise then how important those cooking skills would become to my career.

I also did a typing course in South Molton Street for no reason other than I thought touch-typing might be a useful skill to have. By the end of it I was able to type quite fast, and perhaps that made me ponder the possibility of writing books in the future.

Typing and cooking became two of the most relevant skills I had, but I was also able to transfer most of what I'd learnt throughout my career as a musician and apply it to my business.

From music I learnt discipline. I learnt about being brave and getting up in front of strangers to perform. I learnt how to pitch to strangers and how to avoid panicking and deal with nerves. All these skills proved invaluable when I started my business career. I needed courage when I pitched to the supermarkets. I needed to be brave when I challenged the supermarkets over certain limitations they'd put in place. I needed confidence to get up in front of strangers when giving talks to parents and budding entrepreneurs. Discipline was required as I had strict deadlines for my books, and my experience of dealing with nerves and performance helped me when I filmed my *Annabel's Kitchen* TV series for CITV.

My earlier experience of summoning up the courage to perform on *The Russell Harty Show* was invaluable. Knowing you're going to perform on television in front of 16 million people live on a harp, with all those strings and seven pedals, is incredibly frightening. I realised that if I could do that then anything else was easy – anything was possible. I think mums should take on board the bravery they've had to give birth, because if you can go through that experience, you really can do anything. Many people worry about changing careers, but it keeps you fresh. Someone once told me that everyone has at least three careers in them, and I think that is true. Just because you've put your heart and soul (and even financial investment) into one career, it doesn't mean that you should automatically just carry on with it. You can pivot, change direction and create a new route, harnessing your existing skills, knowledge and experience to positively impact that new direction.

For me, writing was an ideal profession as I could work from home around the children and family life. I was also spending so much time cooking for babies that turning it into a profession seemed like a good idea. So I decided to take a leap of faith, change my career and carve myself a new beginning and ending.

Sometimes we need to take that leap. I'm eternally grateful that I did. I understand that, when you've devoted so much time and energy to your first career, you might be afraid to change direction. But so much of your experience, knowledge, skills and contacts are transferable to your new venture – probably more than you realise.

OTHER EXAMPLES OF SKILLS TRANSFERRED

The collection of super-successful mums featured in this book did not have any formal business training. One or two undertook introduction-to-business classes at evening school, but that's generally the limit. As you'll see in Chapter 5, they all learnt on the job and applied what they'd learnt from previous jobs (and from being a mum) to the task at hand.

So which specific skills did some of these inspirational businesswomen take with them from their previous working roles into running their own enterprises?

Chloe Macintosh, co-founder and creative director of Made.com and mother of two young boys under 10, changed her career twice, but each time has used her creative flair and eye for aesthetics. Having worked as an architect for 10 years, she seized an opportunity to move into home décor when mentor Brent Hoberman was looking for someone to help with the design side of Mydeco.com. 'It was a complete leap of faith. I didn't know anything about interiors and product design but I was also joining a very different type of environment and launching an Internet start-up.'

After gaining three years of online-retail and product-development experience, she harnessed her home décor knowledge and applied it to furniture, when she co-founded Made.com. 'We didn't have a furniture background, and we instead thought of our own complementary skills and experience,' says Chloe. Alongside Chloe's product-development, online-retail and design skills, her co-founder, commercially minded Ning Li, brought his investment-banking background, and experience of start-up management and sourcing products directly from factories. He also brought Julien Callede on board, who had a wealth of operational and management experience. For more on Chloe's story, see pages 57–8.

Sam Roddick, daughter of Dame Anita Roddick and mum of one daughter, took her persuasive and creative skills from her work as an activist and transferred them to her Coco de Mer upmarket ethical sex shops. Providing artisan and handmade products, her brand was about legitimising and promoting positive discussion about eroticism and sex. 'I learnt everything on the job,' says Sam. 'I fire fought my company from not really knowing anything. How I sold people into investing in my company was very much in the same way that I would enlist people [to join the cause] when I was an activist.'

Liz Earle, mum of five, and her business partner Kim transferred their existing complementary skills (Liz's beauty journalism and broadcasting skills and Kim's marketing expertise) to their business. Doing so paid off hugely. 'As a journalist, author and broadcaster on so many aspects of beauty and well-being, I had tested literally thousands of different products over the years, so I had a good idea of what worked and what didn't, which obviously helped enormously when I started formulating the brand's products,' explains Liz. 'Writing and presenting also taught me how important it is to thoroughly research your topic, and this is still an area of my working life that I value – going on field trips to far-flung places to learn about new botanical ingredients, for instance.'

Myleene Klass, mum of two, made great use of her experiences gleaned from being in pop band Hear'Say, a completely unrelated role to the retail ones she later pursued as founder of her Baby K babycare range for Mothercare and her own fashion range at Littlewoods. Says Myleene, 'That pop band experience was my first and possibly most important lesson in what marketing is about.' Myleene learnt that it's not a case of 'build it and they will come', or letting the music or product do the talking: 'If nobody knows about it, it's just going to die a death,' she says. 'That was such a huge lesson.'

Similarly, Myleene was able to draw on her TV presenting skills from fronting *CD:UK* with Lauren Laverne, transferring them to pitching to various countries for her Mothercare brand. 'I do all the franchise meetings now,' says Myleene. 'I was nervous at first, then realised it was like hosting a TV show. I'll say, "Hello Russia, here's the product," and will often have to think on my feet, just like in TV.'

STICK OR TWIST?

Some business advisers suggest you stick to what you know but, while many entrepreneurs do just that, it's not imperative. Many successful entrepreneurs had zero prior experience of working in the sector they are now successful in.

To illustrate this, here's how two women, each with almost a decade working in sales under their belts, took a different approach to using those skills. The first, Fiona Clark, figured out a way to transfer her skills and character strengths into a completely new career, while the second, Liz Jackson, set up a business which was entirely focused on her sales-based skillset.

ANNABEL'S KITCHEN CABINET

UNCOVERING TRANSFERABLE TALENTS: FIONA CLARK

After spending 10 years on the wrong career path, mum of two Fiona Clark didn't think that she had any transferable skills at all. Having worked in sales for 10 years, she thought that sales jobs were the only ones she'd be able to go for. She soon realised this wasn't the case and that her skills and strengths were transferable. In 2006

Fiona set up Inspiredmums.co.uk to coach and inspire women to reach their full potential at work by finding fulfilling careers.

After leaving university with a business degree, Fiona Clark wasn't sure what she wanted to do. 'I ticked a sales box on a graduate recruitment form and off I went into my first career,' recalls Fiona. 'However, after working in sales for 10 years, I realised that, despite doing well on paper, I was not happy, I felt stressed out and knew I wasn't really playing to my strengths.'

Unmotivated and confused, Fiona found herself, aged 31, at a crossroads in her life. 'I couldn't see a way forward because I had been in the same career for 10 years. I found it hard to see my transferable skills,' adds Fiona.

After being given career coaching sessions for a Christmas present from her brother, the seed was sewn that perhaps coaching itself might be a viable alternative career option. 'The coaching sessions made me think outside the box and gave me clarity on what my skillset was, why I was unhappy and what I therefore needed to do going forward. I discovered what my strengths actually were and we talked about how to find roles that played to those strengths,' explains Fiona.

Consequently, Fiona realised that her commercial skills were just one small part of what she was good at. Her skillset was far wider than that. 'My skillset and lists of strengths included empathy, listening and connecting with people,' says Fiona. 'Often, when you are naturally good at something and it comes easily, you assume that everyone is good at it, and therefore undervalue that skill, not realising that that it is a transferable skill you can use in your future career.'

Fiona also realised that a lot of what she had learnt during her sales career was entirely transferable after all. 'I was exposed to a lot of commercial activities, such as selling, negotiating, understanding numbers, profitability … all those skills have helped me set up my business and, in turn, have helped me to coach others to set up theirs.'

With a renewed sense of confidence in what she could do and clarity around what she wanted from her working life, Fiona financed her business by taking on a six-month sales contract while she was pregnant. Eight years later, Fiona has helped hundreds of other women identify their skills and strengths and gain the confidence to find work which inspires and fulfils them.

Understanding which skills were transferable and playing to her strengths has propelled Fiona forward in a career that gives her a real sense of purpose. She didn't need to stick to a sales career after all.

ANNABEL'S KITCHEN CABINET

PLAYING TO HER STRENGTHS: DR LIZ JACKSON MBE

Conversely, Dr Liz Jackson MBE recognised and focused specifically on sales as that was what she felt she was good at and enjoyed most. She used those skills to set up her own business, Great Guns Marketing, and sold those sales skills to paying clients.

'I knew my trade very well before I started up my own company, so I was already a good telemarketer and I had learnt to do that while working for somebody else,' says mum of two, Liz. 'When starting your own business, it helps to do something you are good at, something which you have confidence in and a passion for. Because, if you don't have confidence in that area, the rest is pretty tough,' says Liz.

For Liz, that blend of confidence, belief and passion are what drove her to overcome an obstacle that could have got in her way. Having been diagnosed with a degenerative eye disorder at the age of two, and told she'd be blind by the age of five, Liz got used to playing to her strengths, which include admirable communication and social skills.

Liz didn't go blind aged five but her eyesight did steadily deteriorate, so much so that she lost her sight completely the same year that she set up her Great Guns Marketing business. But she didn't let that stop her. In fact, Liz has gone on to win multiple awards, has spoken at various high-profile events and even made an appearance on Channel 4's *Secret Millionaire* programme.

Using the skills and experience she gained as a sales manager, Liz decided to branch out by herself with a grant from The Prince's Trust. She started her telemarketing business from her living room in 1998. Today she employs a staff of nearly 100 at nine branches across the UK and Ireland, boasting an impressive portfolio of clients including British Telecom, Wella and Lloyds Bank.

'I'd been working as a telemarketer for eight years,' says Liz. 'I never set out to start up a company though.' She explains, 'I was a complete academic failure with no real GCSEs to speak of. My first job at 17 as an office junior was the only thing I had been good at, and I progressed on to become a sales manager.' Liz absolutely loved it. 'I worked for an amazing entrepreneur who showed me that the workplace could be somewhere really rewarding and fun. I realised sales was an amazing career, but after trying a few days in a couple of other companies I felt stifled. I felt like I had been spoilt by having the best possible boss, who nobody else could match, so I decided to do it for myself.'

Not only was Liz able to put her personable approach to good use, she has also trained her staff in those people skills. By doing so, her own strengths have become the strengths of the company. Consequently, Great Guns became the first telemarketing company to be recognised by the Institute of Customer Service (ICS) with the coveted ServiceMark accreditation.

So, you might have industry experience and know your sector, or you may not. Either way, you'll be able to take all of the skills and knowledge you have learnt and apply all of your experience to your venture. You might be great at spotting opportunities and a great listener; you might have operational experience or have well-honed creative skills. You may have been in a certain industry for decades and have a nous for something specific that you could apply, or you may not. Having little experience of a certain industry forces you to get creative with your ideas and commit to learning about the areas you need to; it leads you to be open-minded and see opportunities with fresh eyes so that you are innovative in your application of your ideas.

Indeed, Sir Richard Branson says that once you know how to run one business you can run any business. 'If you can run a record company, you can run an airline. If you can run an airline, you can run a bank. If you can run a bank, you can run a soft-drink company,' he says.

TALENT SPOTTING

There are three actions you should now take to remind yourself of your strengths and weaknesses. This should boost your confidence. You will also be able to see where you need to plug the gaps in your skillset and knowledge base, and we will come to this later in the chapter.

01. **Examine and list what you enjoy doing.** What are you passionate about? Do you have any hobbies? Which tasks do you most enjoy doing as a mum? Which tasks did you most enjoy doing while at work? What topics do you like to talk about? (You may find that these

are duplicated when you list your strengths as we often enjoy doing the stuff we are good at.)

02. Evaluate and list your competencies, skillset and strengths. What have you learnt? What skills have you gained? What experiences have you had that will set you in good stead for running your own enterprise? What knowledge or areas of expertise do you have? What do you know a lot about? What are you good at?

As well as boosting your confidence in how equipped you already are to set up and run your own business, focusing on your strengths from the outset has another benefit. Scientific studies have shown that spending time at work utilising your strengths has a positive impact on your well-being. As Cheryl Rickman, my co-writer, says in *The Flourish Handbook*, 'Identifying your strengths and putting them to good use gives your work meaning and enables you to be more engaged.' And this in turn 'boosts satisfaction and well-being'. She suggests you take this incredibly accurate VIA survey of character strengths to uncover what they are: www.authentichappiness.sas.upenn.edu/testcenter.

03. List your achievements. Jacqueline Gold advises that if you're worried about a meeting you should write an email to yourself listing all of your amazing qualities. She suggests: 'Write down everything you have achieved in your life and keep adding to it over time. If you are going into a meeting where you feel a bit of a wobble, re-read that email to remind yourself about how amazing you are.' Fiona Clark agrees. 'Mums often struggle to be really positive about themselves. They get really modest and shy. So I ask them to talk about what they are really proud of that they have achieved, and it could be anything: mum related or work related,' explains Fiona. 'I then ask what strengths, traits and skills they used to achieve that. Many people find that easier than just saying, "Oh, I am great at this and I am great at that".'

For example, you may be computer-literate with fast typing skills, a good communicator with a good telephone manner, you may be good at writing, coming up with or executing good ideas, you may have qualifications in childcare or marketing or recruitment or sales, and you may enjoy cooking, organising and hosting events, fundraising and so on. You may have been house captain or a prefect at school; you may have trained and run a 10k race or helped to organise the school fete; you may have secured funding for a project at work or received an award for your project-management skills. Each and every achievement listed here would provide you with a wide range of persuasive, organisational and communication skills you could transfer to your business. The process of listing them will give you the confidence that you have shone in the past and will shine in the future.

MY TALENTS WORKSHEET

Please fill in the worksheet below, listing your skills, knowledge, experience, achievements and so on. The aim here is to boost your confidence by making you realise how talented you are, what you've achieved and to see which skills may be transferable to self-employment.

1. From employment I have the following skills:

_____

_____

_____

_____

_____

_____

_____

_____

2. Key experiences/knowledge that I can put to good use are:

_____

_____

_____

_____

_____

_____

_____

_____

3. The sectors I have contacts in include:

_____

_____

_____

_____

_____

_____

_____

_____

4. My achievements include (list everything you've achieved, from being a prefect at school and captaining the netball team to having your children, managing a project successfully, fundraising and so on):

_____

_____

_____

_____

_____

_____

_____

_____

5. I am good at:

_____

_____

_____

_____

6. I enjoy:

_____

_____

_____

_____

7. I know a lot about:

_____

_____

_____

_____

8. Motherhood has given me the following skills that I can transfer:

_____

_____

_____

_____

_____

_____

_____

_____

Aha! Look! See! You are actually rather talented after all!

Now list any weaknesses that are fuelling your doubts. What skills do you wish you had but don't? What are you not so good at? Where do you see potential obstacles and challenges?

9. I'm not very good at (and could do with some help with):

_____

_____

_____

_____

10. Obstacles and challenges might include:

_____

_____

_____

_____

_____

_____

Fret not, because these missing skills can either be learnt or outsourced. Weaknesses can become strengths; obstacles can become opportunities.

LEARN OR OUTSOURCE: FILL IN THE GAPS

Learning is a way to combat your fears and fuel your courage. Through learning we equip ourselves with whatever it is we need to achieve what we set out to do.

Ultimately, there are two ways to learn:

01. Fill in the gaps. Work out where gaps in your knowledge and skills exist and proactively find ways to gain that knowledge and those skills.

02. Learn from your mistakes and strive to do better the next day.

Both methods of learning are equally valid and both should bolster your self-belief as you realise you cannot fail.

You see, it's a very powerful realisation that, should we fail, we have *not* lost out, but have actually gained lessons that we simply wouldn't have learnt had we succeeded. In Chapter 10 we'll explore why failure is one of the most helpful tools in an entrepreneur's armoury and will review what our leading ladies have learnt from their own mistakes, so that you can learn from them too.

I THINK FAILURE IS NOTHING MORE THAN LIFE'S WAY OF NUDGING YOU THAT YOU ARE OFF COURSE. MY ATTITUDE TO FAILURE IS NOT ATTACHED TO OUTCOME, BUT IN NOT TRYING.

Sara Blakely, Spanx founder

THE ONLY REAL FAILURE IN LIFE IS THE FAILURE TO TRY.

George Bernard Shaw

Shifting your attitude to how you perceive failing empowers you. When you realise that you can pick yourself up, dust yourself off and try again, but with more knowledge at your disposal, you realise that making mistakes is okay – worthwhile even, because all learning is good. This gives you courage.

EQUIP YOURSELF BY FILLING IN THE GAPS

You've already bought this book to inform and inspire you to take the plunge, so what else could you do?

- **Train.** Take an online training course, watch 'how to' videos on YouTube or attend an evening class or a workshop. Visit www. bgateway.com/starting-up and www.enterprisenation.com/events to find lists of courses or events. These days you can find out how to do pretty much anything if you search the Internet. You can also find helpful sites in the Useful Resources list on pages 281–5.

- **Read.** According to direct marketing expert Ted Nicholas, 'If you read each day for one hour on one topic for one year, you can become the world's leading expert on that topic.' I'm going to assume, as a busy mum, you don't necessarily have an entire hour which you can devote to reading, but even half an hour every other day would equip you with enough knowledge to fill those gaps. And, even better, if you can improve your expertise on a subject area you are already savvy in, you could blog and write articles on that topic and position yourself as an expert to gain wider credibility and market your expertise and business offerings.

- **Get mentored.** 'Before you say that you can't do something you have got to talk to people who have done it,' advises Sam Roddick. 'The British Library has an incredible mentoring system and department that helps people starting up in business,' adds Sam, who has given talks there herself. 'They do talks, they set you up with mentors, they do workshops for people starting up their own business. My mum used to teach there – it's an incredible resource.' See pages 228–30 for more on mentoring, and visit www.mentorsme.co.uk and www.getmentoring. org to be matched with a suitable mentor.

- **Outsource.** Today, thanks to globalisation and the advancement of web technologies, we can collaborate and pass work across time zones and connect with people from far-flung corners of the globe quickly and easily. This means that we can access more talent and pay affordable prices for work that is outside our skillset and in areas we have no inclination to learn about ourselves. For example, you may need to outsource your website design or copywriting and could therefore post your project on a site such as www.odesk.com or www.elance.com, which enable top-quality but low-cost developers who have expertise in developing websites to bid on your project. You can also outsource a whole range of tasks using sites such as www.freelancer.co.uk, www. peopleperhour.com and www.fiverr.com (for specific one-off jobs).

10 TIPS TO TURN SELF-DOUBT INTO SELF-BELIEF

Jacqueline Gold and Fiona Clark haven't let any insecurities stand in their way. Here are their top tips on turning self-doubt into self-belief.

01. Don't worry about the competition, just do your best. 'The best piece of advice I've ever been given is that "There is nothing more to fear than fear itself,"' says Jacqueline. 'When it comes to the competition, don't become obsessed by them and let the fear of what they are doing distract you from your own business. Success in business is about being the best at what you do. If you do that, you have nothing to fear.'

02. Consider the facts. If you logically check the facts you will probably realise that your worries are unfounded. For example, you might feel you can't pitch for investment now, but then you check the facts: you are presenting investors with a viable opportunity and the numbers add up, you have a good track record and have proved the concept works within your local community. From this, you can see that, once you've practised your pitch, you have just as much chance at succeeding as anyone else. 'If you are having a meeting, remember, these people are meeting you because they *want* to hear what you have to say,' says Jacqueline. We often worry before an event and then realise after that we were worrying unnecessarily as it's normally better than we expected.

03. Find the evidence to back up your positive beliefs and counter your negative ones. 'Write down some positive beliefs about yourself, and your situation,' advises Fiona. 'For example, people might say, "I am hard-working and outgoing, and I have got a good business idea," but might counter it by also saying, "but I can't do this on my own and no one is going to buy my product/service".' She adds, 'It's important to notice and question those negative self-beliefs that hold you back. If one of those beliefs is "I am never going to be able to sell this", challenge yourself to flip that language into something much more positive, such as "My passion for my business will enable me to sell this" and "I have a good track record of being able to influence people". The next step is to reinforce your new positive belief by considering all the times you have successfully influenced and persuaded people to buy or do something. This gives you evidence that you *can* sell and influence people and will shift your attitude from I can't to I can.'

04. Be yourself. 'I learnt early on to embrace who I was and not emulate who I thought a business person should be, which was often the alpha male,' explains Jacqueline, who admits that she was very quietly spoken in the early days and so tried to compensate by attempting to dress the part. 'I used to wear the 1980s power suits, the hair up and

47

the glasses, until someone told me I looked like a politician, and that was enough for me to realise I should just be myself,' she smiles. 'I thought, I am really passionate about what I do, I am proud of what I do and I don't need to be anybody else other than me.'

05. Be proud of your femininity. 'We can be feminine and successful,' says Jacqueline. 'Women are so much more powerful than they realise and yet they often feel uncomfortable being the only woman at a seminar or similar event. This is so sad because women often don't realise the men are more intimidated by her than she is by them.' Jacqueline also advises that women don't have to be aggressive to be successful. She says, 'I am not aggressive. I am firm and relentless and very focused, but I am not aggressive.'

06. Don't be afraid to be assertive. There is a difference between being aggressive and being assertive. 'By the age of 12, girls are three-and-a-half times more likely to have lost their self-esteem than boys, and are most likely not interested in being a leader as a result,' states Jacqueline. She explains that this stems from the classroom. 'Unfortunately, from an early age, girls are discouraged from being assertive as that's seen as being "bossy". The COO of Facebook and author of *Lean In*, Sheryl Sandberg, is running a "Ban Bossy" campaign due to those negative connotations. It is rare for a boy or man to be called bossy. Instead bossy behaviour in men is seen as commanding, assertive or good leadership.'

07. Go it alone. I have to admit that I've taken a female friend along to events where I've known I'd be the only woman and yet, as Jacqueline points out, that can stifle your success and result in missed opportunities. 'It's a great turning point when you get to a stage when you don't need to walk in with anyone else. Instead of talking to a friend, it forces you to engage with others and gives you the opportunity to meet someone who might change your life. The pride you feel afterwards for making yourself do it is huge.'

08. Try role-modelling to fake it until you make it. 'Role-modelling is a really powerful confidence builder,' says Fiona. 'Define what you lack confidence in first. For example, this might be networking … Next, imagine how someone who is confident and relaxed about networking might handle going to an event. It's all about the body language and the tone of voice. They would smile and introduce themselves to people on arrival and ask questions. They'd show an interest in others. By describing what actions that confident person would do, you can figure out which of those behaviours you should try out to appear more confident on the outside. Practise those behaviours when you next go to a networking event and see what reaction you get, and how you feel. Typically it's a self-fulfilling cycle where you will feel more confident and relaxed, and your comfort zone for the next networking event you attend will naturally increase.'

09. Stay in touch. When you are on maternity leave you feel left out of the loop. Jacqueline, who took three months' maternity leave, suggests that you maintain contact, no matter how infrequent, while you are away. 'Keep in touch, go in and see your colleagues again. I carried on the emails. I even see women come back from holiday and feel unsettled because they have been away from the office and feel out of the loop. It's about disciplining yourself to keep that contact going and keep your toe in the water, even if it's just going along to the odd event.'

10. Be bold. Have the courage of your convictions to do things your way. Don't bow to stereotypes or old-fashioned perceptions. From the age of 21, Jacqueline Gold transformed her father's company from a turnover of £83,000 in her first year working for him into an empire with 143 stores turning over £145 million. She did that. 'It wasn't an engaged culture, it wasn't inclusive,' says Jacqueline. 'I admire my father in many ways but the business culture was not something I particularly learnt from. Changing the culture was a good thing to do, and now he works my way,' she says proudly.

🙶🙷
WE WOULD ACCOMPLISH MANY MORE THINGS IF WE DID NOT THINK OF THEM AS IMPOSSIBLE.

Vince Lombardi

ANNABEL'S KITCHEN CABINET

HOW HARNESSING POWERFUL PR SKILLS PAID OFF: CHRISSIE RUCKER

Chrissie Rucker, mum of four, took her magazine and PR experience and applied them to gaining a whole host of valuable editorial and publicity skills when she set up The White Company.

Having spent several years working her way around various magazines, including *GQ*, *Brides*, *House & Garden*, *Vogue* and *Harpers & Queen,* and working in the press office at Clarins, Chrissie gathered some fantastic skills. 'I absolutely loved my time in the magazine world. I learnt how to research, report and write, and I learnt how to organise a shoot. I worked with some incredible stylists and photographers and started to learn the tricks of the trade: how to style a picture and, most importantly, that often simple was the best. The last job I did [at *Harpers & Queen*] was shooting Carla Bruni with two of the top stylists of the time. It was terrifying. But doing something like that takes away the fear.'

That experience gave Chrissie the confidence that she could do anything she set her mind to. When she set up The White Company she was ready to utilise all the skills she'd gathered.

'For the first couple of years, we were helped enormously by PR,' explains Chrissie. With no shopfronts, as a pure mail-order company, she needed to find a way to let people know about The White Company's existence.

'I shot and printed the brochures and used all my money, which was only £6,000,' recalls Chrissie. 'I mailed all these brochures to everyone I knew but I suddenly realised I was in financial trouble. So I wrote my own press release, that's where my experience from working at Clarins came in,' she nods. 'I was very lucky, as, despite not knowing her, Lucia van der Post [associate editor of the *FT*'s *How To Spend It* magazine] wrote a fantastic article in the *FT* after picking up my press release. It was nearly a whole page.

'Many magazines picked the idea up. They liked the idea of everything white. In fact, the piece in the *FT* was the one which launched us,' Chrissie adds.

Chrissie's time working in journalism within the fashion and beauty sector certainly enhanced her creative skills, which came in particularly useful as she began designing and sourcing her own

White Company product range. Her journalism skills also came in handy when she was conducting research to see what was selling and glean information.

Ultimately, you might think on the surface that setting up a mail-order and then multi-channel retailer in the home-furnishings sector would have nothing to do with the experience and skills that Chrissie had gained from her various journalism and PR jobs, except perhaps the stint working for the relevant home magazine. And yet Chrissie was able to use the research, press-release writing and PR skills and the confidence and creativity she'd bolstered through working in those sectors to apply them in a completely unrelated sector.

03

FIND A
NICHE
JUST BE

NICE AND BETTER

Your story and your passion to write your own ending are both crucial ingredients in the recipe for success. However, in order to have the courage of your convictions and persuade customers to buy into what you are offering (and investors or partners to buy into your opportunity), the quality and viability of your business idea is also essential. To ensure this, there are two crucial criteria that all businesses should strive for: first, to challenge existing alternatives and, second, to be innovative in some way.

How can you do this? By being better and by being different.

BE BETTER THAN THE REST

GG JJ
**IT'S NEVER TOO LATE TO BE
WHAT YOU MIGHT HAVE BEEN.**

George Eliot

Most people think that being an entrepreneur means you have to come up with an amazing, entirely unique invention, the like of which has never been seen before – something completely new, pioneering and revolutionary. However, contrary to popular belief, while innovation and creativity are important, it's not necessary to invent something completely unique. What *is* important though is that you find a *better* and/or *different* way of doing something than what has been done before. This is something that challenges and outdoes existing alternatives and services that do not quite meet particular needs; something which provides your prospective customers with a fresh, alternative choice which is more appealing to them than the current options out there. The bottom line is that you need to outshine your competitors, to stand out from the crowd and, in order to do so, you need to be better than the rest.

As ex BBC Dragon James Caan told me, 'Observe the masses and do the opposite. Too many people think success lies in either copying somebody else or being inventive, and that is not the case. To me, success lies in doing something different. You don't have to invent the airline, plane and travel. Take Richard Branson or Stelios, they just took something that was already available in the market but made it more efficient and cheaper.

'There are so many successes out there as a result of people doing things differently. You don't have to invent something, because, actually, you are surrounded by products and services that could be made better.'

Even if you are setting up a trade business, which might not be deemed particularly innovative (although in high demand), such as hairdressing, beauty, gardening or household maintenance, you still need to seek out ways that you can stand out from the crowd.

Think about this: what are your competitors currently NOT doing but should be doing? What's missing? What solution can you NOT FIND already out there in a product or service you are looking for? It could be that you offer a special party package for group bookings or wedding parties in your beauty salon or take away garden waste when other gardeners do not. It might be that you run a childminding service that collects children from their home in the morning, rather than the parents having to drop them off.

The answer to these questions gives you a gap in the market to exploit and, by making sure that you DO offer that, gives you a unique selling point – an enticing and compelling point of difference for your target audience which shouts out: 'Come to us, we do this, but others don't; we provide you with an alternative choice and one which is better.'

For example:

- After a trip to the United States, **Thea Green** spotted that, while American nail bars were culturally accessible to all, there were some flaws. Though fast and efficient, they were NOT providing a nice, relaxing environment and were NOT branded with a clear identity. 'I wanted to take some of the ideas from that, some of the learnings, and then give it a much clearer identity,' says Thea. She opened the first Nails Inc. store on South Molton Street in 1999, offering 15-minute manicures and over 100 shades of polish. Thea has since grown the business into a £25-million-turnover company by opening Nails Inc. bars in department stores. The company now has 50 nail bars in the UK and Ireland and employs 400 people.

- The AVENT brand of baby feeding equipment was born in 1984 when **Edward Atkin** and his wife discovered that standard feeding bottles were simply not up to the task of feeding their baby. The teats were hard, long and narrow, and the small neck of the bottle was difficult to fill. Edward created a wide-necked bottle for easier filling and cleaning, with a larger, more stable base. The teat was the first to be made entirely of silicone and was closer to nature as it was soft and broad in shape. The business was built by the husband and wife team and was sold to Charterhouse, a private equity firm, in 2005 for £300 million. Less than a year later it was sold to Philips for £460 million.

- **Lucy Jewson** and her husband, Kurt, set up organic childrenswear brand Frugi during her maternity leave when they couldn't find clothes to fit over their son's washable nappies. Lucy spent 'huge swathes of time' on mums' forums asking questions. 'It became quite clear very quickly that the only option thus far was to swap info on which brands were more roomy than others,' explains Lucy. Given that those using washable nappies do so due to caring about the environment, she launched her range of childrenswear, which was to be made from 100 per cent organic cotton and made in factories that cared for their workers. Her ethical company now turns over millions.

- When **Dessi Bell** couldn't find a fitnesswear product to help her get into shape for her wedding, she decided to make her own. Her light-bulb moment happened while she was on honeymoon and, a few years of research later, she launched Zaggora – with its signature ThermoFit fabric, which 'gives women better results from exercise' by heating up areas of the body during fitness activities.

- **Shelley Barrett**, founder of ModelCo, spotted a gap in the market for innovative, dual-purpose beauty solutions for women on the go after running her own modelling agency for over a decade. 'LASHWAND Heated Eye Lash Curler was created when I thought about how it would enhance make-up artists' lives if they could instantly and easily curl and coat the models' lashes without the damage,' says Shelley. 'I created this in 2002 and literally had suppliers knocking at my door.' That was also the case for ModelCo's airbrush 'tan in a can': as Shelley says, 'It truly changed the way that women self-tanned, delivering professional results with the convenience of an at-home application.'

ANNABEL'S KITCHEN CABINET

THE WHITE OPPORTUNITY: CHRISSIE RUCKER

It all began over 20 years ago when Chrissie Rucker spotted a gap in the market for affordable but beautifully designed, lovely quality white bed linen. She invested her £6,000 savings to establish The White Company as a mail-order business and started with a 12-page brochure from her boyfriend's spare room. Twenty years later The White Company is one of the UK's fastest-growing multi-channel retailers with 53 stores across the UK and a reported turnover in excess of £150 million.

She told me how she spotted the gap in the market that would change her life forever. Her story outlines how a business often comes from dissatisfaction with a product or service. For her there was a duality in her dissatisfaction. She wasn't 100 per cent happy with her job at the time, which drove her to uncover her passion, and she was also dissatisfied with the availability of affordable, quality white wares.

Having recently met her then boyfriend (now husband), Chrissie jokes that she wanted to show him that she was 'excellent wife material!' 'I suggested that I kit the house out: cutlery, napkins, furniture, you name it! I would buy everything in white,' explains Chrissie. And that was when she encountered the problem. 'Buying everything in white was really hard to do as there were two ends of the scale: either the cheap option that came from China, or the extremely expensive designer options in luxury department stores.'

Dissatisfied with both options, she couldn't stop thinking about it, and decided she would set up a company that did everything white but in the middle market – not too cheap and not too expensive. 'I struck gold when I found a supplier who I went to Portugal with. I found that I could buy the same products as the premium market, and sell them at a lower price. I discovered that the major brands were adding huge mark-ups.'

A year later Chrissie won the Midland Bank Small Business Award and gained a much-needed cash injection. And just one year after that, The White Company got its first office, while Chrissie became the youngest ever finalist for the Veuve Clicquot Business Woman Of The Year Awards and The White Company was listed in *The Sunday Times'* 'Fast Track 100 league table'.

Finding a way to differentiate your business from what is already out there has caused many up-and-coming entrepreneurs to think outside the box and disrupt entire markets by giving existing business models a new twist. From Nakedwines.com (which enables customers to select their favourite wines from independent winemakers, who pitch directly to them) to online furniture retailer Made.com (see box below), these 'me-tailers' have found innovative ways to save their customers money by connecting them directly with makers and cutting out the middleman.

ANNABEL'S KITCHEN CABINET

INNOVATION AND OPPORTUNISM: CHLOE MACINTOSH

Made.com has grown from four to over 160 employees in four years, and gone from being an unknown start-up to a genuine player in the UK's home furniture and fittings market. It has done so by taking the middleman out of the equation by connecting those shopping for furniture directly with the makers and designers.

Co-founder and creative director Chloe Macintosh puts the success of Made.com down to a mixture of innovation and opportunism. The company has gone against the grain by turning the existing business model (of buying furniture from a shop, either flat-packed at the bottom end of the market or incredibly expensive at the top end) on its head and is achieving its aim of bringing original design to the masses by revolutionising the furniture retail market.

Made.com collaborates with designers and manufacturers to create original products not available elsewhere. It creates one sample of a product, photographs and uploads it to the website, and then orders are grouped weekly and only what is ordered is made. If the product isn't doing particularly well, Made.com will remove the product from the site and move on to the next. This approach also reduces risk and enables Made.com to release two new collections per week, compared to the industry standard of two seasonal launches per year. This approach to selling furniture means there is no unsold stock or waste. And, with no inventory or vast warehouse storage, no sales staff or wholesalers, these savings are passed directly back to its customers.

Chloe Macintosh found a gap in the post-recession furniture market for affordable yet valuable furniture and decided to look into it. 'If you didn't want to spend a lot of money, there wasn't a lot of choice in terms of what you put in your home,' explains Chloe. 'Apart from IKEA, there didn't seem to be a lot of alternatives.

'We started to look into an idea which was emerging in France, making products direct with the factory, cutting out everything in between, which meant that costs were minimal as there was no stock,' explains Chloe. 'It was a very clever business model already successfully being used overseas.'

With Brent, Chloe met up with the French founders of this business, and they all came up with the idea of Made.com, and suggested introducing it in the UK. Chloe and her co-founders then set about creating this alternative which gave the consumer the chance to buy high-quality, original furniture at affordable prices, up to 70 per cent off high-street prices.

And therein lies the key to successful exploitation of a gap in the market: providing a worthwhile alternative with plenty of benefits to the customer. Chloe and her team have streamlined a costly and complex process and made great design accessible to all – simply by looking into what *wasn't* being offered, then seeking to be different to and better value than existing alternatives.

FINDING A BETTER IDEA OF YOUR OWN

So now you've read some inspiring but practical examples of successful 'better ideas', it's your turn.

Examine the marketplace you intend to enter into by answering these questions:

1. What isn't being offered?

_____

_____

_____

2. How can you harness your skills, knowledge, experience, passion and contacts to provide an alternative solution?

_____

_____

_____

3. What can you offer people that is better, faster, safer and/or edgier than the rest?

_____

_____

_____

4. What dissatisfies you with existing options? Is it likely that others might be dissatisfied too?

_____

_____

_____

DISSATISFACTION BREEDS OPPORTUNITY

As we've seen, some of the best business ideas stem from dissatisfaction with what's already out there – dissatisfaction with existing alternatives.

For me, existing recipe books for children did not contain tasty, healthy food. My son Nicholas just wouldn't eat the food from these cookbooks. At the time, everyone was saying that babies only liked bland food, but I knew that babies had far more adventurous palates than they were given credit for. So, I decided to write my own book of recipes that was tested by the fiercest panel of food critics: babies and fussy toddlers themselves.

As a start-up, you don't have a track record to shout about, so being better is your route to attracting a customer base. So what can YOU do that is safer, faster, easier, more premium or better value for money than the rest? Can you offer something that is more comfortable, or higher quality and generally better than what already exists? How can you satisfy customers where others cannot? This will be your unique selling point and your competitive advantage.

ANNABEL'S KITCHEN CABINET

A FRESH APPROACH TO FASHION: MYLEENE KLASS

Myleene Klass knows only too well the importance of having a point of difference. Operating her Baby K brand for Mothercare and her own brand for Littlewoods in the excruciatingly competitive fashion industry, being better is often the only way to get ahead – and that takes a lot of hard work, a very firm grasp of precisely who your customer is and what they want, plus a sheer focus on your differentiating factors.

Before embarking on a fashion design career, Myleene had worked in the music, modelling and TV industries. It was when she was working as a presenter for *CD:UK* that she came up with her idea for her Baby K clothing range.

Myleene was shopping for baby clothes with fellow presenter Lauren Laverne, and commented on the lack of edgy girls' clothes which fell in the middle of the price range. She explains: 'I said to Lauren, "I just can't get over these clothes, I don't want to dress my baby like a Victoriana doll. The cheaper clothes feel like they're not going to last two seconds, and the more expensive clothes, I can't justify spending that amount of money on a few pieces of fabric.'''

Lauren suggested that she made her own and they laughed about it. However, Myleene later told her manager about this and he echoed what Lauren had said, suggesting that they go and make some. Myleene wasn't so sure, but he reminded her that if she couldn't find what she wanted, there must be a gap in the market. So the pair set off and spoke to various stores and brands.

Her vision was going against the grain and everybody told her not to do it. 'I wanted to make little black dresses for little babies, so I was going the other way to existing options.' At first nobody seemed to believe in her idea and some of the retailers she pitched to simply didn't get it, claiming it to be gothic or morose. 'The idea was just not going anywhere until I went to Mothercare,' Myleene says.

When she pitched to Mothercare, her clear vision and grasp of her market enabled her to engage clearly with the buyer. She brought in lots of different adult-size dresses and said, 'This is big, because I would wear this, but imagine this in small but in this shape.' She did some sketches as she talked to the buyers and they totally understood her bold vision. Mothercare were in.

The black dresses led to black changing bags and black strollers and set Myleene's Baby K brand apart from everything else out there. 'They couldn't make the black changing bags quick enough,' says Myleene. 'And then we made black strollers with leopard print inside them and the range has grown. It's not just for babies now.'

And Myleene isn't letting the grass grow under her feet. She has now launched her own women's brand for Littlewoods and works hard to ensure that both of her brands continue to stand out in the market. 'I'll go to each country, I'll have a look at what they've got, what they're buying,' says Myleene. 'You need to know what everyone else is up to otherwise it becomes insular. You could be repeating what someone else is doing.

'It's highly competitive,' nods Myleene. 'I'm not saying you need to have the biggest point of difference. But, if you are doing something that someone else is doing, do it better.'

Finding the gap in a niche market and filling it has certainly worked, as Baby K is now in its seventh year, thirteenth season and in 37 countries, while Myleene's Littlewoods brand goes from strength to strength and has expanded from clothing into beauty and shoes.

MYLEENE'S TOP TIPS FOR FINDING A POINT OF DIFFERENCE

- **Go against the grain.** 'I said let's go black, let's go monochrome, let's make clothes that don't look like Victoriana dolls, which aren't beige. And let's try animal print, which is really fun. For me I felt the existing choices if you were having a baby were: pink, blue or insipid yellow,' says Myleene.

- **Identify your niche and gain a deep understanding of precisely what they want.** Myleene has a very clear picture of her Littlewoods market: 'They're working mums who go out straight from the office and want to feel good and be noticed,' she says. We'll explore further how you can find out what your customers want in Chapter 5.

- **Do your best to give your customers what they want.** 'I won't make some kind of wallflower dress,' says Myleene. 'They are bold dresses and they help women to feel good.'

STANDING OUT IN THE MARKETPLACE

Whether you go against the grain and do something completely different or do the same as everyone else but do it better, you need something that will make you stand out, so that you can communicate that difference to your customers and gain a competitive advantage.

Of course, you may not have any competition yet. You may just have something truly unique that you are pioneering as the first to market. In that case you must consider how you can sustain that competitive advantage. Because you won't be the only one in the market for long. Great ideas get copied, quickly. The trick is to let that competition drive you to be consistently at the forefront.

'Don't get bogged down with copycats as it can almost become an obsession,' advises Ann Summers CEO Jacqueline Gold. 'You have to focus on being the best that you can be. Have a clear point of difference and continue to be the best you can be. There is always going to be competition. Innovate, don't imitate; you want to be first to market with everything that is unique about your business.'

As you start to grow your business, competition can really get to you. It's not just the threat of other companies taking the customers you've worked so hard to attract and retain, it's how they can make you feel. It's important not to let the competition get you down, even if they win customers from you with dodgy tactics (as can happen). If you are the best you can be and keep delivering your promises with integrity, you have nothing to fear.

And, if you can be the best within a highly targeted specific niche market, so much the better.

ZOOM IN: FIND A NICE NICHE WITHIN A SIZEABLE MARKET

Uncovering a niche where there's a gap in the market is one of the best ways forward when starting up. Had I chosen to write a book of adult recipes I very much doubt I would have carved out the successful career I have today. Instead, my niche market is parents of children who either have fussy eaters or simply want to ensure that their children eat healthy, nutritionally balanced meals from the outset. My absolute target audience when I started my career was mums of babies and toddlers, as I knew that they were the ones struggling for good food ideas that their little ones would actually eat and enjoy.

While it has been good to have a niche, once you have built a reputation you can branch into other areas. Because I held mums' hands from the beginning, I've ended up supporting them at every stage – from pregnancy to family food. I recently brought out my first cookery book aimed at adults and families, *Annabel's Family Cookbook*, as many people were telling me that they were cooking for dinner parties with recipes from *The Complete Baby and Toddler Meal Planner*! Had I written this as my first book, I doubt it would have sold so well. Thankfully, as I've built up a reputation within my niche market – and mums love my recipes and want to cook for themselves – the book became an instant bestseller.

Many people starting up in business wonder whether they should aim to appeal to the masses or find a niche. Mass-market operations have far less chance of standing out, whereas focusing on a small section of a marketplace helps you to connect and engage with that specific section. Even businesses selling products or services with mass-market appeal often segment them down into niche sections. The Internet helps with this as you can segment your products into various niche markets within your website and devote specific pages (and marketing campaigns) to those particular niches. For example, if you are selling shoes, it's going to be easier to market your products if you focus on one or two related niche markets, such as walking shoes and/or fitness shoes, rather than all shoes, or at least segment your products into those groups on your website.

Of course, your niche shouldn't be too wide or too narrow. You need to ensure that you target a market which has sufficient customers within it for you to generate enough revenue in order to thrive. So, while you should seek out a gap in the market where there is unmet demand, you should also ensure that there is a market in that gap. That means you'll need to do your homework – we shall cover the research and testing processes in chapters 4 and 5.

It's also handy if your idea slots within a niche market that is growing rather than static or in decline. Growth sectors give you potential from which to piggyback off, whereas you might have the best idea since sliced bread but if it's in a sector that is declining you'll be hard pushed to make it work. The same idea in a growth sector, though, and you're likely to see explosive success. Find out in Chapter 4 how to seek out growth industries (see page 101).

The Internet has greatly helped businesses targeting specific niches as it makes the reach of each niche far wider. For instance, if you have quite a small niche, such as selling left-handed products, you may find that within your local vicinity there are only a handful of people who are left-handed and fit into that niche market. However, the Internet opens the opportunity up to the entire world of left-handers, widening your potential customer base and reach.

That's certainly been the case for Wendy Shand, whose Internet operation Totstotravel.co.uk has thousands of customers.

Wendy realised that there was a massive gap in the market for genuine family-friendly holiday accommodation in 2005, when her then two-year-old fell into an unenclosed swimming pool while on holiday in France. In 2007 she launched Totstotravel.co.uk with nine family-friendly villas and cottages in France, which she had personally visited and vetted to ensure quality control, child safety and the provision of all the kit that families with small children need. Seven years later and Wendy has built her team and business into a multi-award-winning brand and leader in the competitive family travel market.

She advises: 'Find and carve out a decent-sized niche within the market you operate in and seek to really understand the pains that these people have and how you can fix them. The opportunities are within the niche markets and, when you look carefully, you'll see that there are plenty of untapped opportunities.'

Operating within a targeted niche market enables you to:

- **Stand out quickly from what's already out there** by demonstrating your understanding of your market's requirements and tailor your offering to suit them, and only them. You can drill down to solving specific problems for a certain set of people. It makes it easier to communicate why people should choose you over the competition.

- **Connect and engage with your potential customers** by pressing the right emotional buttons. Tell them your story, and your business's purpose, which will strike a chord with their own lives. Compel them to take the desired action. This specialist approach creates a better match between you and your market than your competitors and makes conversion from prospect into customer far more likely.

- **Be more noticeable;** you can send marketing messages directly to where your target audience will see them. With a clearly defined target market, you can source publications and websites that they read and visit, you can hone your unique selling point to appeal to them specifically.

- **Be more memorable** (and thus referable), as you specialise in, for example, working with mums or women that want to diet rather than all and sundry.

- **Gain credibility faster** by specialising in a specific area rather than being all things to all people.

- **Be better able to form strategic alliances** with complementary but not competing products or service providers as a result of clarity around your target market.

- **Embrace your nimble and agile nature of being small** so that you can give people what they want faster.

Committing to a niche and carving out your own place within it equips you with clarity (around your offering, your marketing messages, your audience and what problems they have that you can solve) and therefore empowers you to sell more and become known as a specialist provider. It can also de-risk your business, as Caroline Castigliano explains.

ANNABEL'S KITCHEN CABINET

A BRIDE IDEA? CAROLINE CASTIGLIANO

After opening her first bridal boutique in 1991, Caroline Castigliano has been at the forefront of the British bridal industry for 23 years. She continues to run her flagship store in Knightsbridge, offering elegant bespoke wedding dresses, and has 50 exclusive stockists nationwide. Having already run her own business, Survival Kit, in the States – which took advantage of the 1980s aerobics craze, selling sportswear and dumb-bells – she wanted to use her design skills but within a niche, and strive to be better than the rest. And so she did.

'I was trying to find something that I thought was really niche,' explains Caroline of her decision to choose wedding dresses in particular. 'I just think fashion as a whole is a huge risk, because, if you don't actually sell your stock you are left with it, which can bankrupt you very quickly,' she adds. 'In fashion, trends change quite radically, so you just can't sell unsold stock next season like you can with other businesses.'

Caroline wanted to use her talents and combine all that she had learnt about marketing and selling from running her business in the States to create a lower-risk business. 'I wanted to be in something I felt was slightly safer. Obviously doing wedding dresses is wonderful, as your customers are women preparing for the most important day of their lives,' says Caroline. 'It's about dreams and aspirations, but you're not in that same risk factor. If you don't sell out those dresses in that year, you are able to sell them the next year.'

Caroline advises that finding a niche is critical. 'It de-risks you,' she says. 'If you don't find a niche, and choose a mass market instead, your investment becomes quite big, in which case you have got to get the right people in and get orders up front. The market may be larger, but the window of opportunity to buy and sell will be smaller.'

CAROLINE'S TOP TIPS FOR NICHE BUSINESSES

- **Go niche and source niche manufacturers.** 'If I was starting again in the fashion industry now, I would try to find a niche sector. And find out where the manufacturers for luxury items are operating and where they are doing smaller volumes, such as here in the UK, Portugal and Italy,' advises Caroline.

- **Stick to your niche.** 'If you are a high-quality premium brand offering luxury products, market yourself to people who are willing to pay extra for quality and service; don't try and broaden it out to reach another target market. The minute you try to broaden it out, everything comes into a price war and you have lost straight away.'

- **Focus on whatever it is that makes you different.** 'For example, we are using luxury fabrics and it is all hand-cut for every individual person, beautifully finished and all made in the UK. Those are our prime selling points.'

- **Avoid sale-or-return distribution options.** 'Avoid giving your products to stores on a sale-or-return basis, the owner of the store needs to invest in you and your business, and really believe in your product that they are going to be selling. If they have invested into your product it means they believe in it and will have the passion to sell it. Whereas, if they are taking stock merely on a sale-or-return basis, you can be absolutely certain that they are dealing with other companies way bigger than yours who put pressure on them to take stock and sell it. So they will focus on selling those first.'

04

DO YOU HOMEW AND MA A PLAN

❝❞

**I BELIEVE IN INNOVATION
AND THAT THE WAY YOU
GET INNOVATION IS
YOU FUND RESEARCH AND
YOU LEARN THE BASIC FACTS.**

Bill Gates

MARKET RESEARCH AND COMPETITIVE INTELLIGENCE

If you want to create a business that is different, innovative and better than existing alternatives out there – a business which gains and retains competitive advantage offering a continuous point of difference – you need to do your homework. You need to research the market, not just prior to start-up but consistently throughout. Because game-changers, new businesses and shrewd competitors will constantly enter the market and try to get ahead of the game. That's business.

Trends shift and markets change direction, so you are going to need to know about all of this in order to maintain your position and/or market share. Fundamentally, you are only as good as your current knowledge of the marketplace, so you need to be on the ball.

Research is necessary because knowledge is power. Knowledge widens the opportunity. Research informs you about stuff you didn't know – important stuff, such as who the current market leader is, what share of the market they have and what strategy they are implementing to make them so successful. Research will also tell you who the current best performers are and why so. What is their selling model? How often are people buying their product? Research equips you with knowledge about which methods people are using to sell their wares: online? Mail order? High-street stores? Below, I outline the information you should gather and the questions you should get answers for. The point is, if you want to stay one step ahead of the competition and build a successful business, you need to keep your fingers on the pulse of the industry you are entering into.

Ultimately, you can't take the plunge without having the knowledge to support your idea, to estimate sales and, essentially, to assess viability and decide how likely your idea is to actually work. You also need to do your homework before you can populate your business plan with data. You've got to prove the concept works first before you can raise money, or risk not making any.

Your search for knowledge, and thus power, should start with allocating a large chunk of time to digging out facts and figures via a range of sources. For example, if you are launching a business targeting left-handed people, you might uncover that a specific percentage of the UK population are left-handed via a report by a relevant association. Or if you are launching a new piece of camping equipment, you'll need to understand how much Britons spend on camping equipment each year, and you could do this via a camping-industry trade publication.

'Don't just read what's online as there is so much poorly researched information on the web,' advises Liz Earle. 'Reading reputable peer-reviewed factual journals [i.e. those checked by a group of experts in the same field] is a good starting point; otherwise you may be building something on the wrong premise.

'I spent months in the British Library and toured the UK (and USA) talking to academics and leading researchers to really get to the heart of what's important when creating brilliant beauty products,' adds Liz. 'Most academics and researchers are passionate about their specialist subject and welcome the opportunity to talk to interested parties. I don't believe you can do your research properly by sitting behind a desk – I'm afraid it requires a lot more hard graft and effort than that.'

As such, your first task should be to create a list of research sources based on the list below. For example, if you are setting up a new nursery, you should: read nursery-sector media such as *Nursery Today*; visit nurseries to gather information about what is and what isn't available; speak to groups of mums about their nurseries; set up Google news alerts on the 'childcare industry'; and so on.

Next you should create a list of questions. You'll need to gather as much information as you can on the industry sector in which you'll operate, the customers' (target audience's) needs and the competition.

“”

RESEARCH IS FORMALIZED CURIOSITY. IT IS POKING AND PRYING WITH A PURPOSE.

Zora Neale Hurston

RESEARCH SOURCES LIST

- The Internet – type in search terms you'd use to find your own company to find competitors and jot down their web addresses.

- Facebook advert tool. You can use this not only to create an advert but also to gather data and figure out the size of your potential niche target audience on Facebook. For example, if I select women in the UK aged between 25 and 47, who are small-business owners, parents and not connected to my Facebook business page, I have a target audience of 1.28 million. However, if I drill right down to find a niche – such as those who are parents of children aged 0–12 years, are 32–45 years old and have specified an interest in networking, social media, Twitter, self-employed, Internet marketing, etc. … I can discover I have a target audience of just 16 to 40 people.

- Facebook groups.

- Twitter.

- Online forums.

- Office for National Statistics.

- Focus groups (once you have something to show them).

- The Yellow Pages.

- Chamber of Commerce's business directories.

- White papers, government reports and specialist market research on the industry (see Mintel, Euromonitor, Kompass, Business Monitor or iQuest).

- Online research tools such as www.freepint.com.

- Media kits from magazines.

- Trade publications.

- Trade associations and networking groups.

- Trade shows and conferences.

- The library.

- Online directories.

- Google news alerts – search Google News for news stories about your competitors and, even better, set up news alerts for competing companies or industry information. For example, if you set up an alert for 'childcare industry' or 'widgets international', you'll receive an alert via email every time that search term is found on the web or in the news online: www.google.com/alerts.

- Google Analytics searches. You can use Google Analytics to discover the statistics on how many people are searching for particular keywords and phrases. This is very helpful for gauging the interest in a particular niche: www.google.com/analytics.

- Google Scholar – this allows you to search for relevant work in academic literature and research: http://scholar.google.co.uk.

- Competitor websites and brochures.

- Online interviews with your competitors or case studies of their companies online.

- Companies House – you can review your competitors' profitability by downloading their accounts.

- News stories and headlines in online and printed newspapers, national and local.

- The *FT* or financial pages in your daily newspaper to see which markets appear frequently.

- Becoming a customer of your competitor using a different email address.

- Pretending to be a mystery shopper.

- Industry experts.

- Suppliers. Ask them: what are their bestselling items, minimum orders and available credit terms? Delivery payment terms? What changes or trends are they noticing within the industry? What are the wholesale and retail prices for their supplies? What can they tell you about the market in terms of demand? Is it rising or falling?

The ways you can use social media (including your own Facebook profile and business page, relevant Facebook groups and Twitter) are many. Using social media, you can search for your competitors and like/follow them (although remember that people will be able to see if you 'like' a page) to stay up to date on what they are promoting and pushing out via social media.

You can also set up free surveys via social media and ask friends and group members to take part via a simple link. They can share this too. Try using survey tools such as surveymonkey.com or wufoo.com to create surveys quickly and easily. You can also participate in online forums where your target audience gather, or become a customer of your competitor, plus gather additional data via the resources listed above.

Think of yourself as a detective; you want to dig up as much insight on your competitors as possible and use it to your advantage.

RESEARCH QUESTIONS TO ASK

In order to assess the market, the viability of your business idea and get to grips with what your target audience wants and needs, you should split your research questions into three categories:

01. General industry/market.

02. Competition.

03. Customers.

Here is a list of questions you may wish to find answers to in order to bolster your knowledge of these areas and equip your business effectively.

General industry/market research

01. What issues are currently facing your industry? What are the timely topics being reported in the news, featured in industry publications and discussed on relevant forums?

02. Are sales seasonal or affected by any other variables?

03. What costs are involved in the set-up and running of the business? Phone utility companies to get examples of costs for similar operations. Tot up postage costs, web build costs and so on.

04. What is the gross profit and gross-profit margin on items such as yours? (See the box below for an explanation of these terms.) To work out your own gross profit, you'll need to do some digging regarding costs by speaking to suppliers and working out how much your goods and services will cost to make and what your estimated total revenue will be. However, as these figures will be estimations based on how much revenue you think you'll earn, you could find out what the total revenue and gross profit of your competitors are by downloading your competitors' accounts from Companies House. You can also find out average gross-profit margins (percentages of gross profit) in industry white papers and by speaking to industry experts and researching online for 'average industry gross-profit margins'. You need to know total revenue – either of your competitors, if assessing their gross profit, or your estimated revenue, if trying to figure out your own. Once you've estimated your gross profit, you can then calculate an estimated gross-profit margin.

Gross profit is the amount of money you have left from selling your goods or service after you have paid the costs of making your goods or service (including costs of raw materials, labour, factory overheads and so on). Once you have subtracted the cost of goods and services from the total revenue you'll get a gross profit figure. You use your gross profit to pay your fixed outgoings, such as rent and utilities, which then leaves you with a net profit (or loss) figure.

> **Gross-profit margin** is the profit you make for each product sold. To work out this, you divide the gross profit figure by the total revenue. E.g. if gross profit = £45,000 and total revenue = £100,000, 45,000 divided by 100,000 = 0.45. As a percentage this is 45 per cent, so for each product sold you make 45 per cent of the cost as profit (your gross-profit margin).

05. Is certification or insurance required? If you are working from home, you may require a separate business insurance policy; some industries require public liability insurance, which you may also need if you sell goods by taking a stall at local fetes.

06. Are there any news stories about the industry and anything that might be affecting it now or in the future. Technology? Climate? Recycling? Social responsibility? Society? Government? Are government cuts to certain industries (such as children's subsidised activities) leading to more alternatives? Is healthy eating getting a lot of press? Is child safety becoming more of an issue?

07. Overseas – what's happening in US markets? This is worth knowing because commercial trends which start in the States often make their way to the UK.

08. Compare this year's statistical market data to previous years. Is the market growing or static? Is demand sufficient? The Office for National Statistics will be a good starting point here.

Competitor intelligence

By understanding what is already out there, you can determine windows of opportunity and turn competitors' weaknesses into your own strengths. Knowing your competitors bolsters your position in the marketplace.

- Who already exists in the marketplace? Who are the main players?

- Who are the main suppliers?

- Who do your potential customers currently buy similar products in the same category from and why?

- What are they offering?

- What is their USP? What makes them different?

- What are their strengths?

- What are their weaknesses? Are they overcharging and under-delivering in any way? Have they become inefficient with their deliveries or customer service?

- How might you turn those weaknesses into your strengths? (Therein lies the opportunity.)

- What could encourage your customers to switch to buying from you?

- What is selling best (and worst)?

- Through which channels are these products and services sold? For example, do they sell via an eBay shop and through their own online web store or do they have their own retail outlet or distributors who sell their goods on their behalf? Perhaps they sell via the party-plan model via a network of hosts or via a direct-mail catalogue?

- Is there a gap in the distribution chain that you could fill? (E.g. think Thea Green's nail bars in department stores – nail bars existed, but not in department stores.)

- What are your competitors' pricing models? How much are people paying for similar items?

- What are their payment and delivery terms?

- Are certain items not in stock? If not why not?

- Do they get many returns? You can find this kind of information out by asking people in store under the guise of posing as a mystery shopper, someone from HQ or a journalist.

- What is the packaging like on bestselling products? For example, what colours are used and how is the price displayed?

- How many products are you likely to be able to sell per day? (Ask suppliers/competitors.)

- If you are launching your own shop or retail space, what is the décor like in the most successful stores? (E.g. Sahar Hashemi and her brother Bobby noticed sales went up in Coffee Republic when they painted their stark white walls a warm caramel colour and changed their high-class design to a more inviting décor to entice regular people to enjoy luxury coffee.)

- How many items do they keep in stock? (Pretend to be a mystery shopper to see which products are given the most floor space; ask staff about any changes they've noticed in what's selling best and how often products are purchased.)

Customers

Before you start to dig deep for information pertaining to your target audience, you need to have a precise idea of who they actually are. The best way to do this is to create a customer profile based on your competitors' customers and/or on your perceived ideal customer. Trying to be all things to everyone doesn't usually work, as we explored in Chapter 3. Spreading your offerings too thinly waters down and dilutes what makes you unique and interesting. So create a profile for an ideal customer within that niche. Consider:

01. Who are your niche audiences? For example, commuters, mums with fussy eaters, time-starved businesswomen, students, tourists, office workers, law firms, dog owners, farmers, villagers, city dwellers, writers, brides-to-be. Even if you are marketing to a business, you will still sell to a person within that business, so create a profile for them. Are they male or female? What's their job description? How old are they? What are they motivated by? What challenges are they facing?

02. What common characteristics, demographic and psychographic information do your niche audience share? Demographics is statistical information such as age, gender, ethnicity, location, occupation and family status. Psychographics are characteristics such as behaviour, values, personality, lifestyle, hobbies, aspirations, buying style and habits. E.g. do they prefer to buy online and enquire via email, or in person and enquire over the phone? Are they impulse buyers or practical buyers? Are they bargain hunters or is quality more important to them?

03. What are their problems, what do they desire and what do they aspire to be/do/have? Drill the profile down deeper and be as specific as you possibly can. Think of the one person that you want to reach: a representative of your niche market. Consider what they are thinking and feeling, what they are doing and where they are going. What are they 'liking' on Facebook and who they might be following on Twitter (that's if they are social networking at all)? What is your customer most concerned about? What keeps them up at night? It could be that there never seems to be enough time in the day to do everything? That they want to lose weight? Find a better job? Become a better cook, parent, friend? This will help you to define their values and what matters most to them: friendship and family or career and success? Saving money or saving time?

Create a character and give your ideal customer a backstory. For instance, Miriam is struggling because her toddlers are misbehaving and she has no support as her husband is at work. She needs to find an activity which will engage, encourage and reward her children. She needs some order in her hectic life. She ends up having lots of play dates here and there but that's the only time she gets out of the house. She wants to get out more. She needs a community of like-minded people. So, if you are offering a music class for pre-school children, which has its own private Facebook group and organises engaging activities for children, Miriam is an ideal customer. Especially if your business goes the extra mile and provides an evening group for mums of toddlers to get together *without* their kids. By understanding Miriam and the problems she faces, you could win Miriam as a client by speaking directly to her and giving her the solutions to those problems. You could then set about finding others just like her.

By creating a profile it is easier to research where Miriam might go for information and find like-minded people who fit her profile to speak to/survey/find data about. Furthermore, when it comes to marketing, speaking directly to that individual person and understanding their specific needs is a powerful way to communicate and persuade people to choose to do business with you.

Now consider the wider questions to gain knowledge about your customers – questions around the size of your niche market: where they go to find information about products and services such as yours; where they hang out, online and offline; and what their buying habits are.

01. What is the market size? How big is the market?

02. How many potential customers are there within this category that you can serve? (E.g. mums of toddlers aged between one and four years old.)

03. Who are the key influencers of this target market?

04. What publications do these people read? Which websites do they visit regularly? Which social media do they use? How frequently? These are the places you can make your presence felt to reach those who fit your customer profiles. Create a media file listing all relevant websites and publications that you should send press releases and company news to once you are up and running. You will find plenty while you undertake your research. Copy and paste the web and email address for each website into your document.

05. What do customers like and dislike about existing offerings?

06. How much would people be prepared to pay for your product or service? (You can find this out once your product or service prototype is ready to test in a live environment with focus groups, which we'll cover in the next chapter.)

07. How much could you reasonably charge for your product/service, bearing in mind what it costs you to produce or source it, and taking your time, personal service and added value into account? Don't forget to cost in equipment needed, shipping, marketing, Internet and other utilities, wastage, time and an hourly wage.

08. How many would you need to sell each day/week/month in order to generate a profit?

09. Consequently, based on those sums, is this a viable business model? If not, what would need to happen to make it so? (I.e. sell more? Increase price? Decrease costs?)

10. How often do people buy goods such as yours (monthly, weekly, annually, once, as an impulse buy, as a gift)?

11. Do they tend to buy intuitively? Emotively? Technically, based on practical needs?

12. What is the likely footfall of custom in that area (if you are opening a shop)? You can ask other shops nearby but also get a clicker from a stationery store and literally click each time someone walks past your potential location during rush hour to get figures.

13. What exactly do your core customers want? Drill down the precise details. What benefits are they seeking? Do they want to save time and need convenience? Or do they want quality above all else? Do they want more freedom? More privacy? Better productivity? Peace of mind? Are they most concerned about saving money? Making their life easier? Ask customers (during a focus group session or by sending a link to an online survey) to prioritise these benefits in order of importance. (More on that in the next chapter.)

It's essential to find out what customers want. For example do they want quick and easy instant coffee or do they want top-quality gourmet coffee? Martyn Dawes, founder of self-serve coffee brand Coffee Nation, didn't do much research at first. However, he boosted sales by researching the market after his instant coffee machines failed to draw in customers. He conducted some research and realised that customers wanted quality gourmet coffee, not instant. This change, based on customer needs, led him to build a £10 million business.

WHEN IT IS OBVIOUS THAT THE GOALS CANNOT BE REACHED, DON'T ADJUST THE GOALS, ADJUST THE ACTION STEPS.

Confucius

All of this research enables you to a) perfect your product or service so that it is tailored to your ideal customer, and b) focus your marketing messages and distribution of those messages to the right person in the right place at the right time, which is essentially what marketing is all about. Find out more about attracting customers through marketing methods in Chapter 6.

ANNABEL'S KITCHEN CABINET

RESEARCHING THE MARKET: WENDY SHAND

Having spotted a gap in the market for safe places for parents to take their toddlers on holiday, Wendy Shand conducted a significant amount of research before launching her business, Totstotravel.co.uk.

'Knowing how tough it is to start a business, even eight years in, it is really important that you do not enter something without having thought it through properly,' advises Wendy. She joined an online course in enterprise and started developing the idea. 'I did do quite a bit of research, including finding out the size of the market, the scale of the opportunity, looking at competitors, compiling a balance sheet and interviewing potential clients.' Wendy spent a whole year of the course doing research, but after that point realised that she needed to get on with her business idea: 'I did just over a year of that course before I realised that, really, I just had to crack on!'

Her company operates within a two-sided marketplace, so has customers on both sides: 'Hosts (or owners of the properties) and families who trust us with their precious holiday.' When setting up the business, this meant that Wendy had to find people to test the concept from both sides. 'It's a bit like balancing a see-saw,' Wendy explains.

'I did quite a bit of research into whether there was actually demand for hosts to cater for the family market, and in particular for families with pre-school children. My hypothesis was that property owners struggled to fill up their empty weeks outside of peak season and that, if we niche-marketed our concept to families with toddlers, there would be a natural synergy.

'Thankfully the research backed up my hypothesis; owners got the concept straight away and requested my help to make their properties uber-suitable for families like mine. We were off!'

Wendy still continues to research the market to ensure the success of her business. 'Nowadays I look at search volumes as well as competitor intelligence (i.e. how many people arriving on the website are using specific search terms), and the Internet is a fabulous tool for ongoing research to stay ahead of the game.'

CHOOSE THE RIGHT BUSINESS MODEL, STATUS AND LOCATION

Once you've examined the market, industry, competition and target audience, you need to make some decisions about your business. What will your business model be? Where will you run your business from? And what status will your business take – i.e. will you be a sole trader (e.g. Joanne Bloggs trading as Bloggs Copywriters) or an actual limited company (e.g. Bloggs Copywriters Ltd)?

CHOOSING YOUR BUSINESS MODEL

It is important to consider what revenue streams you will put in place. For example, will you charge people a membership fee to sign up to your service? Or will you sell direct to consumers and have an additional revenue stream by hiring affiliates to sell your wares in exchange for commission? What revenue streams do other companies in this sector have in place? In today's business landscape there are many different and new business models emerging. It's no longer just a case of operating a traditional retail model (selling stuff for more than it cost you to make/ source) or traditional services model (selling services to consumers or businesses and charging a flat one-off fee, a monthly retainer fee or regular membership fee).

Here's a list of popular business models, which should give you some food for thought:

- **Me-tail model:** Today you can put the customers in control, just as Made.com has done with their people-powered business model which gives customers the right to decide what the company is selling by voting and, in return for passing on savings and giving them a say, the customers give support by paying upfront for those items. This model has been named 'me-tail'.

- **Freemium model:** Freemium is another business model which means you provide a free version of your product/service and sell a premium version, or offer a free service to generate a large number of users and then sell other services to business customers. For example, Google offers free search, email and so on, and makes its revenue through advertising and selling services to enterprise customers. Various new media companies take this approach, offering free services to generate a large following before monetising the business.

- **Retail model:** With the retail or e-tail (online selling) model you don't just need to sell physical products, you can also sell digital and virtual goods and downloads, from games and apps to information products and expertise. You can sell your products via third-party sites, such as eBay, Etsy.com or Folksy.com, which is a good way to test the market without the cost of setting up your own website.

- **Revenue-share model:** You can choose an eBay-style model by setting up a marketplace and taking a commission from each sale. Or you can share revenue with a third party from whom you gain some sort of benefit, such as exposure to a large number of people. That's how daily deal sites, such as Groupon, work. The merchants selling deals on those sites share revenue with them. You could become a merchant or a marketplace.

- **Subscription model:** You sell a subscription to a product, content or services, whether that's news, information, membership and so on. Magazines operate a subscription model, as do membership networks where you pay a monthly fee to be a member and get various benefits as a result, such as useful content, entry to regular networking meet-ups, free advertising within a monthly members' newsletter and so on.

- **Advertising model:** You sell advertising space/sponsorship. Again, magazines often do this. Some give the magazine away for free and make their revenue through selling advertising/sponsorship. Websites targeting clearly defined niche audiences also choose this model as they can offer highly targeted advertising to companies who want to get their brands and messages in front of that audience. So, if you are running a dog-training business with a targeted audience of dog owners, once you've attracted a reasonable number of visitors to your website, you could sell advertising space on that website to companies who share that audience, such as kennels, dog-walking services, people selling dog beds, dog coats and so on.

- **Licensing model:** You can license your products to create extra revenue, which allows others to sell your product, service or software under their own brand name. They just buy the licence from you, which gives them the right to use your material for their own purposes and repackage your stuff for resale. For example, you might write a booklet on how to eat healthily and license the content to a large grocery chain or juicing company. They could reproduce the booklet with their logo on it and give it away or sell it to customers as a marketing tool to raise brand awareness and gain credibility.

- **Franchise model:** If you create a successful business which can be duplicated, you can establish your own franchise and enable other people to buy the franchise in their region and run that business themselves. It's still your brand, and via training and resources will still be run your way, but they will pay you a fee to buy the franchise and, in some cases, ongoing monthly license fees and/or a share of the profits.

You'll need to provide clear user manuals and have clear processes to give to franchisees, as they'll need to run their franchise effectively in line with the vision of the original. Alternatively, you may become a franchisee yourself. So you buy a franchise and operate a business which has already been proven.

It often makes sense to franchise your business as it grows. I was recently told that Domino's Pizza operated a franchise model, but decided to keep back 100 shops to own and run themselves. In fact, these ended up being the worst-performing stores. They did not compare in terms of service and turnover to the franchised shops, as franchisees put all of their passion into owning and running a successful business.

You don't need to choose just one model; you might choose multiple models. Those operating a subscription model with high numbers of targeted website visitors, for example, might opt to combine this with an advertising model. They might also end up licensing their content to third parties or collaborating on a revenue-share model. If the business is scalable and can be replicated regionally, they may then opt for a franchise model.

Consider the bigger picture and how you might upsell related items to your customers. For example, if you sold web-design services, you might be able to upsell web-hosting services and collaborate with a copywriter on a revenue-share deal to offer a web-page copywriting service as part of a package. Or, if you provide cookery lessons, you could consider upselling cooking utensils and a healthy eating e-book. If you are selling courses or workshops on a specific subject you could sell video products explaining to others how they can profit from their area of expertise in the same way. You could then license your information products to other companies.

CHOOSING YOUR BUSINESS STATUS AND NAME

You can choose from one of three types of business status when starting your own business in the UK.

01. Sole trader: One person owns and runs the business and there are no company registration fees to pay. You simply register with HMRC and fill out a self-assessment income tax form each year. You are liable for any debts incurred by the company as an individual.

02. Limited company: You register your company with Companies House and, in doing so, have limited liability as an owner of that company. So, the company is liable for debts should anything go wrong, rather than you as an individual. You and the company are separate entities, which means that money generated by the company belongs to the company, rather than the owner. As the owner you are a director and shareholder and are paid dividends and/or a salary through the payroll.

03. Partnership: You can either set up a general partnership, which is run like a sole tradership but with two partners, or you can set up a limited liability partnership, which is run like a limited company.

Most businesses start up as a one-man (or woman) band, which is less complex, as you can get on with testing your market while keeping registration and record keeping simple and straightforward. You can still trade under a business name, but it means, in the eyes of HMRC, you'd be Geraldine Brown trading as Wonderful Widgets, for example. It is easy to then transfer your company to a limited one at a later date; you will need to contact Companies House to do so.

Some business owners prefer to set up as a limited company from the get-go. The benefits of doing so include being protected from liability if you were sued. If that happened, the company would be liable, rather than you as an individual. There are also tax benefits to being paid dividends as a director of a company, rather than a salary or taking income from profits, as you might do as a sole trader. Credibility is also a benefit. You tend to have more credibility as a limited company, depending on who your customers are. However, as a limited company you have to pay corporation tax as well as income tax (as a sole trader you only pay income tax on your earnings). You must also register with Companies House and have at least one director and a company secretary to follow the rules and maintain official records. There is generally more paperwork and you are required by law to file annual returns (as well as your tax return). There's less privacy too, as anyone can look at your company accounts, just as you can look at your competitors' if they are a limited company.

The pros of setting up a limited company are your lowered financial liability and the ability to transfer shares easily. The company will be able to continue should anything happen to you.

A general partnership is another option, with each partner taking a percentage of shares and revenue from the business, depending on investment of time and money. Just as with sole traderships, partners are liable for debts, so if one gets into trouble, assets from the business could be seized to pay off debts. Also, I've heard of problems around expectations, when one partner is putting in way more effort than another for the same return, and around decision-making, as both partners need to agree. That said, sharing the vision and having complementary skills can enable the business and boost productivity. You can also set up a limited company as a partnership (or a limited liability partnership, to get the benefits of a limited company and create more structure, equal voting rights and so on).

Once you've decided which entity to set your business up as, you'll need to register your business, either with HMRC only if you are a sole trader or with both HMRC and Companies House if you are registering a limited company. You must do this within three months of starting your business or you will be fined £100. Before you do this, however, you'll need to decide on your business name.

When deciding on a name there are some important considerations. Your business name should:

01. Be short, memorable and easy to spell.

02. Be available as a domain name and company name. Check availability of the domain name (website address) via a registrar such as www.just-the-name.co.uk or www.123-reg.co.uk. Also search the Companies House register to check that your chosen name isn't already being used. You should also check that your name isn't being used overseas as this could cause potential issues as you expand.

03. Fit with your brand personality and customer experience (we'll examine building a purposeful, believable brand in Chapter 6). Consider the benefits people gain from being your customer. Jot down names you like.

Once you've chosen your name and have found out that it is available to register as a domain name, go ahead and register it before someone else does. It's then time for the next step – to put all that you've learnt into a workable plan of action.

CREATE YOUR ROUTEMAP

❝❞
TO ACHIEVE GREAT THINGS, TWO THINGS ARE NEEDED; A PLAN, AND NOT QUITE ENOUGH TIME.

Leonard Bernstein

Busy mums will relate to the above quote – not having enough time does create a sense of urgency, which, coupled with good organisation, can make unbelievable things happen. Whether that's getting all the children out of the door on time against all odds or making it home in time from the office to pick your baby up from the childminder. Yes, as all mums know, there is never enough time in the day. The same can be said for business owners, who understand that everything tends to take longer (and often costs more) than you think it will.

'It always takes longer than you think,' nods Bev James, MD of The Coaching Academy and co-founder of the Entrepreneurs' Business Academy, a joint venture with James Caan. 'And it often takes a bit more money than you think. For that reason it's advisable to add another 10 per cent in terms of money and time when planning.'

Both mums and business owners – especially, mums *in* business – know how helpful it is to have a plan. Juggling various tasks (and children) makes planning an absolute requirement. Knowing where you are going and where you intend to stop en route to your destination is vital.

Just like a foolproof family schedule, a sound business plan helps you to get from where you are now to where you want to be – avoiding as few hurdles as possible along the way. It's like a map which helps you avoid a bumpy road. This written document outlines the nature of your business, defines your sales and marketing strategy and details the financial background and projections going forward, as well as outlining essentials such as how your business will operate and where from. You'll be able to create an action plan from it so you know where to go and what to do next.

Many people think that you only need a business plan if you are approaching banks, investors or other financiers to persuade them to put their hands in their pockets and give you money. However, while deep-pocketed people will always need to see a business plan before funding your dream, you should still write one even if you don't need any external investment.

A business plan is also for you because it's so much easier to be and remain passionate about the future if you can see where you are going and how you will get there. What's more, it's always easier to approach a big project if you tackle it one step at a time. Planning enables this approach. It helps you to stay focused on your objectives and reinforces your belief.

Your business plan is your routemap towards your vision (as covered in Chapter 1). Your strategies are the paths you will take to reach that destination, and your goals and targets are the milestones and signposts that you will reach en route.

So what should you include?

BUSINESS-PLAN TEMPLATE

Here is a business-plan template, which you can use to sketch out notes before creating your own version in a document:

Business details

Your business name, contact information and address.

Contents page

List the contents of your business plan with page numbers.

Executive summary

This is a snapshot of your business which summarises its purpose and unique selling points – what it does, who you will serve and why. Sometimes this is referred to as an 'elevator pitch', as it is how you would summarise your business if you were stuck in an elevator with an influential person who was going to get out of the elevator in a few floors' time. So you might say: 'I run Safer Seatbelts Ltd because I want to live in a world where it is easier for parents to ensure their children travel safely. We supply parents with premium-quality, easy-to-install child seats and extra seatbelts, so that they can get peace of mind. We've already gained positive feedback and have demonstrated market demand by selling [X many] units and securing a distribution deal with [such and such] retailer.'

This summary will also outline when you are starting/have started and define the opportunity in terms of demonstrable demand via testing in the marketplace and gaining proof of concept. While there is a good deal to cover in this summary, it should be kept clear and concise.

Business proposition

- What is your product?

- Who is your product for?

- What made you come up with this idea?

- What makes it different and/or better than the rest? (I.e. what do you offer that others don't?)

- What benefits will customers gain from choosing you? (I.e. will they save time/money, find life/work easier/safer/more enjoyable and so on.)

Business purpose and vision

- Why does your business exist?

- What is your big vision?

- Where do you see the business in five years' time?

Business opportunity

- How big is the opportunity? (I.e. what is the size of the market and the share of the market segment you intend to reach?)

- Who are your main competitors and what are their strengths?

- How are you exploiting their weaknesses?

- Are there any other windows of opportunity within the marketplace?

- Who are the biggest customers of your competitors?

- Why will people choose you over your competition?

- Are there any growth forecasts, trends and/or key market drivers?

- Can you demonstrate demand/proof of concept?

People

- Who are you and what skills and experience do you bring to the table?

- What are you good/best at?

- Who is filling the gaps in the areas you are not so good at?

- What skills/experience do they bring to the table?

- What are they good/best at?

- Do you have any collaborative strategic alliances/partnerships in mind?

Plans

- How do you intend to source/make/develop your product?

- How do you intend to market/promote it? (E.g. PR, social media, TV/radio, email marketing by building a list and submitting a newsletter, telesales, face-to-face, networking, at exhibitions and events?)

- How do you intend to distribute/sell it? (I.e. through which channels – online through your website, via third-party websites such as eBay or Folksy.com, through external distributors/stores, on the high street by having your own store or by mail order?)

Financials and operations

- How much will you sell your product(s)/service(s) for?

- How much will they cost to make (including all costs from manufacture and stock supply to staffing, training and utilities, postage and packaging)?

- How will you pay for your costs and how will you pay those financiers back (grants/loans/your own money/external investment)?

- Do you have any material assets or liabilities? (What machinery/ equipment/premises/IT will you need to buy/hire/rent, or do you own any?)

- How big do you think you can grow the business?

- What are your pessimistic, likely and optimistic assumptions over the next three years?

- How much money will you need to start up and how much credit can you gain from suppliers?

- How much do you need to borrow and how will you afford the repayments? What security can you offer?

Investment

- Do you need external investment? (Start-up capital? Working capital?)

- If so how much do you need?

- What will you spend the money on?

- How and when will investors get a return on their investment and realise value?

- What is the exit strategy for the business?

SWOT analysis

Do a 'SWOT' analysis of your strengths, weaknesses, opportunities and threats. Strengths and weaknesses are generally internal while opportunities and threats are generally external.

For example …

Strengths	Weaknesses
• What are your unique differentiating factors? I.e. what do you do which makes you better than the rest? • What do you have in terms of resources, skills, talent and contacts?	• What could hinder your success? • What do you lack in terms of resources, skills, talent and contacts? • How will you plug those gaps and overcome those obstacles?
Opportunities	**Threats**
• Is there anything timely about your idea? (I.e. news stories or annual calendar events that tie in to your idea and give it a newsworthy angle?) • Are there any emerging or existing trends that your business idea taps into? • Are there any other businesses or technologies which could enable your idea via collaboration?	• Do emerging technologies or other players in the market affect your idea? • How might competition affect your business?

Appendices

These might include additional statistics, CVs of your team and other documentation that bolsters the credibility of the opportunity.

With no track record, your business plan should convey the viability of the opportunity, the passion and talents of the people involved, and research which sufficiently backs the idea up.

CREATING AN ACTION PLAN

The next step is to create an action plan for wherever you are on your journey. This is separate to the business plan and you'll be able to create this once your business plan is produced.

If you are pre-start-up, this might include attending an evening class to learn about social media, researching the market, checking insurance and legislation, buying equipment, sourcing phone suppliers, getting quotes, creating website and marketing collateral, registering with relevant authorities and so on.

Give each action or task a due date and an objective (e.g. to improve knowledge, get ready to launch or prove the concept) and allocate funds or time to it. Ultimately, your action plan will list all the tasks you need to take to stay 'on plan'.

FINANCIAL PLANNING

An essential part of planning your business is working out how much money you will need to finance it – both to get it off the ground and to sustain it. Some start-ups can take a good few months before they see any money come in (and longer before they are able to turn a profit), but there are costs from day one. And for businesses that do manage to bring in money quite quickly, it can still be a while before you, the founder, are able to take any salary or dividends from the business – as some of the profits often need to be invested back into the business in the early days.

If you are married or living with someone and your partner is earning enough to cover your personal expenses, at least during the start-up phase, so much the better. (Personal expenses include rent, groceries, council tax, car, loans, childcare, insurance, utilities, TV licence and subscriptions, clothing, dental, gym membership, travel, birthday gifts, tax and so on.) If that's not possible, you'll need to know precisely how much money you'll need to bring in to cover these costs and avoid personal debt.

So, one of your first jobs when planning is to figure out how much start-up capital you'll need (i.e. money you need to spend in order to launch your business and get your products to market), when you'll need that start-up capital to fund things like buying stock and building your website, and how much working capital you'll need (i.e. money you'll need to ensure that there is sufficient cash flow to pay for ongoing costs and keep the business afloat) and when you'll need it. Lack of cash flow (i.e. running out of cash) is the most prevalent cause of business failure. Even businesses with plenty of customers can run out of cash and be stopped in their tracks. It's worth starting on a shoestring to keep costs down in the early stages.

You'll also need to figure out:

- How many customers/sales you'll need to break even (i.e. to be back to zero again after earning back the money you've spent, after which you'll be profitable).

- How long your sales cycle will be (i.e. how long from first customer contact to invoice and receiving payment), as it may be as long as 60 days or more from when you first speak to a potential customer to securing the sale, invoicing them and being paid hard cash into your bank account.

- How you'll afford to pay back any money you borrow and/or generate a return on investment for investors.

Once you have written your financial business plan *for yourself*, you can then tweak it based on who you're intending to show it to. If you're raising finance, that will depend on how much money you are seeking to raise. The longer the better for a bank manager, but for private-equity investors I recommend drafting a two-pager to get their interest.

Most of the private-equity firms in the City want £2 million profits or more before they even consider talking to you. In general, the first port of call is your own savings, family and friends, then bank funding, and then business angels, start-up loan initiatives, grants and other types of funding.

Here are a few ideas about the kinds of costs you should factor in:

START-UP COSTS CHECKLIST

- Equipment

- Utilities (Internet, telephone, gas and electric usage, etc.)

- Shop or business unit rent/rates

- Postage and packaging

- Stationery

- Marketing materials

- Loan repayments

- Tax

- Parking costs

- Fittings and fixtures

- Stock

- Manufacturing costs

- Import/export costs

- Website design and build

- Website hosting

- Logo/marketing materials/design/copywriting

- Insurance

- Intellectual property costs (registering trademark or patent/submitting designs)

WORKING CAPITAL CHECKLIST

These are ongoing overheads and expenses that you'll need to continue to pay before you receive cash into your bank account from sales made.

- Wages/freelancers' fees

- Loan repayments

- Monthly web hosting

- Monthly utility bills via direct debit

- Postage and packaging costs

- Membership costs

- Marketing costs

- VAT/tax

- Accountancy fees

YOUR ACCOUNTS

While you can outsource the handling of your accounts to an accountant/ book keeper to keep everything in order, you should also gain some understanding of the difference between cash flow and profit and loss (see box on page 94).

Cash flow is the balance of all the money that flows into and out of your business on a daily basis. It's not the amount you've invoiced which is owed to you or owed by you, it's the actual payments that are received and the actual payments that you pay from the business. By the end of the month you may be set to make a profit (your profit-and-loss forecast will tell you this). However, if you are spending more than you are bringing in, you could find yourself experiencing a cash-flow crisis and unable to pay for much-needed stock or similar imperative items. Profitable businesses can go out of business for that very reason.

Avoid this by knowing what income and outcome is coming in and going out of your account on any given day and your cash-flow balance. If required, secure an overdraft to deal with dips. This is particularly vital if you sell on credit. For example, many businesses selling services don't get paid until 60 days after they've delivered that service. They need to ensure they have enough cash in the bank to cover that long sales cycle. Those who earn commission may also find there is a long wait in between securing a customer and being paid commission for that sale. Just be aware of all of this and know how you are going to cover those weeks or months in between.

A profit-and-loss account essentially tells you whether your business is set to make a profit or a loss so that you can seek finance, increase sales, reduce costs or sell assets if you are heading towards the latter.

It essentially provides a snapshot of the actual trading performance of your business over the last accounting period (a year). Unlike your cash-flow account (which records when money is actually paid out and paid in), the profit-and-loss account records when a sale is invoiced, and works out, cumulatively, whether you are spending more than you have invoiced or invoicing more than you spend, and therefore whether you are reporting a profit or a loss, month by month.

Here are some essential tips for keeping your accounting on track:

- Tally up when calculating costs and down when estimating sales, just to be on the safe side.

- Focus on profits rather than revenue. As the saying goes, 'Turnover equals vanity; profit equals sanity.'

- Consider hidden costs and research fully. For example, be sure to know the costs for postage based on the size and weight of the packages you are sending and what minimum stock orders are from potential suppliers.

- Keep overheads down by recycling paper, bartering and negotiating discounts, buying second-hand equipment or furniture, using marketplace sites such as Fiverr.com for certain tasks and using Skype for free phone calls.

- Boost cash flow by leasing or renting/hiring equipment instead of buying it, brainstorming incentives to encourage prompt or early payment (such as discounts or freebies) and focusing your marketing efforts on generating leads rather than building brand awareness.

- Consider costs around location. Where do you intend to work from? If you are working from home, create a separate space or work from the spare room. If you need to lease a shop, consider parking availability, crime rates, footfall, public services nearby, the current business climate based on turnover of neighbouring shops, competitor locations, square footage, costings and so on.

Working out your cash-flow forecasts and profit-and-loss assumptions will help you to decide how much start-up and working capital you need, when you need it and how/when you'll pay it back. Banks will often only lend money if you are committing your own cash into the business. They may match or build on your own investment. They often won't invest if you have no money of your own to invest in the business. After all, why should they risk their money if you are not prepared to?

Long term it is best to use your own money and that from family, friends, banks or government-funded company Start Up Loans. That way you still own 100 per cent of the business. However, if you need significant capital, you can give away equity in your business (if it is a limited company) in exchange for investment.

SOURCES OF BUSINESS FINANCE

Where you source funds from to finance your business depends on how big you are dreaming, how much risk you are taking, whether you wish to grow organically or faster and more manically. We'll explore business growth and growing your team in Chapter 9. For the planning stage, though, you'll need to know how much money it will take to get you to where you want to be. If you have big ambitions, and aim to open five stores within five years, you are likely to need to find a venture capitalist or business angel. If you need £10,000 to pay for your equipment, stock and website, you are more likely to be able to get the money from family, friends, the bank or Start Up Loans, or mix that up with grant funding and your own savings.

Here is a list of veritable sources of cash, from traditional bank finance and private equity to alternative sources, from crowdfunding to corporate venturing. James Caan advises: 'Find out which category the amount of money you need fits into … It's important to research all of your options first and find out which one you are best suited to.'

Friends and family and your own resources

The cheapest way to raise finance is through family and friends, although this can be fraught with difficulties, for instance in terms of damaged relationships if the business fails. As long as expectations are clearly defined and tax implications – if you choose to pay interest on any money raised – are known, the interest-free or low-interest rates involved may be attractive. However, if things go wrong you need to be sure that whoever lends or invests the money is able to bear the loss. Friends and family should therefore be made aware that they should only give or lend what they can afford to lose, because any investment in business is a risk and there are no guarantees on getting a return on investment.

Your bank

Going a more traditional route, you could persuade the bank to give you a loan or overdraft to cover those first months of start-up. Your bank can help benchmark what kind of amount of finance may be available to you based on the financial situation of your business. Generally they can provide a loan and/or overdraft facility, but you should talk through the rate of interest, repayment period, plus any set-up fees for these options.

Overdrafts charge interest on the amount used, whereas loans charge interest on the full amount borrowed, so, if you need cash at specific times of year, using an overdraft may be preferable. Debt financing such as this lets you get your hand on the required cash pretty quickly too. The main advantage is that it doesn't require you to give away any of your equity. The disadvantage is that you will most probably be asked for a personal guarantee, which could be secured against your home, and we wouldn't recommend that, even if this strategy has worked for some passionate entrepreneurs.

The Prince's Trust

If you're aged between 18 and 30 and are unemployed or working less than 16 hours per week, you can apply to The Prince's Trust Enterprise programme. It offers start-up business finance including low-interest loans of up to £4,000 for a sole trader and £5,000 for a partnership, with some business grants on offer too. As well as funding, the Enterprise programme can help you to work out if your business ideas are viable and whether self-employment is the right option, with mentoring as an added extra.

Credit cards

You should only finance short-term expenditure on credit cards as interest rates tend to be attractive initially but become a good deal higher than the bank financing options over the long term. If you know you can easily pay off your monthly credit-card balance and accrue no interest, credit cards can be useful to finance emergency purchases. But be careful – examine this option for hidden charges.

Asset finance

If you need to buy or hire a piece of machinery or equipment, you can secure such a loan on the equipment you are borrowing against. Opt for 'HP' (hire purchase) if you wish to own the asset at the end of your payment term, or 'lease' if you want more flexibility, want the lending company to be responsible for its maintenance and don't wish to own the asset. While HP deals are generally less flexible than leasing, the benefit is that you own (and could sell) the asset once you've finished paying for it.

Public-sector grants and loans

There is public-sector money available via grants and loans. Grants don't need to be paid back and are often for a specific use (such as to pay for training employees or marketing costs), whereas loans are repayable with interest added to the repayment.

If you have an especially innovative idea, you could try getting a grant from the government. Use j4bgrants.co.uk to search for grants. Start Up Loans (startuploans.co.uk) provides loans (generally under £10,000) and Virgin StartUp (virginstartup.org) can help with the application process.

EIS and SEIS investment scheme tax breaks

The Enterprise Investment Scheme (EIS) and Seed Enterprise Investment Scheme (SEIS) are government initiatives designed to help small, higher-risk start-up or early-stage companies, based in the UK raise finance by offering a range of tax relief to investors who purchase new shares. Setting your company up to qualify for EIS or SEIS is a good way to make investing in your company even more attractive.

Investors in an EIS will get income-tax relief of 30 per cent, although to be eligible for the tax relief an investor generally has to hold the shares for at least three years before selling. An SEIS is very similar to an EIS but designed for investing in even smaller companies and provides an even more generous 50 per cent tax break. For information on these schemes, see SEISwindow.org.uk and www.gov.uk/bis.

Private equity from venture capitalists or business angels

You could also try seeking private money by pitching to venture capitalists (VCs) and business angels (BAs). This is known as equity finance as you give away a percentage of equity in your business in exchange for money and (ideally) industry contacts.

Some business owners give away equity to people for services provided, not just in exchange for cash. So you might be able to persuade a web or software developer who believes in your idea to accept equity in your business rather than payment.

Early-stage businesses will find it very difficult to secure investment from private equity as the model and business is unproven. The investment usually depends on how profitable, successful and valuable your business already is. See pages 231–2 for further information on these forms of investment, especially regarding financing in the later stages of your business journey.

Funding initiatives such as Seedcamp

Seedcamp (seedcamp.com) is an initiative supporting start-ups. It generally gives away 25–50,000 euros for 5–10 per cent of the company and enables early-stage companies to compete for cash and advice via its Mini Seedcamps and annual Seedcamp Week.

Corporate venturing

This is a way for large companies (often listed corporations) to invest capital in exchange for equity. The company provides resources, such as office space, back-office support and access to skills and personal assistants, as well as financial capital in order to give growing businesses the credibility and clout of the larger business while retaining the flexibility and agility of a small one.

Sponsorship

You could even be innovative and try to gain sponsorship to help fund your launch. That will give you credibility as you can say you are sponsored by such and such a company when you approach other financiers or potential partners, as well as cash. But you will only be able to gain sponsorship if there is something in it for the sponsor – generally if you are certain you are going to get in front of a lot of their target audience or do something that fits with their own strategic objectives.

Philanthropists

If you have a social enterprise or are running a not-for-profit organisation or charity, you should seek out those who may wish to invest in your business. Even if you are not, if you have an ethical purpose it may be worth finding philanthropists who have put money into ventures such as yours. For example, will your business improve society? Improve a community? Improve people's lives or self-esteem or health? When it comes to philanthropy, people like to get involved with projects rather than a business.

Crowdfunding

This deployment of the crowdsourcing phenomenon has become a popular method of raising finance for start-ups. By pitching to the crowd, i.e. thousands of 'micro-investors', and harnessing potential customers' enthusiasm via your crowdfunding campaign (often a video and campaign page, sometimes listing extras you will give those who pledge) you can raise funding when lots of them make small pledges to back your project. It used to be preferred by creatives and social enterprises but has become more mainstream. You can harness the viral power of the crowd who have backed you (and their networks); however, the crowdfunding platforms generally stipulate that you have to raise all the money you need within the timescale of your campaign in order to be successful, and it can take a long time.

The benefits of crowdsourcing finance is that you get a bunch of avid brand ambassadors with all sorts of business and other experience who can help you to achieve your goals.

Try:

- Crowdcube.com – the world's leading investment crowdfunding site.

- Crowdfunder.co.uk – one of the largest reward-based crowdfunding platforms.

- Kickstarter.com – a crowdfunding site for creative projects, not just businesses.

- Mumsmeanbusiness.com – a global platform specifically targeted at supporting aspiring and established mums in business.

- Seedrs.com – an equity crowdfunding site that supports early-stage and pre-revenue start-ups.

- Seedups.com – a site with an investment crowd of high-net-worth individuals rather than the British public, but charges a small finder's fee.

- Microventures.com – a site that allows investors to invest between $1,000 and $10,000 online.

- Kriticalmass.com – this site goes beyond funding and also offers 'supporters' the chance to offer their skills, time or network to help a business.

- Fundingcircle.com – a crowdsourcing site that allows you to access debt financing instead of equity (borrowing money rather than giving away shares in exchange for cash).

For information on extra funding options for later business growth, see pages 230–4.

SECURING THE RIGHT INVESTMENT

To determine which type of financing is right for you, ask yourself:

01. What do you need money for and how will that help you to achieve your goals?

02. Which added-value extras would you find useful? Be specific. For example, introductions to manufacturers or distributors within a certain industry? Industry contacts? Mentoring?

03. Which sources of finance may provide these? List the ones that appeal to you most.

04. How do you intend to gain such finance? What actions do you need to take? Plan them.

You don't have to compromise to find the right investor. It's a marriage so you need to find the right match. You are likely to be with that person for a long time. So make sure that you like being with that person; don't just take their money and think they're going to go away.

TOP TIPS ON PITCHING TO SECURE FINANCE

- **Be prepared.** Dale Murray, a seasoned investor, suggests that you have a number of pitches ready: 'your 10-minute formal pitch, your 30-second elevator pitch and a 2- or 3-minute one which follows the elevator pitch, when someone wants to know more.'

- **Get proof of concept.** Prove viability on a small scale, so that any financial input will simply increase the volume of sales and enable you to scale up. A big mistake that many entrepreneurs make is to be seduced by their own idea. You need to prove that there is a market for it, and the only way you can do that is to get out there and sell it, even if it's just a prototype. James Caan suggests that you can use a prototype to get a letter of intent from anyone interested in buying. For more on testing the market, see Chapter 5.

- **Communicate your 'why'.** Persuade investors with your passionate purpose, your cause and why you are devoting your life to this business. Sharing your passion will make others want to get involved.

- **Communicate your 'why you'.** Explaining why you are well positioned in terms of your skills, situation and track record is vital in terms of bolstering credibility.

- **Communicate your 'who'.** Clearly sketch out the person that your business serves. Quote testimonials from customers you've delighted, reveal logos of brands who are using your products or who have featured your articles or blog posts.

- **Be clear about what you want and why.** Work out what you want the money for, how you're going to invest it and how you're going to turn it into a profit so you can share it with your investors. Also be clear if you want strategic help (such as introductions to key contacts within the industry or media contacts) as well as money. Telling the investor what added value they can offer helps them to make that link in their mind. If you are seeking mentorship, be specific about what you need – i.e. half an hour per month to act as a sounding board for strategic decisions.

  James Caan advises, 'if [an investor] brings value, I would give him more of the equity than I would a passive investor who is just providing capital.' He adds, 'I would not haggle with that investor, because they are already adding a huge amount of value.'

- **Demonstrate progress.** Who is already on board and how long has that taken to achieve? How many people – be they customers, partners, team members or investors – have joined you?

- **Be clear about where you are headed.** Clarify and communicate your preferred exit route. Investors, especially venture capitalists, will be looking for some kind of exit to give them their return on investment, so they'll want to know when you intend to exit and who to. See Chapter 11 for more on this.

- **Don't overvalue your company.** In order to win investment and convey your value, you need to demonstrate that you have customers and are in a growth sector. Look at your forecasts and seek a business in your sector which is comparable. Find out what they're worth by downloading their filed accounts from Companies House or reading up on trade press about them. If you can demonstrate that you are likely to be as valuable as they are and are able to back that up, you can put a figure on the value of your business and work out what a percentage of that business is worth for how much investment capital. (For example, if, based on this method of valuation, the business is worth £1 million, a £250,000 investment would be worth 25 per cent equity in your business.)

- **Reduce the risk for the investor by suggesting a ratchet deal.** James Caan explains: 'When an investor puts money in and wants a return, they have made that decision based on how much risk they think they are taking. If you can demonstrate that they are not taking on the full extent of risk that they are priced at, you can negotiate.' He says, 'For example, you want to give 15 per cent equity, they want 25 per cent equity; the reason why they want 25 per cent equity is because they do not think you are going to hit your numbers.' In this situation James advises that you tell the investor: 'If I achieve over the next three years the number that I have said, I will give you 25 per cent today but I would like 10 per cent of it back over the next three years.' He explains, 'That way you have got to where you want to be, and they are not taking on that huge risk.'

- **Dress smartly and memorably.** Consider how you wish to be seen. If you are a creative thinker, dress smartly but with a bold and brightly coloured belt or accessory as you will stand out more (and remove your badge or lanyard if you are one of many pitchers seeking finance, so that you look more like a speaker than a delegate).

- **Remind.** Tell the investor the company name again and where they can find you online or at a pitching 'event'. Say thank you at the end of your pitch and invite questions.

BUSINESS PLANNING: TOP 10 TIPS

01. Take ownership. 'Make your business plan a working document that you take ownership of. Get help if required but don't delegate it,' advises Bev James. Write it yourself and then use it, work out your monthly targets and your marketing strategy based on your business plan.

02. Break it down. 'It can feel overwhelming to start a business, so I suggest breaking everything down into manageable chunks so you don't get overwhelmed and paralysed at the beginning of the process,' advises Fiona Clark of Inspiredmums.co.uk. 'Set your three-, six- and nine-month journey goals and for each big task, like setting up a website, write a detailed action plan … By breaking it down you feel like you're making progress each day and week, rather than feeling like there are a million things you haven't done yet and getting overwhelmed by that.'

03. Pivot if necessary. 'Be willing to tweak your plans on the basis of research,' Fiona Clark says. 'Some people have a really fixed idea of what they want to do, but you might need to be flexible about that as you research more into it … You have to adapt to what you find the reality to be.'

04. Be open to opportunities. 'Sometimes, you may be offered a lifeline from a completely different angle to the goals you've set for yourself,' says Myleene Klass. 'You shouldn't stifle progress because you are too fixated on taking a certain route.'

05. Don't let your goals become limitations or boundaries. 'People often say you should have a three- or five-year plan of where you want to be.' says Myleene. However, she adds: 'If you set too many boundaries (not goals) and it doesn't work out, you can feel like you're failing.'

06. When pricing products, do all you can to make the product great and the rest will follow. 'I think customers always want value for money, but this doesn't necessarily mean making something as cheaply as possible,' advises Liz Earle. 'Obviously, a business needs to be profitable in order for it to flourish, but my partners and I never sought to solely achieve profit. The key is to achieve happy customers – then profit should follow if you're running your business properly.'

07. Understand how many sales you need to break even and become profitable. If you are priced at the bottom end of the scale you'll need high volume, whereas a top-end product won't need so much volume. 'Knowing how many customers you need, on a daily, weekly, monthly basis – in order to make the business profitable – is essential,' says Bev James. She says that the way to do this is to take all costs into account and consider how much you need to earn per year. That's what you are aiming for after you've subtracted all the costs from a total figure.

08. Be ready to take payment as soon as you've written your plan. 'One of the first things I did was go to the bank and make sure I was able to take credit cards and debit cards, so I had the facility set up straight away,' says Jennifer Irvine. 'For some reason many people are scared to think about the money side before they have started, but it is really important to take payment; it's one of the most basic things you can do.'

09. Create a Plan B. Business plans help you to consider the 'what ifs', so be as prepared as you can by creating a Plan B for those possibilities. 'Look at worst-case scenarios,' advises Jennifer Irvine. 'These are the parts of the business plan that have come in most useful for me. For example, I put in a scenario of the whole business burning down, so when someone just came and stole our computers we had them backed up and secure. So, no matter what happens, we have another plan.'

10. Assumptions are just that. Don't panic. 'Don't agonise too much about the figures because with your projections you are usually guessing them,' says Jennifer Irvine. 'Once you realise that you will probably relax.'

ANNABEL'S KITCHEN CABINET

PROVING THE CONCEPT AND BEING CASH-FLOW POSITIVE: JENNIFER IRVINE

Jennifer Irvine's entrepreneurial instincts run deep – growing up on a self-sufficient farm, she sold eggs at farmers' markets. In 2003, she created The Pure Package, the ultimate food-delivery service for the health-conscious. Her chef-produced, nutritional meals have attracted a small army of devotees, including celebrities as diverse as Linford Christie and Ruby Wax. Turnover hit £500,000 in little over a year, and the company now turns over £2 million, with Jennifer still owning 100 per cent of the business herself, having never opted for external investment.

In fact Jennifer settled on the idea for The Pure Package because it ticked the positive cash-flow box. 'I came up with lots of business ideas, and I was very conscious of cash flow. I knew that, if someone is not going to be able to pay then you're not going to be able to pay other people, and so, out of the dozens of ideas that I had, one of the things that made me want to do The Pure Package was that I recognised that clients would actually pay me in advance for it.'

Jennifer didn't fancy pitching to investors about the opportunity. 'I'm not good at blagging and realised that I'd struggle to borrow money from a bank – not only because I was child-bearing age and they'd probably ask me all kinds of questions about childcare but also because I didn't have a clue about what my cash flow would be, didn't know whether I was going to pull it off and I'm a terrible liar. Based on that realisation, I knew that I should have a concept where seeking finance was not necessary.'

So Jennifer built her business based on existing skills and resources without the need to fundraise. 'I literally started at the kitchen sink with what I already had,' she smiles. 'I already had my fridge-freezer, I already had my oven and a computer upstairs in the spare bedroom, so I was able to start with that.'

Since 2003, The Pure Package has grown from Jennifer's kitchen table to an innovative space based in New Covent Garden Market, which has grown organically alongside the business. 'New Covent Garden Market is the biggest fruit and vegetable market in the UK,' adds Jennifer. 'That's why I chose this location as it makes it easy for us to get most of our fresh produce. We are within 200 metres of where the produce comes in from everywhere. The farmers pick the fruit and vegetables one day, it arrives at the market that night and my guys will start prepping it first thing.'

The Pure Package is now a multi-million-pound, award-winning business, and in 2013 Jennifer expanded her business by starting Balance Box, nutritious food packages for those looking to lose weight.

05
LEARN DOING, AND LIS

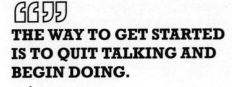

**THE WAY TO GET STARTED
IS TO QUIT TALKING AND
BEGIN DOING.**

Walt Disney

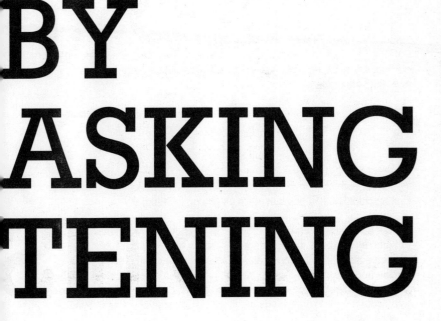

BY
ASKING
TENING

You have already learnt a good deal about the viability of your business idea from researching the market, competition and customers. Now it's time to get on with the process of doing (building, making, sourcing), asking (establishing proof of concept) and listening (gathering feedback). In this chapter we'll examine precisely how to do all of these things effectively.

HARNESS YOUR AGILITY AND TAKE ACTION

When you are small you have something that big businesses don't have: an ability to harness your agility. Being equipped with agility means you can move fast. Unlike large companies, you can react to a rapidly shifting marketplace, you can manoeuvre into position, make decisions quickly and put new ideas into practice instantly.

You don't need to wait for lots of department heads to sign something off or have multiple meetings to agree a certain strategy; you can just get on and do it. You can innovate and move fast. This also means you can fail fast – and this is actually what many entrepreneurs advise as it allows you to learn from that failure to know what to do next (and, more importantly, what *not* to do). 'If you are going to fail, fail quickly' is a common dictum used by entrepreneurs and investors alike, or, as business writer Tom Peters suggests, 'Test fast, fail fast, adjust fast.' Corporations don't have that freedom to perform, test, fail or learn quickly. They are bogged down with office politics and efficiency requirements, which leads to risk-aversion and innovation inertia.

So, while it's essential to think your idea through and do your homework before you launch forth, as outlined in the previous chapter, it's also important that you:

- **Act.** Take action; create, build or source your product or service, even if it's a prototype or 3D design, so that you have something tangible to show people, and you can learn as you go, on the job.

- **Ask and listen.** Test out your idea or product in the marketplace and listen to feedback to secure the validation you need to prove that the idea outlined in your business plan works. You need to demonstrate demand by gaining proof of concept and, if you find less demand than you thought and cannot prove the validity of the concept, you can tweak it accordingly. Whether you prove or disprove your concept, feedback is incredibly valuable.

In business, it is very rare for everything to work 100 per cent perfectly. I believe there is always an element of risk-taking as an entrepreneur, because you can't always wait for every single box to be ticked. If you did that you'd never set anything up or move forward. So, while research is a vital component of business start-up and should be done thoroughly, following your own belief and instinct and being prepared to take risks are also paramount.

To take advantage of being small and nimble you need to be a doer. Remember the Nike slogan 'Just do it'. It is very easy to sit around talking about an idea for a new business, but until you take action it will never get beyond just that: an idea. If I say I am going to do something I always do it. This is common among entrepreneurs – they act on their ideas. Together, passion and action are the fuel which drives business owners forwards.

66 99

INACTION BREEDS DOUBT AND FEAR. ACTION BREEDS CONFIDENCE AND COURAGE. IF YOU WANT TO CONQUER FEAR, DO NOT SIT HOME AND THINK ABOUT IT. GO OUT AND GET BUSY.

Dale Carnegie

LEARN ON THE JOB BY DOING

There is a lot to be said for launching a lean business (one that strives to minimise expenditure and waste in product and processes while satisfying customer demands) and learning on the job as you go.

I learnt a lot about the importance of doing – of getting out there and taking action – from my mother. My father had an industrial rubber company but he went through a difficult time when I was young and had to sell the business. I remember we were on holiday in France and our mum bought us a Yorkshire terrier to help us get over the disappointment of only spending two days on holiday when we were supposed to spend two weeks. That's typical of a good mum – trying to find a way to sort everything out. And sort things out she did.

Subsequently, my mother became the breadwinner. She had trained as an architect but had not worked for some time as she had been raising a family.

My mum has amazing energy and she opened an interior design and antiques shop in Mayfair's South Audley Street, which was a great success. She was very inventive and would make amazing tables out of old doors and lamps out of architectural salvage like French balustrades. Alongside the antiques shop, she worked for a number of clients decorating their homes. One of these was a well-known fashion designer. He was so enamoured with how she had decorated his apartment, he asked her if she would design and build his concessions within department stores. So she started designing shop fittings for Harvey Nichols and Harrods, and was soon building concessions for Estée Lauder and Clinique in Harvey Nichols and Selfridges, then entire shops in Bond Street and Knightsbridge, and became a very successful shop fitter.

My mum's experience taught me that I never wanted to be left in a vulnerable position if I left work to become a mother and that I should always be able to rely on myself. Ever since, I have been conscious of this enormous insecurity, yet, through channelling it to create positive energy it has been liberating, it has become a forceful self-reliance.

I have huge admiration for my mother's 'get on with it' attitude. She was incredibly resourceful. Many people would have buried their head in their hands when their spouse's business failed. She did not. I'm so grateful to her for showing me the importance of boldly taking action, of getting on and doing it. My mum taught me that anything is possible if you put your mind to it and have the passion to carry it through.

ANNABEL'S KITCHEN CABINET

LAUNCHING LEAN: JENNIFER IRVINE

Jennifer Irvine spotted the gap in the market for a nutritious food-delivery service for busy Londoners after sending her husband off to work each day with a healthy packed breakfast and lunch. She decided to crack on and take action by starting small, launching The Pure Package from her kitchen table.

Within three days of launch, Jennifer had to start a waiting list to cope with demand, and had celebrities on the phone asking for her fresh and convenient gourmet-food packages tailored to fit all needs, from weight loss to pre- and post-natal packages.

So how did Jennifer bring her idea to fruition with such effectiveness?

Jennifer explains: 'My degree is in food marketing economics and, from that, I know that there is only so much research you can do, and that you have to go with gut instinct a little bit. And, if you are starting very small, you're not taking big chances.'

She called her local environmental health officer, who reviewed her kitchen and qualifications and gave her the go-ahead. Jennifer then attended a week-long Business Link start-up course and used their mentoring programme.

'It was four days long and cost £50 and I think it was one of the best things I ever did. They had some great lecturers that came in to teach us about HR and employment laws, and they were very honest. They said, "These [are] the things you actually do need to know, but don't try to know it all. If you try to learn too much about too many things, you are going to become overwhelmed and you probably won't even get going."'

Jennifer did get stuck into doing some market research and decided early on that she should focus her research time on getting out there and testing the product to get genuine feedback and prove there was a market for the concept.

Initially she tried testing the product on her friends, but she found they were far too nice. 'They only gave me positive feedback, which is, quite frankly, useless,' Jennifer says. She wanted to find people who wouldn't just tell her what she wanted to hear, so decided to ask people who she didn't know and yet trusted. She decided that the most opinionated people were the press so she reached out to them. 'I would read something really competent a journalist had written and think, "I like this person, I'll ask them,"' Jennifer recalls. 'So I would phone them up and say, I'm starting a new business, I honestly am not looking for any editorial, I just want your honest opinion.'

Jennifer sent out samples along with a nine-page questionnaire with a variety of questions such as what they thought of the cutlery, the temperature of the bags, the quality and taste of the food, and so on. 'I targeted publications from *Tatler* to *Good Housekeeping* to the *Evening Standard*,' she says. 'They would leave comments such as "the fork broke", and their genuine feedback was really helpful.'

As well as getting honest feedback about her product and packaging there were additional benefits to having journalists test and prove The Pure Package concept. Not only did they give her some fantastic constructive feedback and suggestions, they also wrote positive articles about the concept.

'By being the first to try our product it gave them a kind of ownership of the brand so, when we launched on 1 March 2004, I got a completely unexpected full page in the *Evening Standard* and the phones rang off the hook. Then within weeks we had a full page in *Tatler* magazine and so I immediately had more clients than I could handle,' explains Jennifer.

Despite no advertising, phones were ringing constantly and Jennifer soon decided if she couldn't handle the numbers she could put them on a waiting list. 'I had Patsy Kensit on the phone saying, "Please don't put me on your waiting list, I'll pay extra," so that was amazing. Celebrities just found their way to me.'

She advises: 'I think if you do too much planning in business, you think too deeply, and sometimes you actually don't get started as soon as you could. So, while research is important, you learn on the job by testing real products with real people and continuing to learn from there.'

🖎🖎

THERE IS NOTHING BETTER THAN LEARNING FROM DOING. THAT IS THE BEST EXPERIENCE.

Dessi Bell, Zaggora

TOP FIVE DOS AND DON'TS FOR LEARNING ON THE JOB

- **Don't wait for perfection.** There's no point waiting to launch your business until everything is absolutely perfect. Equip yourself with knowledge, gather data and write your business plan to back up your idea, and then get on and test the idea live in the marketplace so that you learn on the job. 'There comes a point when you just have to do it, for it will never be perfect,' says Bev James, MD of The Coaching Academy. 'If you do get bad feedback it's about how you respond to it.'

- **Do get as much practical experience as you can before you launch.** Remember that learning is the operative word. So, make sure you have armed yourself with enough knowledge through research and learning on the job. Bev James says, 'I know someone who loved eating out, loved restaurants and food and wanted to set up their own restaurant. But if you don't have the know-how, and no time to learn on the job, you could run into problems, as this person did … So go and learn first; go and work in a restaurant.' Thomasina Miers says, 'Prue Leith told me early on, "Learn on someone else's time. If you feel you are an entrepreneur, learn by working for other people.'" She adds, 'I know Linda Bennett worked for many other shoe shops before setting up L.K. Bennett.'

- **Don't be afraid to step outside of your comfort zone to learn.** That's what Myleene Klass did when she learnt on the job with Baby K. After all, she had no experience of making or selling clothes for young children. 'I learnt to tweak my vision,' says Myleene. 'Mothercare said, "Well, you can't make the black dress in broderie anglaise because a little baby's finger will get caught in there …" and suddenly you're learning on the job about the safety elements.'

- **Do ask advice.** I have often found that some wonderfully experienced people are happy to help and actually really enjoy giving someone with a young business a bit of advice. 'I definitely learnt on the job,' says Chrissie Rucker. 'We just made it up as we went along, but I was never afraid to ask for help or for an opinion when I felt unsure about something.'

- **Do seek out experts to learn from.** 'I have always had good mentors,' says Bev James. 'In the early days, I would find someone who I felt I needed to learn from and I would offer to help them in some way.' Bev even offered to work for free for several weekends at The Coaching Academy (which is now her company). 'That gave me the opportunity to learn the ropes on the job. I was planning to own the business at that stage, so by helping out I could watch the speakers and observe how they engaged with people.' She adds, 'Those trainers became my mentors as I was learning so much from them.' See Chapter 9 for more on finding a mentor.

TEST YOUR IDEA'S VIABILITY IN THE MARKETPLACE

Another vital way to learn is to ask questions and listen to the answers. You will have already done plenty of asking during your research, as covered in detail in the previous chapter. However, now that you have taken action and have something tangible to show people, you can take that product or service out there into the marketplace and test it. It is only through taking this action and inviting feedback that you can gain proof of concept to demonstrate genuine demand.

Before you can do that you must research precisely who the buyer is – who is most likely to buy your product and who your ideal customer is – so you should use your customer profile, as outlined in Chapter 4, and find people who fit that type.

For me, both when I decided to start selling food as well as writing books, I felt it was very important to talk to my consumer. I couldn't loiter around the supermarket talking to people, so I started to attend all the baby shows around the country while I was writing for *Practical Parenting* and *Prima Baby*. They would have these huge baby shows with 30,000 people attending. So I would take a stand and spend three days just talking and listening to all of the mothers. What do you like? What products have you not got? What products do you wish you had? It was an amazing environment for my research which helped me to discover what mums were buying and why they were buying it.

When it comes to testing the marketplace, you should aim to carry out a mixture of both quantitative and qualitative research. Quantitative involves gaining a snapshot of consumer needs and opinions by surveying a large number of people, either via an online survey, over the phone or in person. Often it can be a good idea to provide multiple-choice answers to your questions and ask those you are surveying to choose the answer which applies best to them (and leave space for 'other' answers). These will provide you with statistical information to help you suss out your audience and make more informed decisions about how to progress with your idea within the marketplace. A more detailed picture can be gained by using qualitative techniques, which include one-to-one in-depth interviews and focus-group discussions.

The kinds of questions you might include in a survey are:

Quantitative survey questions

01. Where do you look for a product/service such as this (e.g. online, asking friends, Yellow Pages and so on)?

02. When do you find yourself buying this product/service?

03. How often do you make such a purchase?

04. What are your primary reasons for buying?

05. What benefits do you aim to gain from buying such a product/service and why?

06. What problems does it solve?

07. Which brands have you bought these kinds of products/services from in the past?

08. Which magazines/newspapers/websites do you read/subscribe to?

09. Which benefit from the following list is of most importance to you? Please list in order of importance … (E.g. Saving time? Saving money? Good quality? Makes life easier? Other?)

You should also ensure that you retain each individual's name, age, email address, occupation and postcode/location. This is especially useful if you are surveying a large number of people as you can see which areas of the country are in need of your product or service the most.

The kinds of questions you might ask individuals/focus-group members are:

Qualitative focus-group questions

01. What is your first impression of this product/service?

02. Would you buy it?

03. Why/why not?

04. What changes could be made to it to persuade you to buy it?

05. How much might you be prepared to pay for such a product/service?

06. Why might this product/service not work?

07. What kinds of things do you see going on in the industry?

08. What features/components do you like most about this product/service?

09. Where, when and how would you use this product/service?

10. If you could add any feature/benefit to this product/service, what would it be?

TESTING THE IDEA: SCHOOL-RUN SAMPLES

Many mums who start their own business find that they have a ready-made focus group that they can enlist: other mums on the school run.

When investor and entrepreneur James Caan's sister was starting a food business, he advised her to seek proof of concept before moving forwards: 'I said to her, "Look, you have a great idea, a great food product, but will anybody actually buy it?"' He suggested that she test the product with people aside from family and friends. 'In her particular case she was a mother with three children and she would meet lots of mums on the school run. She got chatting to some of the mums and told them she was thinking of launching this product and asked them what they thought. They asked if they could try the product, so she made 100 samosas in a kitchen and sold them to the mums,' explains James. 'Some of the 20 or so mums who wanted them bought 25 and some bought 50, and the feedback she got was amazing.

'Fast forward and today my sister employs 36 people and has a workshop where they make half a million samosas a week,' says James. 'But she needed to gain that proof of concept by getting somebody to test or buy or to say they would pay for it, which transferred her idea from being a cooking hobby into a real business.'

Similarly, when new mum Katy Hymas designed Mumlin – a stylish and practical alternative to a muslin to protect clothes when burping babies – she was constantly surrounded by her target audience: other new mums. 'Every coffee shop, baby group or weigh-in became an impromptu focus group, and prototypes and business cards were constantly being handed out,' smiles Katy. 'I learnt early on the value of watching how people interact with your product … I had not designed Mumlin with the intention of it being used for baby, but consistently mums would place it over baby as a bib … This extended the life of the product beyond that which I had anticipated.'

James Caan suggests that if you can't make an example of your product at the testing phase you can print a prototype using 3D visuals on 3D printers and take that into the market.

Determining demand and knowing that there is a market for a product minimises your risk as someone starting a business and gives you the confidence and courage of your convictions.

Before Frugi had customers, founder Lucy Jewson spent a good deal of time getting out there and proving her idea was worth pursuing. 'I hung out all the time on cloth-nappy and mum forums on the Internet,' says Lucy. 'I also asked anyone and everyone I knew about how they found clothing around cloth nappies.' However, Lucy adds, 'Never just rely on your family and friends. They love you and may shield you from the truth if you have iffy ideas. Go to the most critical plain-speaking people you can find. I used my own experiences to guide me in new-product development all the time, but then checked to ensure I wasn't alone.'

For me, I continually test out my recipes on children. Having initially tested out my recipes for my books with my son Nicholas and his fellow fussy eaters at the Babes In The Wood toddler group, I still rely on families for their input for my food ranges. I send recipes and products to families and give them over a week to try them. They then fill out an online survey to record their feedback. It's easier for them to test something in the environment of their own home, because it's real, so that customer panel is very useful to us.

Our research has been interesting. For example, fish pie came up top as the favourite recipe. I couldn't believe that children, especially those who'd been deemed 'fussy eaters', liked eating my fish pie. I love that.

And the research has proved to be true in the marketplace too, as fish pie has been the bestselling recipe in our range.

That's one of the reasons that you should watch as well as ask, because if you said to a small child: 'Do you like fish? Would you like a fish pie?' they'd say 'No!' But if they taste the fish pie, they love it. Children don't lie about taste. If they don't like something, they just spit it out. They don't tell you what you want to hear, they'll just tell you, 'Yuk! It's horrible!' The child is our ultimate consumer and if they like what we provide them with, their mums will buy it for them. So what I think isn't what's important, it's what the child thinks that's important. I let the children's tastes guide what to include.

ANNABEL'S KITCHEN CABINET

UNDERSTANDING CUSTOMER NEEDS: SHELLEY BARRETT

Aussie beauty mogul Shelley Barrett ran her own successful modelling agency for many years before taking her understanding of the beauty market, industry and products to launch ModelCo. More than a decade on, Shelley Barrett is as much a household name as ModelCo. Her brand is stocked in over 3,000 stores internationally as well as shipping globally from modelcocosmetics. com and draws attention from celebrities, make-up artists and industry experts alike. And the company's growth has had a lot to do with listening to the needs of its customers.

'I knew there was a gap in the market for quick-fix, smart beauty solutions for women,' says Shelley. 'I knew there was high demand because I was close to models and beauty editors.' That close proximity to the industry enabled Shelley to assess the demand and act swiftly to supply it.

'The crux of my business is innovation, so I am always looking for solutions to everyday beauty problems that my staff, models, friends and family all face,' says Shelley. 'For example, I was driven to enter the skincare beauty category when the results from a survey we conducted showed more than 89 per cent of the 8,000 respondents wanted to see a natural skincare line added to the ModelCo range.'

Shelley listened to that feedback, which came via surveys from the website and social media, and created the natural skincare range, which is an extension of the existing self-tanning, cosmetics and sun-care offering. 'Our customers are a significant part of our development strategy,' says Shelley. 'We listen when they tell us what they want and we make it happen.'

TOP FEEDBACK FUNDAMENTALS

- **Don't be visible at your focus group.** (You can be within earshot but not visible.) If you do a focus group and you're there, people will often say nice things to you as they don't wish to be rude. 'I think focus groups are really useful providing you don't have "yes people" who are just doing it for the money,' says Bev James. 'You need people who you know will give you really honest feedback.'

- **Do send products out.** It's often better to send something to a customer panel so they can use it at home in their real environment and supply feedback online via a survey or in an email. They will be more truthful that way.

- **Do target your niche but gather feedback from a wide range of socio-economic groupings.** Don't just send it to your friends; send it to all sorts of people, from different backgrounds and different ethnic groups.

- **Do use all the tools at your disposal.** For example, we attend baby shows, use social media, and you can get reviews on apps, on Amazon and so on. There are plenty of places for people to comment on products and services. I have a stand at all the baby shows and I ask people what their favourite recipe is and learn from that.

- **Listen carefully and proactively put feedback into action.** What would people like which would make their lives easier? With my company, people gave us feedback about it being difficult to get the food out of ice-cube trays, so I invented the first flexible ice-cube tray for the company. I put that design into Boots. Then I created mini ice-lolly moulds to put fruit purees in. The lollies are great for teething babies and are easier for them to hold. We also had feedback from parents who said they were tired of spaghetti, so we made tiny organic pasta shapes.

- **Don't take criticism personally.** 'Focus-group feedback is gold dust; it's really special. If you are offended you are missing the value of what you are being told,' advises Myleene Klass.

- **Don't always believe what people say; watch what they do.** If you ask people whether they prefer organic fruit and veg, many will say 'yes', but the truth is, when it comes to the crunch, they don't want to pay the extra money and will opt for the non-organic items. So watch behaviours as well as asking. You can do this by watching how people shop in retailers and asking for real purchase habits (via statistics, asking suppliers or organic food retailers vs non-organic food retailers).

- **Do ask the WHY question.** People normally just ask, 'Do you like the product?', 'Would you buy the product?' and 'How much should the product cost?' People generally follow these specific research questions. The important questions are: 'Why would you buy this?', 'What would make you buy this product instead of this [competing] product?' and 'What's missing from existing solutions?' That way you find out not just what people think about the product but how the product would fit into their purchase habits.

- **Don't ask friends for their opinions (unless you are sure they'll be completely honest).** But do ask friends for their help instead. They may be able to introduce you to a group of people to ask within their own contact network, which could prove very useful.

- **Incentivise people.** 'Offer people the chance to win vouchers or a cash prize,' suggests Mumsnet's Carrie Longton. 'If someone knows they have a 1-in-200 chance of winning something, they are more likely to spend the time answering your survey.'

- **Do invite companies as well as individual consumers to join your focus groups.** For example, if, like wedding-dress designer Caroline Castigliano, your customers are shops rather than people, you should seek their opinion. 'You have to get people outside your immediate circle,' says Caroline. 'Because people love being flattered, you could say, we are doing this in your area, and we would like to invite you to a "research event", and we know you are a really big seller/important shop in the area and would love your opinion on our collection.'

- **Ask potential buyers how much they'd sell an item/service such as yours for.** Some retailers would want to make a 50 per cent profit, while other larger stores, such as supermarkets, would expect to make a 100 per cent profit, so they would sell it for double (or sometimes even triple) what they paid you for it. So, if the wholesale price is £4 they might sell it for £8 or £12. Of course, you need to make a profit too, so, based on this knowledge, you'd figure out how much you'd need to make it for. If you want to make 100 per cent profit, you'd need to make it for £2 including all costs. You would then approach a manufacturer and tell them this is the cost we need to make it for and we can't spend any more on it than that, to see if that is possible. It's vital to know the end price so you can determine what you are able to spend on the cost of making your products. Sometimes there's a balancing act between maintaining your point of difference and your profit margin. For example, sometimes I make less margin because I want to use vanilla or blueberries, which cost more than apples and pears. However, using these types of delicious, quality ingredients gives me that point of difference, so I'm prepared to make slightly less margin as customer demand will be higher, as I have something quite different to my competitors. The same goes for my fish pie. Because I want to have a good amount of salmon in it to offer plenty of omega-3, I'll make less margin on that.

- **Don't just ask customers; ask suppliers and even competitors for their advice too.** 'Be bold and keep asking questions,' advises Caroline Castigliano. 'Ask the British Fashion Council or try the Chambers of Commerce. Ask suppliers to show you things they've already made for others, ask about guarantees that they have in place and find out minimum quantities.'

ANNABEL'S KITCHEN CABINET

TAKING LISTENING TO CUSTOMERS TO ANOTHER LEVEL: CHLOE MACINTOSH

The founders of online furniture brand Made.com devised a way to put customer feedback at the forefront of their business, to give their customers control over what is actually made.

Chloe explains: 'We always test our products with the customers. It is my absolute conviction that the consumer has the input. They have the answer; they have problems in their home and we just need to find out what those problems are and solve them. Every time, I put something in front of them and I get them to tell me exactly what they want.

'We often use our social media channels to gauge the opinions of our customers on our products. We ask: is that something you like? Is that something you would buy? The first time we do a product, the interest we get will give us an insight into what future sales will be. We also learn a lot about the needs of our customers using the photos they share with us of their homes on our social platform made.com/unboxed. It's a great insight into how people are living across the country.'

This different business concept means that Made.com does not hold stock so there can be a longer waiting time for the product. However, the business is very transparent about the process, and its customers are saving so much for such good-quality furniture that they are happy to wait.

Chloe Macintosh came up against many naysayers. One of the objections that industry experts gave was that it is so impersonal doing business online. They wondered how the Made.com team would talk to their customers. But, on the contrary, Chloe discovered that online communication can be far more open and honest than face-to-face communication.

MYLEENE KLASS

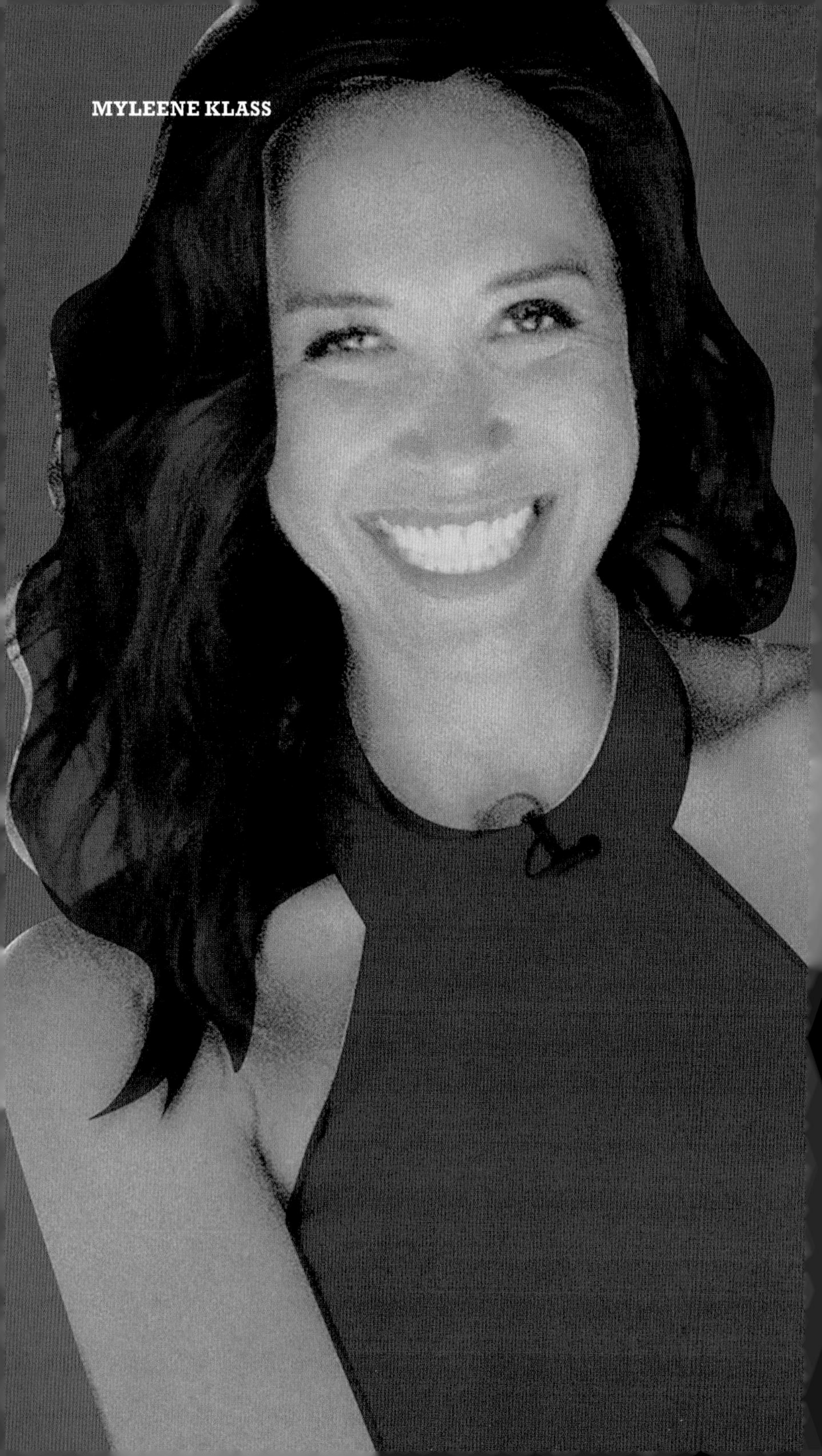

ALEX POLIZZI

CHRISSIE RUCKER

CHLOE MACINTOSH

THOMASINA MIERS

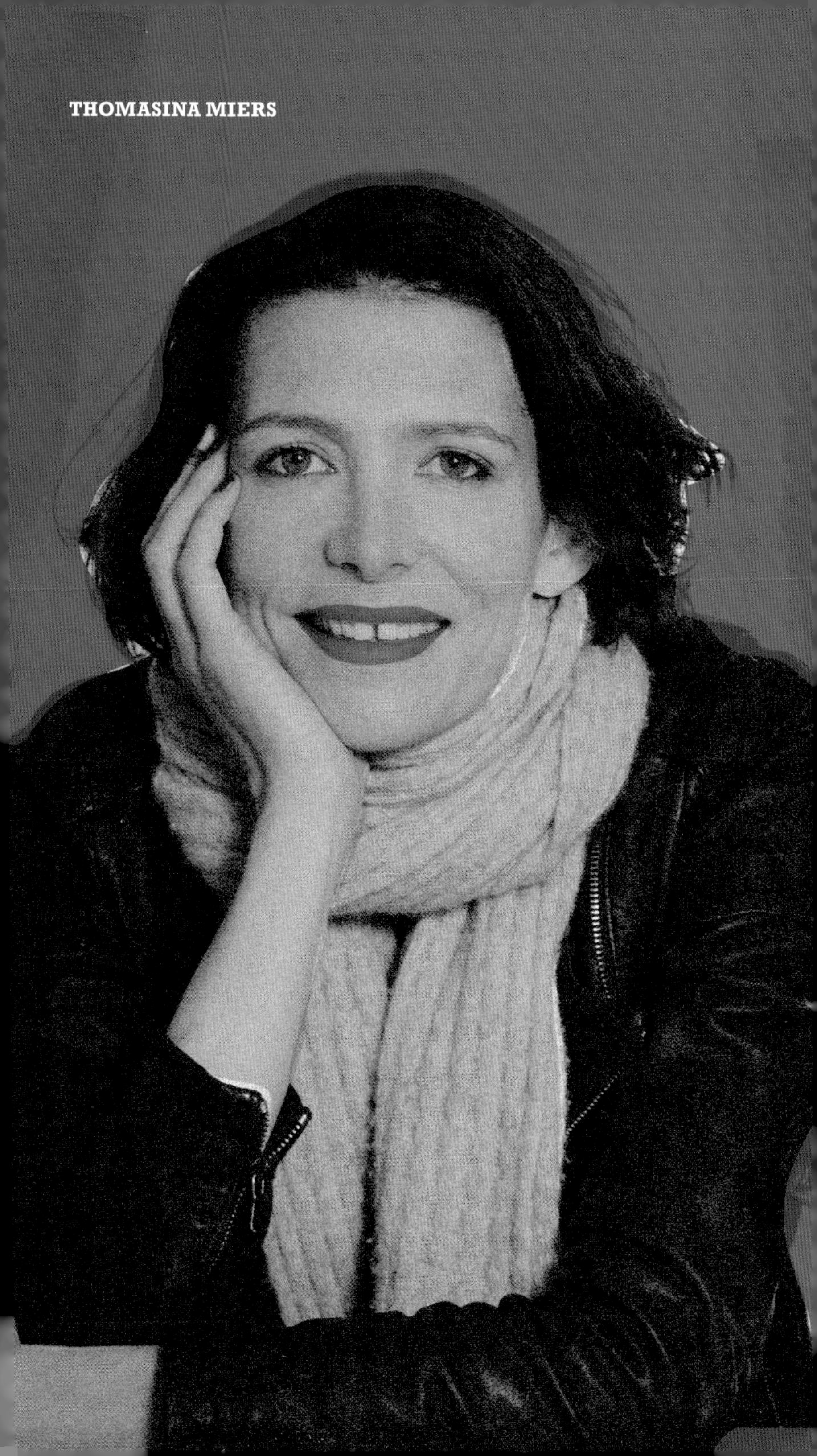

JACQUELINE
GOLD

LIZ JACKSON

CAROLINE
CASTIGLIANO

THEA GREEN

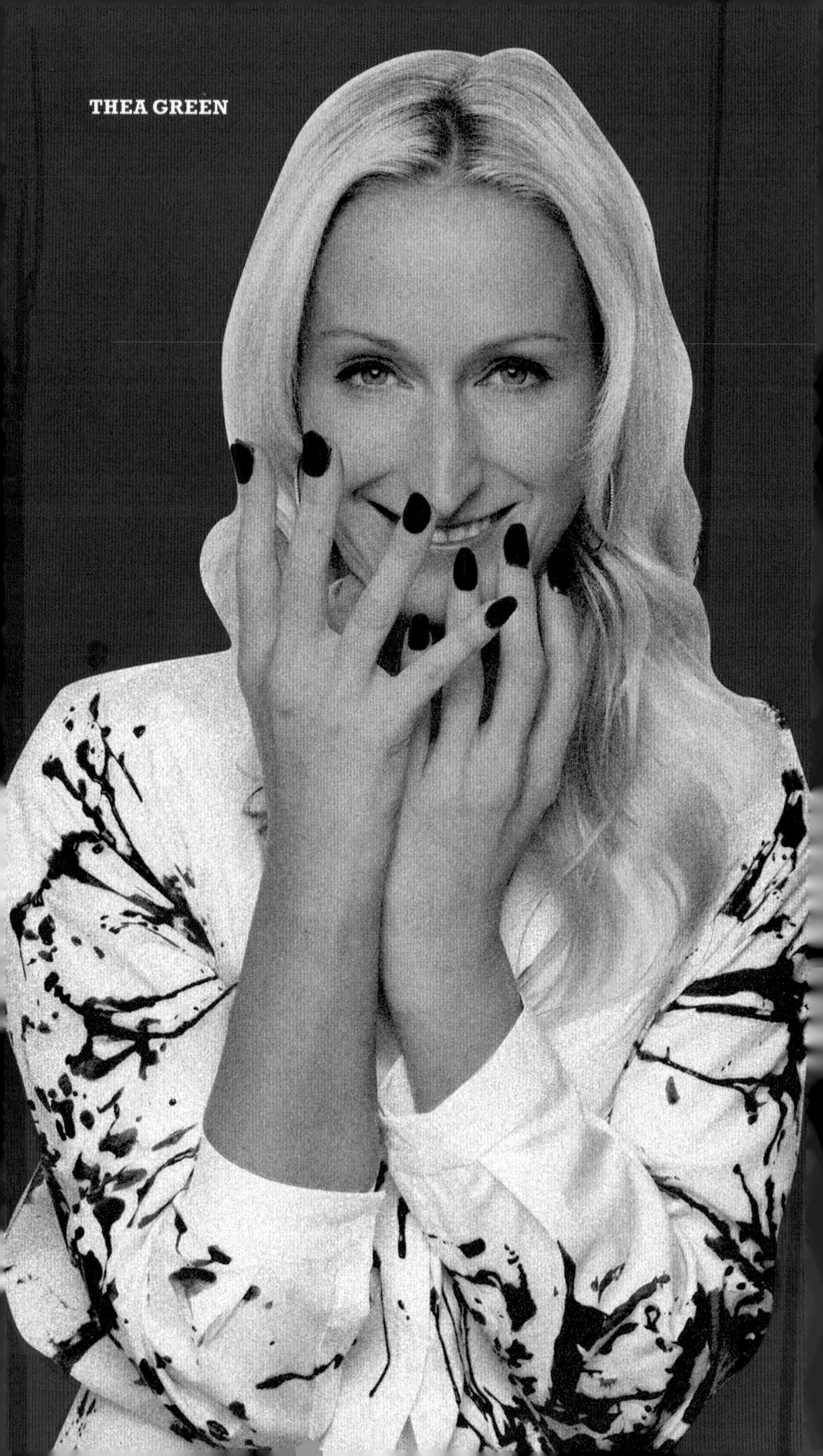

GAIL REBUCK

KATY HYMAS

LUCY JEWSON

BEV JAMES

BAUKJEN DE SWAAN ARONS

CARRIE LONGTON & JUSTINE ROBERTS

LYNNE FRANKS

DESSI BELL

SAM RODDICK

SHELLEY BARRETT

FIONA CLARK

'What I quickly realised is that you tell a lot more about yourself when you don't meet the people,' explains Chloe. 'We have people telling us what they need, and telling us their life story, *because* they don't meet us. The communication through live chat and direct online communication is fluid.'

There's much to learn from Chloe. Firstly, that we can gain so much valuable knowledge and feedback through online and social media channels; secondly, that innovation unlocks potential that may have previously been limited; and, thirdly, that putting customers in the driving seat enables you to get on and learn on the job, create a more sustainable business model and maximise valuable feedback about customer needs and wants. As she declares, 'The difference between a crazy idea and a brilliant idea is how many people you can get to agree with you.'

THE IMPORTANCE OF LISTENING

There's a famous saying, 'You have two ears and one mouth for a reason.' Good listening at pre-sales stage will skyrocket your sales when you enter the market because you'll have a firm understanding of what your customers really want. But it doesn't stop here. You need to continue to listen while you are selling, after the sale and beyond.

'Hearing what customers think is very important to me,' says Baukjen de Swaan Arons, founder of clothing brand Baukjen and maternity brand Isabella Oliver. 'Things that I have learnt include how women feel about the cuts and fabrics of the clothes, how they like to wear colour, what models appeal to them, what styling works and what tone of voice works for them,' adds Baukjen. 'Even after 10 years I still learn from every focus group and other research that we do.'

Lucy Jewson's organic babywear company Frugi recruits 12 ambassadors each season to act as a parent's voice. These Frugi crusaders even have their own secret Facebook page where they can chat and provide feedback. 'We tweak our designs all the time as a result of customer feedback,' says Lucy. 'They tell us what they like, what they don't like and what they wish we did. Being the brand that our customers want us to be is the lifeblood of Frugi. If we didn't listen, we wouldn't be successful.'

'These days customers are very vocal about their needs,' says Alex Polizzi, hotelier and co-owner of Millers Bespoke Bakery. 'Customers have more ways than ever before to let you know what they think of you. The rise of the Internet means that your failures are trumpeted as loudly as your successes. There are forums for every single business. So go there, look and listen because your customers will tell you more than anyone else will about what you are doing right and what you are doing wrong.'

'Listening to customer feedback isn't just important, it's vital,' says Liz Earle. 'At Liz Earle Beauty Co., the customer is king (or, more often, queen!) and the company's customer service has repeatedly been voted number one by *Which?* magazine, which is a wonderful accolade for the team.

'Aside from hearing what's gone well or what you could be doing better, customers also have many great ideas if you give them the time and the right platform to express them,' says Liz. 'Their feedback was the inspiration behind many of the beauty company's products.' For example, the brand decided to produce a Cleanse & Polish for men after many requests from wives and mums fed up with having their own cleanser 'borrowed'.

Learning from and listening to customers should be at the forefront of your strategy because times and trends change. By listening to your customers you can stay ahead of the curve and implement changes internally to reflect external market shifts. That's what Jacqueline Gold, CEO of Ann Summers, did when she made the decision to rebrand in 2011.

'It's such a fast-moving space,' says Jacqueline. 'It was at the middle of the recession when most people were reigning in their spending. I thought it was a good time to do some research about what our customers were doing. I wanted to know every intimate detail about what they were and were not spending money on and what they wanted.' Their customers gave feedback that they wanted the brand to be 'sexier, and edgy at the same time', so Jacqueline implemented changes across the brand, including product, branding, store concept and more on the back of that research.

TOP TIPS FOR LISTENING TO YOUR CUSTOMERS

- **Learn how the customer shops.** Don't assume anything. 'Some people like to buy unisex, so you might assume that you could double the orders by making everything unisex, but it doesn't work like that,' advises Myleene Klass. 'You have to understand how the customer shops. When they're buying for babies they like to buy for girls or boys.'

- **Keep asking *why* even once you've started selling.** 'I get a stocktake every Tuesday from Littlewoods and every Thursday from Mothercare. I read everything through and I think – why?' says Myleene. 'I think about the weather and I know what I want the weather to be doing. I think about why this dress is a bestseller, and we can use the answers to those questions to our advantage.'

- **Keep an open dialogue with your customers.** Justine Roberts, CEO and co-founder of Mumsnet, says that everything they do results from conversation with their Mumsnetters. 'We listen to their views on everything from the campaigns we run to the advertising we carry,' she says. 'Our users are stakeholders; it's a collaborative effort.' She adds, 'In this world of social media, feedback will be immediate and constant. Brands should see that as an opportunity to refine and hone their message rather than as criticism.'

- **Make the most of social media.** Social media is a great way to open dialogue with your customers and create customer communities. Jacqueline Gold has harnessed the power of Twitter to engage in direct conversation with her audience, open up collaborative opportunities and to champion female entrepreneurship. 'If I thought 10 years ago that I could speak to tens of thousands of customers personally, I would never have believed you, but now with Twitter it's possible,' smiles Jacqueline. 'Small-business owners should harness that power to have conversations with their customers.'

- **Make your customers feel valued.** As well as requesting feedback, if you can demonstrate that you have listened by implementing changes and tweaking products specifically as a result of listening to them, you prove to your customers that their opinions matter. 'Our customers have been tremendously valuable for us, even in educating us about what products we should launch,' explains Dessi Bell, founder of activewear brand Zaggora. 'They told us they wanted something with sleeves so we brought out the hot top, which has been successful. They told us they wanted hot pants with high-cut waist bands, which has also been tremendously successful. I think listening to your customers can only help you. Even customers who are unhappy with your service, if you manage to listen to them and turn them around, they can become your biggest advocates.'

PRE-LAUNCH BUSINESS VIABILITY CHECKLIST

Once you have listened sufficiently, you will have proven (or disproven) the concept. You will know how viable your business idea is. So, before you launch the business, run through this quick business viability checklist. If you can answer yes to the questions below, you're ready to launch.

01. Do you believe in the idea? Are you passionate about making it work?

02. Does the opportunity sit within a growth market?

03. Have you found a niche?

04. Have you found a gap in the market? Is there a market in that gap (i.e. a big enough niche to generate revenue from)?

05. Do you have proof of concept (by making and testing a prototype in a live market situation)?

06. Have you uncovered a genuine demand for what you will offer?

07. Do you have honest feedback from focus-group participants or surveyed prospects (that is, prospective customers)? Does your market research say 'yes'?

08. If the idea is not pioneering or disruptive, is it better than existing alternatives?

ANNABEL'S KITCHEN CABINET

NAILING IT: THEA GREEN

Thea Green set up Nails Inc. in 1999, when she was in her early twenties. She'd been working as the fashion editor of *Tatler* magazine and, after raising £250,000 from private investors, opened her first store on South Molton Street in London's West End. Nails Inc. is now the UK's largest nail-bar chain and turns over £25 million. In 2011 its product range launched in the USA and Canada through Sephora.

Thea had spent years working hard to achieve her dream of becoming the fashion editor of *Tatler*, but once she'd achieved this she was inspired to set about exploring other opportunities and possibilities.

At *Tatler* she had worked on a number of fashion shoots in the States and had loved that she could get her nails done with such ease. 'I noticed that everyone in the fashion world, regardless of their salary level, would get their nails done when they went over to the US.'

So Thea talked to her friends back home. She found that they only got their nails done as a treat in the UK but they would definitely have them done regularly if they were in America. Having found a gap in the market, Thea built on that realisation by doing research and organising focus groups to prove the concept and raise finance.

Thea spoke to a number of entrepreneurs and even her competition. 'People are nervous of talking to their competitors or other entrepreneurs because they are nervous of them stealing an idea. The idea is such a small part of the business. Don't be afraid of the competition, speak to people, go and get advice. We're all in this together,' advises Thea.

A friend, MT Carney, was working in advertising and had a lot of experience running focus groups, so Thea asked her to become her business partner (which MT did for the first 18 months until she moved to the US with her family). MT helped her run professional focus groups to take those initial conversations with family and friends to the next level.

Thea explains: 'Talking directly to potential customers via well-organised focus groups was immensely helpful. Not only because of the value they brought through their feedback, but also because of the value their proof of concept gave the company – something which persuaded investors to put their hands in their pockets … we had these great statements from the focus groups – women saying, 'I have never had my nails done, but I would use Nails Inc. weekly.'

Thea was able to use her network of contacts, gained from working at *Tatler*, to secure investment. She gathered £250,000 through small investors, with investments ranging from £15,000 to £50,000. 'There were venture capitalists who were prepared to back us for more money, but they wanted a higher percentage of the business, and to skew it to a web business, but we were convinced we should be more of a retail business, so we stuck to our guns.'

Their resolution and determination paid off. 'The great thing about Nails Inc. was that it was busy from day one and it continues to be very busy,' Thea says. 'We opened with a full range of nail products, and that gave us an edge: we were a brand with product. A large percentage of the £250,000 investment was to develop a range of 60 to 70 shades of polish.'

Learning on the job was Thea's philosophy throughout. 'Working on magazines taught me all about a can-do attitude and doing everything at speed. You need to get on with it and learn,' says Thea.

And learn she did. 'It was a business I knew nothing about but I just learnt as I went along.'

Thea believes that ability to get up and go, to learn on the job, to be happy with a varied role, is very much part of being an entrepreneur. 'I do think you have to be someone who is comfortable saying I am happy today doing this creative thing, I will be happy tomorrow checking the text on the packaging, happy the day after sitting in a lawyer's meeting and still happy the next week deciding where to warehouse the product,' says Thea.

Taking action as soon as she'd had the idea, researching the market, using focus groups and even asking advice from industry experts and competitors has set Thea in good stead. Now she does the same to help others who are starting up. 'I have been helping somebody with a hair brand. Should I be doing it? Not really. But I remember the help others gave me,' smiles Thea.

06

DEVELOP

VALUE YO

BRAND A

“”
**A BRAND IS A VOICE AND A
PRODUCT IS A SOUVENIR.**

Lisa Gansky

AND

UR

ND TRIBE

WHAT IS A BRAND?

It's a common misconception that a brand is just a sign, symbol, slogan or a tag line – these are merely a signature. A brand is so much more than this: it's a 'promise of an experience' and conveys to consumers a certain assurance about the nature of the product or service they will receive, and shows the supplier or manufacturer the standards your business seeks to maintain.

For example, a brand might focus on uniqueness of design, simplicity and ease of use, or perhaps excellence of customer service. This guaranteeing function is not created overnight; it is usually hard-won in the marketplace and develops over time.

Brands are therefore reputational assets based on powerfully held beliefs and a strong set of values. They drive the understanding of perceived value in a product or company, and, perhaps most importantly, customer loyalty.

Great brands stand out and stand for something. They don't toe the line and do what's expected; they dare to be different and take a strong stand for what they believe in. They don't try to please everyone because they know who their audience is.

It is, therefore, vital that you have a clear vision of how your brand will act, feel and look from the very beginning of your journey. And, as you grow, how new products or services will fit into that core brand identity, which is driven by your purpose and values.

VALUE YOUR BRAND

I've spent a quarter of a century building my brand name, Annabel Karmel.

My brand name came about effectively by default. I was an author, and my name was naturally featured on my books; Annabel Karmel became my brand name. It was not a conscious decision, but it turned out to be the perfect one – especially in terms of getting my supermarket products stocked.

Building a strong brand requires a lot of thought and effort. Competition is in abundance. It's especially challenging nowadays with so many of the major retailers and supermarkets building their own brand labels. Major sums of money are being spent by these key players testing the market and promoting their own ranges to customers, which, in turn, makes it difficult for small companies with minimal marketing spend to create that same impact – no matter how unique or different they might be. Luckily there are two areas of the supermarket where own brand doesn't work so well – pet food and children's food. That's because the emotional attachment you have for your pet or child means you look for a brand that you trust.

The cut-throat nature of Britain's supermarket-dominated grocery industry means that, as a brand, Annabel Karmel has to be fiercely competitive; and having maximum control over the running of my business means I can keep my eye on the ball.

For starters, when it comes to pitching our products to buyers or meeting new suppliers, who better to pitch the range than me? I can share my story first-hand and create that important emotional tie between my personal journey and my delicious food range.

And the hard work doesn't stop once you're in the aisles. To stay well-placed on a supermarket shelf and secure a good level of distribution, brands have to meet sales targets. Having volume allows you to become more efficient as it increases your gross margins, which allows you to fund further marketing, which will drive volume up again.

However, I have absolute faith that I have created the very best products I can, and Annabel Karmel stands on its own merit.

Having helped Marks & Spencer launch their children's food range in 2000 and then working with Boots on a branded range of foods and equipment for babies and toddlers, I gained valuable knowledge in how to produce my own food range under the Annabel Karmel brand name. Yet I initially felt that I should take the safe route of working with a company who already had a presence in the field to turn my recipes into meals. I held discussions with companies like Premier Foods (who had successfully worked with Loyd Grossman on his range of sauces, as well as OXO, Ambrosia and Mr Kipling, among others). However, meetings with these large organisations spurred me on to 'go it alone' and take full control of my destiny. I realised that I could not just hand over everything that I had worked so tirelessly on for someone else to have control over it. Decision made; I was going to produce my own food range under the Annabel Karmel brand name. I have kept it safely guarded ever since.

PROTECTING YOUR BRAND

When it comes to protecting your brand, you can register designs and pay to register your trademark. You can use ™ simply by using your brand name, as this stands for 'unregistered trademark', but you can only use ® after your brand name if you have officially registered it.

You can file a patent if you have something truly innovative, but it costs a great deal to both set this up and to police it once your patent is approved. The website Own-it.org provides a comprehensive guide to protecting your intellectual property.

But protecting your brand means a lot more than safeguarding its intellectual property. In order to safeguard your brand, you need to be at the helm; you need to be in control, so that you are in charge of decision-making. Your brand is valuable so you must retain ownership of it.

Jacqueline Gold, CEO of Ann Summers, advises: 'The one thing that you as leader of your business has to do is to own your brand yourself. You don't give that brand protection to anyone else; it has to be owned by you. I have that vision of where I want the brand to go, where I want it to be right now and it is ever evolving.'

Jacqueline needed to stick to her guns to stay true to her brand: 'Years ago I was trying to open up a retail store at The Glades shopping centre in Bromley, but they would not let us have the shop unless we changed the name, which I refused to do.' Jacqueline adds, 'Good branding is about consistency and I would never compromise the power of our brand for one retail location.'

Changing your brand name often isn't worth the risk. However, when I launched my first food range, Eat Fussy, the branding company we used thought that Eat Fussy should be the overall brand name. It was supposed to signify that you should be fussy about what your children eat, but I think some people thought it was a range for fussy children. On the original packaging design 'Eat Fussy' was prominent and underneath was my signature.

I soon realised that the Annabel Karmel name had a pretty loyal following so we dropped Eat Fussy and simply made the Annabel Karmel logo larger and more prominent. This was not an ego trip on my part, but made good, practical, commercial business sense as I had built up my brand to be recognised by mums as someone they could trust when it came to feeding their children. Changing or minimising that would dilute the credibility I'd spent years growing.

Everybody identified me from my books. So we started to expand that brand recognition by putting a message from me on the back of the packaging saying, 'This is one of my favourite recipes from my books.' We essentially made the most of the connection between me, my books and my recipes.

As such, to preserve the integrity of my brand name, I have consciously stuck to what I am good at. While diversification can bear fruit, it can also dilute the integrity of your brand. If you have some success and achieve a good level of brand recognition, it can be tempting to slap that name on products or markets that do not fit with your brand purpose or where you have no credibility. For example, if I suddenly ventured into sweets or chocolates, or if Liz Earle Beauty Co. started selling skincare creams that didn't have the ethical botanical element, we'd be compromising and potentially destroying the brands we had spent so long building. If the resulting product is not good quality, and not in line with your audience's needs, or not innovative enough, it can be fatal for your brand.

When Britain's largest retailer, Tesco, opened in California seven years ago, there was talk of this major retailer revolutionising the way Americans shop. Its 199 'Fresh & Easy' stores were smaller than a typical American supermarket but larger than a convenience store – a model more in keeping with British tastes. The chain's line of 'ready meals', popular in the UK, failed to resonate with US shoppers. Neither did the fruit and veg, which tended to be wrapped in cellophane bundles that meant shoppers couldn't inspect fruit for bruises or buy a single apple or onion.

Similarly some didn't find it that 'Easy'. 'Fresh & Easy' relied on self-checkouts, and shoppers found them complicated. Often the self-checkout lines got clogged as the customers needed to wait for store staff to assist with problems like barcodes or payment issues. Critics say Tesco had miscalculated the market and failed to cater to American tastes. The 199 stores across the US lost money since opening, so Tesco exited from the US market in 2013, selling the majority of the stores to Yucaipa and closing down the rest. This cost Tesco dearly to the tune of £1.2 billion. In this case, diversification did not work.

The other, more viable, way to protect your brand is to raise awareness and shout from the rooftops about it. Pottery designer Emma Bridgewater advises: 'You can't protect ideas and, ultimately, if your product is good, you'll be copied. Your only weapon is ruthless showing off. Publicity and marketing is your best protection.'

HOW TO BUILD A STRONG BRAND

WHO ARE YOU AND WHAT DO YOU STAND FOR?

We touched on the importance of having a purpose in Chapter 1. Being purposeful is what branding is all about. As Liz Jackson, MD of Great Guns Marketing, says, 'For me branding is not really what we look like, it's more about who we are. Brand is like the blood in your body that pumps around.' She adds, 'It's how you answer the phone, your values and your culture.'

Sometimes who you are changes and what your customers want from you shifts. While consistency is vital, it's important that your brand reflects who you are and what your customers expect right now. Liz Jackson had the Great Guns logo redesigned a few years ago to reflect how the company had moved on.

The key here is to know, understand and then define through your branding precisely who you are and what your purpose is. This will define your strategic direction and actions and will shape how you communicate and who you communicate with. Hence why your brand should be at the heart of all that you do. It should be interwoven into your branding, your culture, your customer-service policy; everything.

Sam Roddick launched her erotic boutique brand with a very clear vision. 'Coco de Mer launched in 2001 with a private reception hosted by the former Eurythmic Dave Stewart. Ad agency Saatchi & Saatchi, working for free, had also come on board with a campaign that involved taking photos of a dozen or so people at the point of climax. The Coco steering committee took the courageous stand that, if this were to work, it would have to be real rather than simulated. From the outset, I already had the people and purpose in place to create a strong brand identity,' says Sam.

'Everything had to be ethical and conceptual around the ethos of consenting,' she adds. 'So, while the business concept was very difficult and the financial reward was extraordinarily tight, it was still a huge marketing success.'

One of the strengths that Liz Earle recognises she had, having built her beauty company into a multi-million-pound firm, was the clarity of her branding. She'd long been an advocate of using organic, botanical, sustainable and ethically sourced ingredients, which enabled her and her business partners to build a trustworthy come-to brand. 'From the outset, the management team and I established a clear philosophy for the beauty company that is still in place today – a set of core principles that defined who we were and what customers could expect,' explains Liz. '[This] helped build up not just a very strong brand, but customer trust and loyalty. You can't buy these – they have to be earned.'

And there it is – the best thing that you can do for your business is to create a strong purposeful brand, because in doing so you can build trust, credibility and keep customers coming to you as THE solution to their needs, time and time again. Without that, the fickle customer will simply go to whichever brand best serves their needs at any given moment and you could lose customers. Conversely, if you know who you are and why people come to you and create a strong and trustworthy 'come-to' brand based on that, you can grow by exceeding expectations and building on those firm foundations.

WHO DO YOU SERVE?

In order to present your brand opportunity to your customers, you need to communicate with the right people with the right message at the right time. But, before you create that clear message, you need to know who your market is.

Often, you are your own customer. For example, I was a mum with a fussy-eater child, so I was my own customer. Similarly, Chrissie Rucker, founder of The White Company, wanted to find white bedding and furnishings that were neither too cheap nor too expensive. 'New products have often come about from my personal experience,' says Chrissie.

Being your own customer, you can create products which appeal to you, which provide solutions for you. However, you need to extend on that. You'll have already created customer profiles and have considered why someone who fits within those profiles would want to buy what you are offering (see page 77). You may well have more than one audience across multiple age groups or niche sectors.

To effectively engage with your customer you need to know who they are (and create strong customer profiles). 'Work out how to be engaging,' advises Liz Jackson. 'Learn about the buyer personas for your ideal customers. Understand who they are first. Because, if you don't understand who your customer is, you are not going to be able to talk to them in the right way.'

Liz also advises that you need to optimise your website, social media and whole digital presence for your market. 'Understand the words they are going to use to find you online. Do some "keyword research" considering search terms your most likely customers would type into a search engine to find your products or services. Ask them,' she advises. 'You'll need your website optimised for search engines (i.e. making sure your website follows certain rules around its content, keywords and authority to appeal to search engines when they choose how to rank websites; see page 158). But none of those things will work until you understand those keywords that people will use to find you.'

You need to know who you serve, who they are, what they are seeking, where they go, what media they engage with and which words they use to find you.

'Once you know exactly who you are and exactly who you are speaking to, you create the brand to resonate with that market,' says Wendy Shand, founder of Totstotravel.co.uk. 'This comes about by asking what your brand stands for in the marketplace, what's your take on your industry, what is it that you have done to address your customers' needs and wants? Do this with integrity and authenticity, creating win-wins for customers and partners along the way, and you'll begin to get traction,' adds Wendy.

Building a brand is about linking who YOU are to who THEY are – it's about relating, engaging and empathising. To do this you need to take that understanding and create your voice and your image to speak to that niche audience.

BUILDING A RELATIONSHIP WITH YOUR CUSTOMERS

It is vital to build trust by engaging with your customers regularly and consistently. One of the most powerful factors in branding is developing an emotional relationship with them. In my own case, we want our target consumers to feel like they are part of a community that they can rely on for support, inspiration and a bit of a giggle! We frequently communicate with our audience via social media, monthly newsletters, blog posts, forums, web chats and live events.

Look after your customers by delivering a top-notch customer service. Exceeding expectations is what enables your business to nurture relationships and retain custom so that you generate repeat business. Ultimately your reward for wowing your customers and keeping in touch with them is their loyalty. Sometimes businesses get so focused on getting new customers and attracting new business that they forget about existing customers, who are the most important base they have. Not only have they already bought into you, but if you look after them they'll stay.

Added to that, good experiences are shared, so you want to keep your advocates on side to attract new ones. We're constantly in touch with our customers through Twitter, Facebook, our website and telephone contact line. Whether they are happy, confused or a little frustrated, our team are always talking to them. See the next chapter for customer service and connecting with customers via social media.

MY BRANDING WORKSHEET

Revisit Chapter 1 where you considered your purpose, vision and reason for existence as a business (see pages 12–25). Also recall your own personal strengths and talents you uncovered in Chapter 2 (see pages 39–44). Use these to create your branding.

Jot down your notes about your brand here:

Who are you?

_____

_____

Who are you speaking to?

_____

_____

What do you stand for? What do you love to do?

_____

_____

What is your purpose? What happens because of your
existence? What is your mission statement? (This is simply
your statement of intention which answers those questions. For
example, TED.com's mission is to 'spread ideas' and Lego's is to
'Inspire and develop the builders of tomorrow'.)

_____

_____

What behaviours might you instil within your company culture
which represent the brand personality?

_____

_____

What are you contributing to the world?

_____

_____

Why might people (ideally the press) want to talk about your brand? What's the angle of interest?

_____

_____

Consider the characteristics of your brand personality, based on the above information you've written down.

WHAT'S YOUR HALLMARK?

Your job is to package up your brand – your purpose, vision, strengths, characteristics – and articulate, communicate and reinforce those through your brand identity (i.e. via your brand name, logo, slogan, font, style, website, marketing communications, packaging and so on). Consider the following questions:

1. Which words characterise your brand? Are you:

- Bold, brave and spirited?

- Confident and charismatic?

- Stylish and sleek?

- Reliable and traditional?

- Creative and cheeky?

- Fun and sunny?

2. Does an animal, plant or shape spring to mind when you think of those characteristics? (This is helpful when considering your logo.)

3. How might people describe you? Because you are your brand's spokesperson, if your brand can personify you and your character, that's a great start. What three words might people use to describe your personality?

4. And how might you describe the personality of your ideal customer?

- Time-starved, busy, frantic?

- Happy, positive and helpful?

- Environmentally friendly, genuine, kind?

5. Are there characteristics which overlap?

6. Which colours spring to mind when you put those characteristics together? Colours have connotations linked to them, so it's worth looking into what these are when choosing the colours for your brand identity. For example, many brands targeting time-starved people use bright primary colours because, according to studies, people who are in a rush respond positively to primary colours. Think McDonald's or easyJet. And The Body Shop logo is green, signifying environmental friendliness and strong ethics.

These characteristics, colours, shapes and other features can come in useful when choosing your font and type styling to create a unified style guide for designers to use when creating branding documents, letterheads, logos and so on. Your brand identity – which includes your logo, colours and styling – will be used on your website, in your store, if you have one, and at all the various points where you engage with your customer.

GAIN CLARITY IN YOUR SALES AND MARKETING MESSAGES

There are many rules when it comes to creating clear sales and marketing material which relates to, attracts and engages with your audience – whether it's a potential customer, client, distributor, partner or investor.

RULE 1: WHAT'S IN IT FOR THEM? SPELL OUT THE BENEFITS!

Anyone you are trying to persuade to get involved with your business will want to know what exactly is in it for them, and what they will get out of their relationship with you. So you must have complete and utter clarity when it comes to communicating the answer to those questions.

'Focus all of your communications on "What's in it for them?" and "Why should they believe you?"' advises Liz Jackson. 'You need to build your credibility and make all communications benefit-orientated rather than features-heavy.'

Wendy Shand concurs. 'After identifying your niche and the problems people have and determining how you can fix them, the next step is to understand why your offering is different from any of your competitors and promote that, by speaking in terms of the benefits you offer. Having a niche is gold dust in terms of uniqueness, expertise and marketing potential. So create your story around why you are the perfect person/ have the perfect product to service this niche that will really resonate with them,' advises Wendy.

So forget about the features of your product – the fact that your T-shirt range is tumble-dryable or your IT solution has more security measures in place than any other cloud-computing. It's the benefits that those features provide that are important – whether that's making mums' lives easier (in the T-shirt example) or giving customers complete peace of mind (in the cloud-computing example).

People don't care about you; they care about what's in it for them. It's important for you to know what you do brilliantly and better than the rest, but *how* does that positively impact your customers? And how can you prove those benefits?

As a start-up you may struggle to include testimonials or case studies to prove how you've solved problems for real, although you may be able to include focus-group feedback from those who've tested the product and agreed to let you share their positive words. The point is, you will need to craft your marketing messages around those benefits.

List them here.

---

1. The benefits customers get include:
(E.g. saving time, saving money, making their lives easier, becoming more productive, more organised, healthier or fitter, less stressed, less anxious, gaining peace of mind, feeling empowered and so on.)

_____

_____

_____

---

2. The problems my product/service solves include:
(E.g. fussy eating, wasted time waiting for clothes to dry, concerns about security or safety, not being able to find what they need and so on.)

_____

_____

3. Which of these benefits do your customers value the most? (Refer back to your survey responses and focus-group research to prioritise benefits in order of importance.)

_____

_____

You should flag up these benefits in the headline and body copy of your marketing messages and on your website.

RULE 2: CREATE A CLEAR AND CONCISE STRAPLINE AND 'ELEVATOR PITCH'

One law of marketing is that you have only a matter of seconds to persuade a potential customer to buy, to click a link or to opt in, or to continue to listen to what you have to say. That's partly due to the information overload and the sheer amount of choice consumers have today. You need to grab their attention quickly. So you need to be clear, concise and compelling. With that in mind, you need a strapline (which summarises what you do and why you do it) and an elevator pitch (see page 87; this pitch extends on your strapline and gives a 30-second summary of your business opportunity).

The best brands nail their unique solution within their strapline. They summarise their USP (unique selling point) and solution in one snappy sentence, usually only a few words. From Sainsbury's 'Live Well For Less', which focuses on quality and saving money to Tesco's 'Every Little Helps', which focuses on bargains. Saga's niche-focused strapline is specific: 'Providing high quality services for people 50 and over'; and Climbing Trees Clothing, a T-shirt brand aimed at girls, 'Provides active girls with more choice; because girls like dinosaurs and pirates too.' This is your opportunity to connect with and relate to your audience and compel them to act.

Brainstorm some straplines here. Try to limit yourself to between three and six words:

_____

_____

_____

_____

_____

Your next task is to write your 'elevator pitch', outlining your idea for your product, service or project. So what's your hook? What's your USP? Why should they be interested? Give them one good reason to take your business card and connect with you. (Refer back to your branding notes on pages 136–8.)

Use the following as a template and then see if you can improve on it to make it as clear and compelling as possible:

We [insert your purpose]. We do this by [insert what you do] and work with [insert your target niche audience] who have a problem with [insert problem]. We solve that problem by [insert solution], so they can [insert benefits in order of priority]. And we now have [insert investors/partners/distributors] on board. We'd love to talk more to you about this so that we can [insert how they might be able to help].

_____

_____

_____

_____

_____

You can also use this for the introduction on your 'about us' page on your website or a shorter version as the description on your social media pages. 'Your brand has to be screaming from every page on your website as to what you stand for,' says Caroline Castigliano, 'whether you sell directly to consumers or not.'

RULE 3: SPEND TIME ON YOUR HEADLINES/SUBJECT LINES

Your headlines, especially your subject lines when sending an email, can make the difference as to whether a campaign gets opened and read or ignored and discarded. They are what creates that first impression. It makes sense therefore to devote sufficient time to brainstorming powerful headlines, subject lines and opening paragraphs. Keep them concise and benefit-rich, enough to entice the reader and make them curious to read on. And never ever end your headline with a full stop, as stop is the last thing you want your reader to do. You want that headline to compel them to read on and take action, to be so irresistible that they can't resist.

Try some of these techniques:

- **Use a 'How To' headline** to give advice about something relevant that you are an expert in. For example, I might use: 'How to Cook Food Your Baby Will Eat, Every Time'.

- **Ask a question to engage your reader instantly.** Often people will want to read more to uncover the solution/answer to that question. For example, I might use: 'Are You Worried About How Little Your Fussy Eater is Eating?'

- **Use a testimonial as your headline.** People will always believe genuine results more than any sales copy. For instance, 'My fussy eater's favourite foods are fish and vegetables thanks to Annabel's recipes'. You'll need to include the full name and location of your happy customer so it's clear you haven't made it up.

- **Reveal a secret.** For instance, 'Revealed: How the fussiest eater became the healthiest eater in just two days'.

- **Make a promise.** For example, 'Give me two days to turn your child from a fussy eater into a healthy eater'.

- **Provide benefits.** Focus on the most important benefits in your headline, such as 'Make Meal Times Happier' or 'Make More Time for Your Family'.

- **Announce interesting news** if it will improve the life of your customer. For example, 'Introducing Our New High-in-Omega-3 Dish'.

- **Use a number of tips.** For example, '7 Ways to Ensure Your Child Eats Enough Fruit and Vegetables Every Day'.

RULE 4: INCLUDE CALLS TO ACTION

It's important to tell your potential customer exactly what it is you want them to do, how to do it and when. For example, 'Learn more by clicking this link' or 'Call today to claim your special discount'. This means that your momentum isn't lost.

RULE 5: REMOVE THE RISK

How can you remove or at least minimise the risk of doing business with you? Can you give a money-back guarantee or offer them the chance to read reviews and testimonials? Can you give them some way of having nothing to lose? Money back within a certain time period or if your product doesn't do what you promise it will do? If your product really is as good as you say it is, you will see far more additional sales as a result of implementing a guarantee than you will receive returns.

RULE 6: GATHER PROOF

Provide your prospects with proof. Shine a spotlight on customer reviews and testimonials from happy customers (or, at start-up stage, from a product-testing panel/focus group). Reveal how you have solved real-life problems and given people the solution they were looking for. Include positive comments from focus-group participants until you start to get real customers with stories of how your product/service has positively impacted their lives.

RULE 7: SEND YOUR MESSAGE AT THE RIGHT TIME

Timing is crucial with marketing: you need to get your messages in front of people when they are most likely to need your products. So I need to be in front of mums when their children are babies and, ideally, when they've tried other solutions which haven't worked. If you have a product targeting parents going on holiday, you need to be there when they are planning to book their holiday.

'Attention is the most valuable commodity today, and getting people's attention is the hardest thing, which is why story-telling is important. For us, there is a very practical aspect to respond to a need at the right time,' says Made.com co-founder Chloe Macintosh. 'The right time in our customer's life is when they are either moving house or something is changing in their life. So we need to capture their attention at these times. However, we also need to be aware that becoming front of mind for our future customers is also a very important part of our growth, and so we make sure to give non-customers interesting storylines and an aspirational environment to give them ideas.'

HOW TO PITCH PROPERLY AND PERSUASIVELY

Creating marketing messages for consumers – on your website, in brochures, via emails and so on – is just one part of the marketing and sales process. You also need to know how to pitch your products or services to customers face-to-face, whether that's to get your products into retail partner stores or to sell your services at a meeting with a potential client.

Here are some top tips for pitching well enough to close the deal and sell your products:

- **Capture hearts.** Share your story enthusiastically. Tell them your 'why'. Giving a reason why you are embarking on this venture helps people warm and relate to you.

- **Capture minds. Demonstrate your credibility.** Why should your audience listen to you and trust you? Win their trust by sharing impressive facts about yourself. Explain how you are well placed to deliver what you intend to; what research you have done to prove your concept; what experience, passion or transferable skills/knowledge you have; who has written about you; what your customers or focus-group participants are saying about you.

- **'Put yourself into it,** your personality,' says Myleene Klass, who does all the pitches for her brand Baby K around the world. 'People buy from people, so they are buying you.'

- **'Question your pitch,'** suggests Myleene. 'Before you go in and deliver your pitch, imagine you're listening to it. Would you get engaged by it? Think about your audience. Imagine being them.'

- **'Keep it short.** Nobody has ever in their life begged for a longer speech,' says Myleene.

- **Harness the power of a pause.** Mark Twain once said, 'No word was ever as effective as a rightly timed pause.' If you pause for a few seconds straight after delivering some powerful insights and facts about your business, you give the audience time for the information to sink in.

- **'Create visually appealing tangible material,'** recommends Caroline Castigliano. 'Rather than having to read something, you need something visual to land on someone's desk, or gain their attention when you are standing in front of them; something they can see, touch and feel.' John Lewis buyer Edward Kelleher agrees: 'Ensure your product stands out. We receive lots of phone calls, emails and samples – make sure it's you we remember.'

- **Define your ideal customer.** Paint a picture for your audience to see 'the stressed-out mum', 'the ambitious student' or 'the well-paid executive who is eager to please'. Bring your product or service to life by showing who will use it.

- **Know your place.** If you are pitching to a retailer, know where your product will fit within their existing categories. Which block will it sit best within?

- **Build momentum.** Explain how many people are already on board. From team members to customers, retailers, partners and investors, explain who has joined you to demonstrate early progress if you can.

- **Define what you want to come away with.** This could be an order, a trial, a monthly retainer (where the customer pays you an agreed fee each month for you to carry out a service). It might be funding, access to media contacts, access to their customers. Spell out what you are seeking.

- **Define what they will come away with.** Get them excited about your opportunity. For example, if you are pitching to a supermarket, show them what their margin is at the first meeting. They are interested in the bottom line, in what's in it for them; they want to know how profitable it will be and the page showing your projections and their margin is the page they get really excited about. Explain through your marketing plan how you will raise awareness about your product. Don't rely on shops to market your products; that's your job. They are simply giving you shelf space. And don't promise the earth, moon and stars. Make promises that you can keep.

- **'Create a sense of urgency to get an actual signature on the dotted line,'** says Justine Roberts, CEO and co-founder of Mumsnet. 'Always try to put a time limit on an offer or create another good reason for the client to act NOW.'

- **Prepare for questions.** Make sure you have done sufficient groundwork to be able to answer anything they may ask. Know every detail about your product, including where everything comes from. Never wing it because savvy buyers will ask you all sorts of searching questions. 'Have sales data, business plans, know your market and ours,' advises Edward Kelleher.

- **Dress professionally.** Don't turn up in jeans if you are asking for an order, an investment or are pitching to potential clients. Don't give people grounds to remember you for the wrong reasons.

- **Make people feel good about this opportunity.** Remind people who you are, what's in it for them, where they can reach you, and end with a thank you.

- **Don't try to be perfect.** Don't worry if you don't know something; say you don't know it. There's nothing wrong with showing your vulnerabilities, because that's what people like. People don't want someone who's 100 per cent perfect. If you do try to be perfect, people might in fact envy and resent you for it.

GROW YOUR BRAND: HOW TO BUILD YOUR TRIBE

You should now know how to identify your niche and what to say to that audience. But how will you reach them? When it comes to finding customers, where do you start?

There are so many marketing methods to choose from – so many ways to tell people of your existence. And it doesn't end there; once they know about you, it's important to keep them informed consistently and constantly. So how do you choose which mediums and methods to use, to reach the right people with the right messages at the right time?

One way is to see your marketing activity as a pie, with four slices based on your objectives.

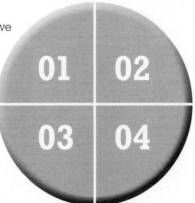

01. Gather leads, attract prospective customers, collect referrals and contact information.

02. Get their attention and persuade them to take action, whether that's signing up for your newsletter or agreeing to a meeting.

03. Closing the deal and getting the sale.

04. Providing the product or service and following up to deliver excellent customer service, then requesting a referral or testimonial.

Once you've completed slice 04, you will return back to slice 01 as you gather more leads, and so on.

Slice 01 will be your initial focus as a start-up. To attract prospects and generate leads, your marketing will need to include tasks such as building a website and driving traffic to it by distributing press releases to announce your launch, inviting buyers and press to a launch party, writing guest blogs with links to your website, distributing flyers, posting Facebook ads, speaking on the radio or appearing on TV, and so on.

For slice 02, you'll then qualify leads by getting in touch to see if they might, in principle, be interested in buying/stocking/distributing your goods and persuading them to have a meeting with you or join your mailing list. You'll use methods such as telemarketing, email marketing, social media marketing to contact prospects via LinkedIn, Twitter or Facebook, and will continue to write blogs with calls to action to persuade those leads to do what you want them to do.

To close the deal and get the sale (slice 03), you'll need to remind them about your special offers via email and social media, through special offers included in your press releases, as well as pitching face-to-face and over the phone.

You'll follow up with a phone call or email or by sending a catalogue or thank you through traditional mail (slice 04), and will then begin the cycle again, raising awareness about your brand to gather more leads. You can pick and mix your marketing strategies depending on your objectives at the time – depending on which slice of the marketing pie you are on.

Here's a list of marketing methods:

- **PR** – submission of press releases to targeted publications and websites to gain editorial coverage.

- **Content marketing** – via blog posts on your own and other people's websites, articles, reports, videos, podcasts, e-books, audio, etc., to establish yourself as an expert.

- **Trade shows** – having a stand to promote your wares, gather feedback and collect business cards.

- **Social media** – using Facebook, Twitter, LinkedIn, Pinterest, Google+ and Instagram to connect and engage with potential customers, partners and other stakeholders.

- **Public speaking** at workshops, seminars and conferences to build credibility and make contacts.

- **Telemarketing** – contacting and following up with prospects/ customers over the phone to qualify leads and book appointments.

- **Email marketing** – creating useful content to give to subscribers and distributing it to them regularly via email to build relationships over time and promote special offers.

- **Networking (online and offline)** – connecting with like-minded people at events or via online communities and swapping details/advice/contacts/information to build relationships and gather knowledge.

- **Generating word of mouth.** My career grew from word of mouth; one mother saying to another that they had my book and the recipes were easy to prepare and their children loved them. Jonah Berger, author of *New York Times* bestseller *Contagious*, said, 'Word of mouth is probably more effective than any other form of advertising.' It tends to reach people who are actually interested in the things being discussed. You can try to generate word of mouth by sending products to key influencers. So, for example, when I write a book on feeding babies I will often send copies of the book to paediatricians, mummy bloggers, journalists with babies and celebrity parents.

- **Online competitor marketing** – online retailer Ocado is a great example of this. They enable you to find out who is buying your competitors' products, allowing you to target these customers and send them a free sample of one of your products with their usual Ocado order. There is a cost attached, but it is a clever way of reaching your target market and challenging their usual purchasing habits.

- **Traditional advertising** – paid-for-promotion on social media, in a targeted publication or on TV/radio to raise brand awareness and promote offers.

- **Display advertising** – advertising on targeted websites.

- **Facebook advertising** – we use this regularly, and in conjunction with TV and wider marketing activities, as it's highly targeted and cost-effective. Facebook adverts can be targeted to specific groups that are segmented by age, gender, personal likes and interests. More specifically, Facebook can search through profiles and cherry-pick those profiles that have specific keywords and phrases, so your ads land on their page and sponsored posts show up on their feeds. It's also not bank-busting: Facebook offer a variety of bundles for impression-based campaigns (paying based on the number of times an advert appears) or cost-per-click (paying based on the number of times somebody clicks on to the ad), which gives you the option to tailor your campaign based around either budget or other choices.

- **Direct mail** – sending printed materials and letters through the post to raise awareness and promote special offers.

149

- **Customer-led endorsements** – introductions to other prospects from happy customers and positive reviews of your products/services by customers to persuade people to buy.

- **Celebrity-led endorsements.** Shelley Barrett has secured some very high-profile 'faces' to endorse her brand ModelCo, such as Elle Macpherson and Rosie Huntington-Whiteley. To find the best 'ambassadors', Shelley does her homework to find celebrities who fit well with her brand, then sends samples through the agencies representing them. 'I am always generous with my send-outs as I believe in growing the brand awareness organically, so the more product VIPs have to use and work with the more chance they will come across something they genuinely love,' says Shelley.

- **Face-to-face pitching** – persuading a prospect to buy via a pre-booked appointment.

- **Website/app** – promoting special offers via your website, running giveaways via your app, selling directly via e-commerce or through a PayPal link and so on.

- **Competitions and giveaways** – a means to collect data by offering a prize in exchange.

- **Local directory listings** – such as 118.com and yell.com.

- **'Organic' search-engine marketing** – not paying for search-engine listings but following SEO rules so you are listed reasonably high up in searches; see page 158.

- **Link development** – exchanging links with relevant websites to drive traffic to your site.

- **Paid search-engine marketing.**

- **Printed materials** – distributing flyers, putting up posters and giving out business cards.

- **Affiliate marketing** – recruiting 'affiliates' to promote your products or services. They earn commission on any sales which come through their tracked web link.

- **Daily deals** – using sites such as Groupon, Highlifedeals and LivingSocial.

- **Awards** – entering or creating awards to gain publicity and credibility.

- **Cross-promotional activity** with complementary companies who share the same audience as you. They promote you and vice versa for mutual benefit.

- **Appearances on TV and radio** – raising brand awareness and positioning yourself as an expert (see below).

POSITIONING YOURSELF AS AN EXPERT

I have been fortunate enough to be able to further grow my brand through television. After a series on *This Morning* called 'The Gurgling Gourmet', with my then six-month-old daughter Scarlett, and a strand for *Richard & Judy*, the 'Foodie Godmother', for which I travelled round the country helping persuade children who were incredibly fussy eaters to change their eating habits, I finally had my own series, *Annabel's Kitchen*, on CITV.

I was able to do this because of my positioning as an expert in my field, due to my knowledge of feeding babies and children and the number of books I'd written and sold on the topic of feeding them.

If you are an expert in a specific topic there are many ways you can get yourself on the radar of producers, journalists and editors. They are constantly seeking expert guests, contributors and presenters to bring authority, passion and credibility to a topic or programme. As well as signing up to a speaking agency, you can register on websites such as findatvexpert.com and beatvexpert.com for a fee.

You can also spend time writing expert articles, blog posts, e-books and making informative videos, webinars and podcasts on your topic of expertise. Or you might strive to get booked as a speaker at events and workshops.

Once you've created some worthwhile content to position yourself as an expert, you should:

- Submit that content to targeted publications and use social media and other mediums to promote your content links and engage in conversation about those topics.

- Email editors and journalists with your comments/responses to articles whenever you see an expert quote on your area in their publication – something which you could have said.

- Include links to your content in your email and social media signatures. So, when you post on a forum about a similar topic, links to your relevant content are included at the foot of each post.

- Become active on targeted forums by joining in the conversation. Seek out questions and requests for advice that you can answer and respond to. Don't try to sell your products and services, simply become known as the person to go to about a certain topic.

While you focus on giving, you should also be mindful of your objectives. Do you want more customers or affiliates? A new supplier? A venue? Let these goals guide the media you choose to use, what metrics you measure, the conversations you have and the marketing tactics you deploy.

Positioning yourself as an expert on a topic is one of the most fruitful ways to enable your business to flourish, as you can use so many marketing strategies to push your expertise out there and promote yourself and your brand: from PR and content marketing to radio/TV appearances and public speaking. (Note: if you're not already an expert, by devoting one hour each day to learn you will soon become one!)

GENERATING COLUMN INCHES

As with many of the women featured in this book, Wendy Shand says one of her most successful marketing strategies for promoting her business Totstotravel.co.uk has been PR. 'One day I wrote a couple of press releases and these were picked up by *The Times* travel section and *The Times* business section. I remember those first enquiries coming in on the back of those articles, catching me completely unawares!' recalls Wendy. 'I was lucky. I had a good story that resonated at that time.' And PR is still vitally important for Wendy today, as she makes the most of her position within the media as an expert commentator on family travel.

ModelCo founder Shelley Barrett advises that you research the media you would like to be featured in first. 'Tailor your pitch according to the style, content and needs of the outlet. It makes all the difference when a journalist feels that you have taken the time to understand the content that he/she needs for the article,' says Shelley.

PR tips from Katy Hymas

As well as running Mumlin, Katy Hymas runs her own PR agency, Cherry Pie PR, which she launched in 2008. Her PR expertise enabled her to get great press for Mumlin, including a mention on *This Morning*. Here are Katy's tips for creating newsworthy events which don't cost the earth.

- **'Work out the angle that makes you of interest,'** advises Katy. 'You don't have to be gimmicky or spend lots of money to secure coverage … Think what makes you newsworthy; is it your background, your personal life, your product? How are you different and interesting? Draft a release and invest in networking with the press you want to impact.'

- **Build a steady feed that builds your brand awareness.** '[This] is a cost-effective way to build momentum around your business,' says Katy. 'Unlike advertising where spend guarantees you space, PR is a bit less certain. Keep knocking opportunity dominos over in the direction you want to go, as each small step has the potential to take you somewhere exciting, like a spot on national TV!'

- **'Get the balance right between not being forgotten and not being a nuisance,'** advises Katy. 'What you send out will depend on what your product is but where possible product samples are a good idea, along with engaging, informative and concise copy.'

- **Network with journalists.** 'Ideally if you spend time networking with key press contacts they will come to you when you are relevant to a feature they are working on,' Katy says.

- **Ensure you have good product photography** to show your business in the best light, as most press opportunities will require a high-res image.

- **Enter awards.** 'Awards are a great way of adding prestige to your brand, and they give you something new to talk about too,' says Katy. 'Pick the ones that would add the most value, perhaps ones that your competitors have, so that you can show your customer base that you are a worthy alternative.'

DON'T BE AFRAID TO STEP OUT OF YOUR COMFORT ZONE

Lisa Barber, founder of RootsandWings.biz, runs kitchen-table retreats on growing a business for heart-centred entrepreneurs. She advises that you focus on stepping out of your comfort zone to reap the best results.

'Like it or not, the most impactful and cost-effective method to embrace in your SME [small- or medium-sized enterprise] is usually the one that scares you the most!' says Lisa. 'The reason it scares you is usually the reason it would also be the most powerful technique for you to be using in your strategy,' she adds. 'For example, presenting as a speaker at an event can be some people's worst nightmare … And yet the very fact that you are forced into the limelight is exactly the reason why embracing public speaking would be a really effective way for you to communicate your message.

'The same is true of writing an opinionated blog post,' Lisa explains. 'It can be really daunting to be authentic, to say what you really think … Yes, some will disagree with your viewpoint and may even vocalise this but this is actually a really good thing. You want to focus your time, effort and energy on those customers you're a perfect fit for – your niche.'

Similarly putting yourself forward for awards may seem daunting but can be very valuable. Liz Jackson has benefitted greatly from the many awards she's won (including Great Guns Marketing winning 'best female-led company in the UK' by T-Mobile and the *Sunday Express* and winning the Customer Focus Award in the National Business Awards), as they've led to valuable editorial coverage and PR. These, in turn, have led to Liz being regularly asked to speak at corporate dinners, conferences and events – raising her profile and reach even further.

Often women in business can be fearful of picking up the phone. They don't want to annoy anyone or waste their time. However, as Lisa Barber explains, 'Having a one-to-one conversation about the product or service you offer with a key decision-maker or prospect is one of the best ways for your company to win business. You've got so much more to win than lose in picking up that phone.'

Liz Jackson's cold-calling tips

Picking up the phone is something that Liz Jackson has never been afraid of. In fact, telemarketing is the foundation that Great Guns Marketing is built upon. Here are Liz's telephone tips on getting appointments.

- **'Stay professional and treat people with respect.** We would never call someone by their first name unless they gave us permission to.'

- **'Put yourself in the decision-maker's shoes and make the conversation relevant to that individual.** If the focus of the conversation is around how you can resolve any problems they have, or help them achieve their own objectives, then you're much more likely to progress the relationship. Identify the need and demonstrate how your solution can add value and meet that requirement.'

- **'Build rapport quickly.** Ask open-ended questions. If you don't tell somebody what the call has got in it for them within a very quick period of time, then you lose that opportunity, so you generally have about 20 seconds to make it worth it for them.'

MARKETING DOS AND DON'TS

- **Don't forget to create a strong email signature.** Every time you send an email, you have an opportunity to share your web address, contact information and compelling strapline. You can even include links to your social media profiles and recent blog posts.

- **Do blog.** It's a great way to build a tribe by encouraging the reader to sign up to your mailing list and position yourself as an expert. Make your blogs valuable and useful and publish blogs with consistency, to pull readers back frequently. Always ensure that you include a short bio

at the end of your blog outlining your expertise, strapline and a link to
your website.

- **Do incentivise people to sign up to your mailing list.** You could offer a
free report, e-book, tips sheet, webinar, worksheet or printable poster.
Consider what your ideal customer would find useful, create it and offer
it as a freebie to entice sign-ups to your mailing list. Once people have
joined your list, you can develop relationships with them by sending
useful information or links to blog posts including discounted offers.
Mailchimp and Aweber have good newsletter templates and enable you
to create sign-up forms and set up autoresponders.

- **Don't be afraid of making videos.** If you have a phone that takes
videos you can harness this powerful visual medium to connect
directly with your customers and provide them with a strong insight
into what you are all about. Vimeo and YouTube enable you to post and
host your videos on their sites, and embed them into your own website
and link to them from your social media profiles. Just remember to
include your web address and call to action at the end of your videos.

- **Do go local.** If your business sells to local people only, list your site on
Google Local and free classified directories such as Yell, The Best Of,
Thomson Local and so on.

- **Do go global.** If you have a website, you can in theory get subscribers
to your newsletter and customers from all over the world. To improve
your chances of success, though, you could provide translated pages
and product information specific to the territories you wish to focus
on, with prices in the local currency. This is ideal if your products
require no demonstration or face-to-face explanation. Alternatively
you could license a foreign company to pay you a royalty for each sale
along with a licensing fee in order to produce the product and use your
brand name.

- **Don't advertise unless you have a specific niche, and try PR first.**
For example, if you target vets or cookery students, it might be worth
advertising in a publication which targets them. However, advertising
in the media can be expensive, so aim to get editorial coverage first via
PR, as that's free. Facebook advertising, however, is a more affordable
way to get your messages in front of people who fit into your niche
audience (see page 149).

- **Do get organised.** Get a wall planner or create a PR calendar which
indicates when to send out press releases with specific angles. For
example, if your business has an angle on being kind, you might
submit PR to publications ahead (three months ahead if targeting
glossy magazines) of Random Acts of Kindness Day.

- **Do be clear with your goals.** 'Aim to do two to three tasks per day towards achieving that goal, whether that's making two phone calls and asking for a testimonial from a customer or preparing materials and practising your pitch,' advises Lisa Barber.

- **Do understand where the stories are in your business to make the most of PR.** What are people talking about on social media? What's trending? What are industry publications covering? What is being debated? How might you add to the debate?

- **Do get creative.** For example, if you are promoting a new spa product you could hire a masseur and send them to all the glossy magazines to deliver your press release and give the editor a back rub (if they can get through reception).

- **Don't think you are too small for TV.** Look for new Sky channels and offer them competition prizes in exchange for a free advert.

- **'Don't leave a bad comment unanswered,'** advises Frugi's Lucy Jewson. 'Never remove a negative comment, just show people you've listened and take their concerns seriously.

- **Don't forget to measure your marketing and track responses.** This enables you to know which marketing methods, headlines, audiences and other variables are working best and which are not working so well. You can measure your marketing by outlining the measurable components, such as split-testing two different subject lines in your email campaign (you can do this using Mailchimp) or having customers quote a source code depending on where they heard about you. Always ask fresh leads where they heard about you – from a friend, website link, search engine or flyer? 'We use something called Act-On, which tracks digital footprints,' says Liz Jackson. 'It's a great way of tracking your digital marketing spend. Say you have a 100,000 email addresses, Act-On will tell you who opened the email and so on. It scores everything based on behaviour.'

CREATE A CREDIBLE, CLICK-WORTHY WEBSITE

You can sell online via eBay or Amazon, and possibly Etsy.com or Folksy. com, so you don't need to have your own website to test the market. However, if you do, once you have secured your domain name (the bit after the 'www') from a site such as 123-reg.co.uk or http://uk.godaddy. com and have found somewhere reliable to securely host your site for a few pounds per month, you need to carefully plan your content.

This topic is a book in itself, but here are five vital elements to get right when it comes to creating a good website:

01. Shop around to find the right website platform/theme or designer/ developer for you. If you are opting to use a platform such as WordPress.com, you will need to choose a theme. Some themes (what the site looks like) are free, and others are available for between £50 and £100. Other low-cost DIY website options include Create.net, Joomla.org, Wix.com, Moonfruit.com, plus webstore.amazon.com and pages.ebay.com/storefronts/building.html. Alternatively you can have your website designed and developed by a bespoke developer.

02. Look at other websites for best practice of where key content elements are positioned, such as logo, header, footer, contact info, navigation bars, drop-down menus, buy buttons and so on. If you opt to use a platform such as WordPress.com (which has all kinds of plug-ins to add functions to your site, from adding PayPal buttons to inserting sign-up forms), you can download templates which have everything positioned well for optimum usability.

03. Outsource your design, development and even copywriting if it is not your strength. Your site should be visually enticing, so, if you don't have a big budget for logo design or other imagery for your site, take a look at GraphicLeftovers.com and GraphicRiver.net to see if any logos there suit your branding ideas. Alternatively you can get a reasonably priced logo from smallbusinesslogos.co.uk; you can crowdsource for various people to pitch ideas to you via crowdspring.com or 99designs.co.uk; or you can hire a designer for $5 at fiverr.com. See pages 44–6 for more on outsourcing.

04. Make your words web-friendly. Focus your home page text on what's in it for the customer and address the reader with 'you' rather than using 'we'. Leave 'we do this' text for your 'About Us' page.

05. Ensure that your site is optimised for search engines. You can learn a lot by typing 'search engine optimisation tips' into Google (and see box below). I didn't believe in search engine optimisation (SEO) until my web team made some quite simple but effective changes to our website content. We now attract millions of people to our site. Search engine optimisation is absolutely key.

Once your website is live, make use of Google's free tools such as Google Webmaster Tools and Google Analytics to gain insight on what is working and what needs attention. For example, these tools will show you which keywords and search terms are driving visitors to your site, as well as the websites that are referring traffic your way.

SEARCH ENGINE OPTIMISATION (SEO) TIPS

In a nutshell, SEO is about ensuring you create a positive search loop. The better your content, the better your click-through rates (the number of people who click on a link to your site) and the lower your bounce rates (those who click straight off your site). SEO is the process of improving the visibility of your website on search engine result pages. Internet users rarely click through pages and pages of search results, so you want your site to rank high in the list to improve your chances of being visited. The consequence will be happier (returning) visitors and a higher perceived authority, and thus a higher ranking in Google.

These tips show how you can please both search engines and visitors.

- Create unique, authentic, fresh, quality content which is first published on your site (as opposed to duplicate content) and gains citations and inbound links from other reputable, authoritative sites. Content that is linked is perceived by search engines as having more authority than content that is not.

- Ensure that your site is relevant (by examining text, headlines, titles, page descriptions) and important (by examining authority of those pages via the number of quality links to your site).

- Consider the words and terms that users type into search engines to find your web pages and related content. Then ensure that your site actually includes those keywords within its pages, in your URLs, page titles, meta tags, main headlines, blog-post titles, video/image captions and navigation, so that keyword and page content is accurately reflected.

- Ensure that search engines can easily crawl your pages. For instance, use Google Webmaster Tools (GWT) to identify any errors.

- Break news stories where possible. Being first gives you a window of time to be indexed before competitors.

- Minimise bounce rates and maximise user dwell time by making sure that content is user-driven and delivers on promises it gives in its title and description. Ensure content is interesting, useful and engaging. Write content for your users not for search engines and deliver a diverse range of content across multiple formats.

ANNABEL'S KITCHEN CABINET

BRAND AMBASSADOR: MYLEENE KLASS

Back when she landed the coveted place in the pop band Hear'Say, managers and agents were in the driving seat of Myleene's destiny. These days Myleene has regained full control of her future and her business empire. She is involved in every decision for her hugely successful ranges Baby K for Mothercare and her clothing line at Littlewoods; consequently she's learnt a huge amount about building a global brand.

'For Baby K, I own the brand as I wanted to own the rights, so I'm fully involved in every aspect … My range is my own vision,' says Myleene. 'I see myself as an ambassador for the brand and know how strong the brand is.'

The same goes for her brand at Littlewoods: 'There's not a thread that I don't know about, not a single thing,' she says. 'Today, on the way to this interview, I've been testing the make-up for my Littlewoods brand. I've got everything in my bag from sample stage, because I get the final say on everything.'

And Myleene's products have such a distinctive look, which just say 'Myleene'; her brand has that much clarity. That's because Myleene knows exactly who her customers are. 'If you tell me to give you a profile breakdown of each of my customers, my Baby K customer all the way through to my Littlewoods customer, I can do it,' she says.

Knowing who your customer is, what they desire, what benefits or solutions they are seeking, literally supercharges everything else. By knowing this you provide products and services that solve their problems and satisfy them.

'I've just launched my bedding range, despite there being a lot of bedding out there. So how do I differentiate? By knowing who my customer is. My customer wants something that is effective, something that stands out, that is as quirky as their personalities but is affordable and has to go through a 40-degree wash; they are mums.

'As I have various different brands and am constantly diversifying and trying new things, there are different challenges in each area,' admits Myleene. 'For example, with my children's brand, safety is my key asset, but with my online fashion brand, it's value for money while oozing fashion at the same time. I feel extremely satisfied that mums know I've done the groundwork so that they don't have to and they can hold a product in their hands which they can trust.'

That strength of brand identity leads to strong brand *integrity* too. It makes it easier to know which partnerships and opportunities to pursue and which to relinquish.

'Five years ago I was offered a deal that my 13-year-old self would never have believed,' recalls Myleene. 'It was to sign up for five years to a huge international brand and more money than I could have ever imagined, but I turned it down, because it wasn't right for where my brand needed to be,' explains Myleene. 'It didn't fit with my brand values.

'I felt the company offering the deal was shotgun. It didn't have class, or the prestige that I wanted,' she says. 'You can always step down the ladder, but you can't climb up it again once you've descended in terms of how your brand is represented.

'So ask yourself, what do you stand for?' she advises. 'You can't stand for everything. You have to have brand integrity. And that's not cutting your nose off to spite your face. Yes I did lose a huge cheque and security of five years, but what is five years compared to a lifetime of work and all the work I have put in, plus the fact that they could bring my brand name down?'

When you have that clarity in your branding, its perception, and the brand's overarching purpose, you know which route to take to give your wares the best chance of success. Myleene hasn't done a couture Dior collection; she chose Littlewoods, she chose Mothercare, because she knows who she appeals to. 'I know exactly where I stand in the market. The quality has got to be correct. I've always wanted to be an affordable range. I'm a working mum. I didn't want to price mums out of the market,' says Myleene.

With sales at an all-time high, by creating strong brands which tap into what mothers want, both here and overseas, the Myleene Klass brands look set to grow from strength to strength.

07
MAKE T
MOST O
NETWO

HE
F YOUR
RKS

NETWORKING KNOW-HOW

Networking is a vital skill for anyone in business, but it's especially important in the early days of a start-up. As a business owner you must be active, not passive. That means not only relying on your existing connections – though of course they can be invaluable – but also being willing to go out into sometimes unfamiliar situations, being unafraid to talk to people who have knowledge and experience and, above all, being prepared to listen, share and give.

When I started writing my first book, I was able to test out the recipes I was creating on babies and toddlers that were coming to my playgroup. I suppose I've always had that entrepreneurial spirit in me, as I set up Babes In The Wood before I ever wrote my books or produced supermarket food ranges, because I recognised a problem – a lack of decent playgroups in the area – and wanted to solve it. The other mums I knew had talked about wanting to get together, so I took a stand and made it happen. The group provided me with a network of mums who could relate to each other and it was this fantastic group that gave me the honest feedback I needed for my recipes and that inspired me to write a recipe book in the first place.

I still use the same philosophy of listening intently to feedback from my target audience. For years, I have been going to baby shows up and down the country – huge events with tens of thousands of visitors. I host talks on the main stage, where mums have the opportunity to put their questions to me, and then I plant myself on the Annabel Karmel stand so I can better understand exactly what mums' and parents' needs are. We talk to everybody who comes by: 'What are the best things you've bought? Which are the favourite recipes you've used?' And it's not just about what they like about Annabel Karmel; I want to know which of my competitors' meals they prefer and why, or what they'd like to see more of from me. Getting feedback from all types of parents is invaluable and I always come away with an agenda of new ideas and new areas to research.

Using your networks and networking isn't only about gaining feedback and conducting research, it also provides you with a platform on which to build relationships and advocacy for your business, to tap into communities and to connect with people locally and globally. From those relationships you can gain:

- Contacts and introductions

- Business referrals

- Word-of-mouth recommendations

- Sources of suppliers, partners and collaborators

- Custom

- Information

- Inspiration and encouragement

Personal contacts are a great source of information, but if you can grow that network you will open yourself up to an even bigger hive of activity and knowledge. By getting yourself out there and meeting friends of friends, or contacts of contacts, you'll find cheerleaders who get your idea and want to support you. They'll want to help you share your business idea and may be able to point you towards people who can assist you in achieving your goals.

You'll be able to do the same for other people, which is equally – and in many cases even more – rewarding. You need to start by showing an interest. My attitude is that you need to be a friend to have a friend. When I meet someone, I think about whom I might introduce them to who might be helpful or mutually beneficial; it's a gift rather than a trade.

YOU CAN MAKE MORE FRIENDS IN TWO MONTHS BY BECOMING INTERESTED IN OTHER PEOPLE THAN YOU CAN IN TWO YEARS BY TRYING TO GET PEOPLE INTERESTED IN YOU.

Dale Carnegie

I also realised the power of digital communication early on; I would use my website and social media channels as a means of connecting with mothers and linking them with each other via forums and chats. The Annabel Karmel website now receives millions of hits a year, and we are more active than ever on our social platforms. With good-quality, relevant content, we've built up a fantastic loyal following of parents, who we can tap into for honest feedback, reviews and ideas. Mums play a vital role in helping to shape everything we do, whether it's feeding back on a new recipe or telling us what they want from a new app.

From that initial Babes In The Wood group to the people I've met at exhibitions and from those I engage with via social networking, I've gained so much: opportunities I wouldn't have been privy to had I not participated in a conversation, introductions to key people who have helped me to achieve my objectives, partnerships I'd not have thought of. It all began with that initial connection and conversation leading to collaboration. Today, that's what business is all about. This is great news for fledgling start-ups, as the playing field has been levelled. It's far easier today to connect and engage in conversation with influential people than it has ever been before.

One of my most successful collaborations came from tapping into the network I had just been introduced to at Disney. I had been approached by Disney to help them develop a parenting website called Family.com. I had always thought that it was a shame that, more often than not, cartoon characters were used to promote *un*healthy foods. I asked the people I was working with on the website who the food-licensing contacts at Disney were and subsequently arranged a meeting with Dan Dossa, who was in charge of Disney's food licensing. One contact led to another.

I remember us both being sat at this very large boardroom table at Disney. I explained that all the healthy snack ranges for toddlers were pretty tasteless and asked whether he would be interested in developing a range of wholesome snacks that tasted fantastic, using Winnie the Pooh and Mickey Mouse. I believed that the Annabel Karmel brand would provide trust for mums and the Disney characters would deliver child appeal.

I thought it would take forever to get a huge corporation like Disney to agree, but at that meeting Dan said, 'Let's do it, it's a great idea.' I didn't expect that. Yet, after conducting some research and working with Mary Brazier from the Disney food-licensing department, who was as passionate as me about the range, we discovered that the Disney brand didn't have as much perceived integrity as the Annabel Karmel brand, so my brand had to be stronger on the pack than Disney, which was interesting.

I also said 'no' to a lot of the samples, which were bland, until they finally came back with something really tasty. There are now 17 products in the Annabel Karmel Disney snack range, which is stocked in all the major supermarkets and which won the Halo Award for outstanding product range at Disney's annual conference.

The supermarkets like the range because it has longevity. They are ideal for ages one to four years (in fact, older children love them too), whereas most toddlers' snacking ranges go up to 18 months, so they stay longer in the baby aisle. It's a successful partnership for all involved; and having Disney on the pack means that I can now export to almost any country, because everybody knows and loves Mickey Mouse.

It all started with a connection at Disney via the parenting website and then a conversation with Dan. Connection and conversation led to collaboration.

OPPORTUNITY KNOCKS AND OPENS DOORS

According to Richard Wiseman, author of *The Luck Factor*, networking actually makes you luckier. His research showed that lucky people tend to network more, stay in touch with contacts, listen, use eye contact and open body language and smile more than their unlucky counterparts. The more people you meet, the more chance of bumping into someone who'll positively affect your life, so networking widens your luck. By striking up a conversation with someone, you instantly open the floodgates to many new possibilities and opportunities.

As Richard Wiseman explains, 'By chatting to Sue, you are only a handshake away from the 300 people that she knows on first-name terms. But it doesn't end there. Each of Sue's friends also knows 300 people on first-name terms … You are only two handshakes away from roughly 300 x 300 people – 90,000 new possibilities for a chance opportunity, just by saying hello to Sue.'

I might never have had my first book published if it wasn't for me getting out there and making the most of my networks. It was quite random how it happened. Somebody I played tennis with suggested I speak to a book packager they knew of, Eddison Sadd. They design, print and package books and then sell them to publishers all over the world, so they are effectively the middleman between the author and the publishing company. This does mean that royalties are reduced. However, if they can generate interest, the book can lead to something far bigger, as it did for me, and an international audience.

I had tried so many publishers prior to meeting with Eddison Sadd that I didn't have great expectations of the meeting. However, I was as passionate as ever about my book mission and they immediately believed in me. Almost 25 years on, my *Complete Baby and Toddler Meal Planner* has sold 4 million copies worldwide, becoming the number-one parenting title in the UK and the bestselling children's cookery book by volume of all time.

It was a contact that served me well. The point is that, through being open and having a conversation about my dream to be published, I was introduced to one of the biggest publishers in the world who kick-started my career as an author.

I learnt from the relationship that, when somebody believes in you, you should show them the respect that they afforded you. Even though I signed a one-book deal with Eddison Sadd and worked directly with Ebury and Random House afterwards, I certainly felt a loyalty to Eddison Sadd and so I let them handle the foreign editions of all my books. We are still working together. In fact, just over a year ago, I published 10 mini cookbooks with them for Sainsbury's. I think if somebody believes in you at the beginning, think about them when things are going well, and give them something back if you can.

My belief is that it's important to talk about your idea with as many different people as possible. This will offer you a different perspective on things, and could fuel an idea or string of thought that you hadn't originally considered. It's also that passion for what you do that will get others talking – and connecting you. If I hadn't mentioned the book to the guy I was playing tennis with, who knows … I may never have got a publishing deal and be where I am today.

As well as informal networking through friends and their networks, official networking events can be very fruitful. There are regular networking events being run all around the country: from those targeting mums in business to formal Chambers of Commerce ones, and from speed-networking to three-minute pitching gatherings. You never know when you might meet someone who could have a positive impact on your business. You'll be more likely to make that happen if you get out there and network at events like these, both on your home soil and abroad – whether industry-focused or general.

For me, networking abroad has proven as fruitful as connecting nearer to home. While I was at the Dubai literary festival, word had got around about my work through talking to other authors and various different people, and on the last day I was told that one of the world's largest global airlines was interested in talking to me. I arrived home to find an email from the head of food and beverage for a leading Middle Eastern airline, who was in fact English. He said they'd be interested in us designing their food for children on the plane. A few weeks later, I was returning to Dubai to meet with this amazing global company, and a year later we were developing airline food for children which would be served on all of their planes across the world. We now also export our organic baby purees and snacking range to the Middle East, which is something we simply wouldn't have done had I not seized the opportunity when it was presented to me. Once again, connection led to conversation, which led to collaboration.

TOP TIPS FOR EFFECTIVE NETWORKING

It is important to dedicate time to both face-to-face networking as well as online networking, as relationships can be built faster and cemented when you meet in person. If you don't do either properly it can be a drain on time, so follow these tips to get the most from your networking efforts. Find opportunities to talk, connect, interact and go with the flow to see where it takes you.

01. **Prepare and be clear about your objectives.** What do you wish to achieve from attending this event/connecting with these people?

Perhaps you'd like to find a venue for an event? A publisher for a book? A joint-venture partner to collaborate with? Retailers or distributors to sell your products? Team members to recruit? Set networking targets – what you'd like to come away with. For example, to gain introductions to 10 potential new stockists by the end of the year or find someone who can swap knowledge/skills (e.g. social media training for bookkeeping). Focus on those objectives.

02. Give, contribute, support and share. Focus on the other person's needs first. How can you be the link in the chain for someone? Successful networking is about mutual gain, collaboration, community and sharing. It's about connections and community rather than transactions and commerce. What you give is what you get with networking, so it should not be used simply as a lead-generator. Uncover people's objectives and consider whether you know anyone who can help them. Match and introduce people. Tweet about them. Offer advice. 'I am very proud of the WOW (Women on Wednesdays) competition that we run on Twitter,' says Jacqueline Gold, CEO of Ann Summers. 'Every week hundreds of women tweet me their business idea and we then trawl through these entries and choose our top three. What I love about it is they are very supportive of each other; they interact with each other, they do business which each other as a result of WOW. I profile their website at the same time, so they get a drive in business and offer advice and support. Once a year we pick our top three and organise a mentoring lunch. In addition, we also invite those three down to our head office and have a mentoring day that they find really helpful. Everyone is really supportive.'

03. Tell people what you are looking for. Share your objectives with those you are networking with. Be specific. For example, if you are looking for an event venue or have a service for pre-school children, say it out loud to your networking group as someone in the room is likely to give you relevant contacts. Don't forget to return the favour by asking them what they are seeking.

04. Harness your existing contacts. LinkedIn is great for this. Send a quarterly email seeing if you can help anyone by asking them to reply to your questions: 'What are you trying to achieve right now? Who would be your ideal connections/in which industry? Try me to see if I can help.' Then they might be able to help you in return. You could also try going to a school reunion. As well as reminiscing about old Mr Price's high trouser line, ask your old mates what they're up to and then tell them about your work too. You never know when an opportunity will present itself. 'Recently I went to a school reunion,' says Fiona Clark of Inspiredmums.co.uk. 'Two of the people worked in law firms, but had children and were asking me if I help people get back to work. It's tough for the law firms to retain female employees and it is hard for mums to re-enter. That conversation led to a meeting about maternity coaching at a law firm, simply from networking with old school friends.'

05. Match your existing network contacts to your objectives. Do you know anyone specifically who could potentially help you? For example, Thea Green secured £250,000 for Nails Inc. through a range of investors who came from her own personal network of contacts and introductions from those contacts.

06. Have something to talk about. 'I used every networking opportunity possible, whether it be online or in person, to get the word out about my new career as a coach,' says Fiona Clark, who attends women's networks such as Athena and WIBN. 'I also started to run workshops myself for mums returning to work or considering starting a business, so that I had some news to talk about at networking events and in the local press.'

07. Have questions to ask, then listen. After asking people who they are hoping to connect with and what their goals are, ask them how they got into what they are doing now and what they are looking for from this networking event. Listen intently to responses. You learn far more from listening than talking. Many people make the mistake of using the time when the other person is talking to think about what they want to say or look around the room to find the next person to talk to. Active listening is a skill that can have a really positive impact on all relationships.

08. Focus on quality rather than quantity. 'Networking is about the amount you give,' says Chloe Macintosh, co-founder of Made.com. 'Brent Hoberman taught me that. I don't look at people as assets first; I think, what can I give them? I then create a bond, not so that they owe me, but because it creates a transparency and enables both parties to be clear about what they are looking for. That is how I created my network in a way that I am comfortable with.'

09. Identify your ideal connections and be tenacious about connecting with them. 'Networking is very important,' says Wendy Shand, founder of Totstotravel.co.uk, who uses social media and regularly attends focused networking groups and 'meet the media' events, which she regards as crucial. 'More and more I am being strategic about the connections I make, so am less shy about identifying somebody that I would like to get to know better and then asking them out for lunch. It pays to be tenacious!'

10. Become a networking detective. Devote an hour to reading comments and tweets, following conversations, finding out what others are saying and which topics are generating the most interest and response.

11. **Be yourself, be *natural*.** Develop conversations about shared interests, from being a dog-lover to enjoying a good book. Build relationships by being you and connecting with like-minded people.

12. **Ask for advice.** People often like to give advice so feel free to post that you are new to networking but would love to get advice on how to do something or other. You'll get a good response and will be able to then engage in conversation. Give advice too. Participate actively and you'll get more out of networking.

13. **Avoid trying to sell at every opportunity.** Sure, outline what you do and why you do it, but don't try to sell to people.

14. **Consistently network as often as you can.** 'Realise that everywhere there is an opportunity,' says Caroline Castigliano. 'Through networking you get invited to events … so you meet more influential people. You just have to constantly keep that whole networking thing going to seize those opportunities.'

15. **Harness your feminine power of talking openly and sharing to open the door to endless possibilities.** '[Women] do business in the way they do everything else. We'll sit down, we'll share, we'll get to know each other, take the mask off and we connect,' says Lynne Franks, founder of the SEED Network (Sustainable Enterprise and Empowerment Dynamics). 'Women are naturally open. In fact, somebody who used to work at Shell told me that they had done research which revealed that women connect and build relationships by sitting down with each other and talking, whereas men find it very difficult, so that's why men do most of their business standing up – either on the golf course, in the pub, walking to the coffee machine or in the urinal – whereas women find it more comfortable to sit down, talk and create something together. It just flows naturally. I embrace that.'

16. **Find and become cheerleaders for other mums in business.** 'Get out there and find out what the industry is all about,' says Lynne Franks. 'There are so many women's networking events now so I advise you go to as many as you can. You'll find a lot of support out there.'

HOW TO CREATE A BUZZ WITH SOCIAL NETWORKING

As we've learnt already, business today is more about connection, conversation and collaboration than ever before. It's therefore important for small-business owners to go where the conversations are, which is generally on social networks. But as there are so many people using these mediums (over 1 billion active Facebook users creating 41,000 posts per second, over 280 million active Twitter users tweeting 500 million tweets per day and 300 million business contacts on LinkedIn), it's critical to get your social networking strategy right. Contributing actively in group discussions on Facebook, tweeting with hashtags (#) about topics which are relevant to you and connecting with industry contacts on LinkedIn enables you to connect and engage with potential customers, partners, suppliers, investors … people who like what you are doing.

Dessi Bell tapped into social media to create a buzz for her Zaggora fitnesswear products. She gave away 500 ThermoFit products to bloggers and influential people and then built on that.

'We took to Twitter and literally searched for people who might be interested,' explains Dessi. 'We sent out thousands of tweets before we got our group of samplers. It was hard work. Then it was about getting them to spread the word and leverage the buzz we were getting with retail relationships.'

Growing such a big online community of advocates was a core secret to the success of Zaggora, and building a community of half a million women from all over the world who love their products is what Dessi considers to be her greatest achievement to date. 'We continue to utilise social media for marketing to over 500,000 followers through various social media networks. Word of mouth is such a powerful tool.

'You have to give your customers the power to share, which means giving them the right incentives. In our case it has been about making weight loss fun and focusing on the positives, which is a great message.'

USING INSTAGRAM TO PROMOTE YOUR BUSINESS

Instagram is another form of social networking that is becoming very popular. On Instagram you can post images and short 15-second videos. I've been using it a lot. Here are a few tips on getting the most from it:

- Choose an account name, ideally your business name.

- Consider how Instagram fits into your overall brand-marketing strategy. For example, is your objective to increase awareness, shift perception or reach a new audience?

- Choose posts that will appeal to your followers. I post lots of recipes, fun food photographs, pictures of me with my children and my three dogs and behind-the-scenes photos. It's a snapshot of your life.

- Keep posts personal and not corporate. Balance fun images with pictures about your business. Keep captions short and incorporate a few hashtags – preferably not more than three.

- Reward your followers with discount codes, promos or 'money can't buy' opportunities.

- Find the brands and people you enjoy and can learn from. Look through your followers and follow back anyone of interest. Through Instagram I have found people all over the world who are passionate about food and I've connected with people I haven't seen for years. It's also a great way of keeping in touch with my children!

TOP TIPS FOR MAKING THE MOST OF SOCIAL MEDIA

In general, to get the most from your social media endeavours:

- **Go where your audience is.** Create profiles on the social networks that your audience are most likely to use, whether that's Facebook, Twitter, Pinterest, Instagram, LinkedIn, Google+ or all of the above.

- **Focus on your purpose.** To tap into communities and connect with individuals within that community, you need a cause. So connection comes back to having that all-important purpose again, the passion behind your business.

- **Consider whether you are broadcasting or networking.** Count how many people converse and interact with you once you've reached out to them via various channels (whether that's through forum and group posts, Twitter/Facebook/LinkedIn updates, blogs, YouTube videos and so on). How many people are you actually passing opportunities to and sharing thoughts and ideas with? If the answer is a high number, you are networking effectively. If the level of actual conversation is low, then you need to stop broadcasting and start networking. Make sure you give ways to enter into conversation with you by including your contact information wherever you post, along with your links.

- **Know who your customers are and find out how they tell your story on your behalf.** It is far easier for your story to go viral if you target the right customer to share that story.

- **Identify influencers.** Create remarkable products or services and content and it will be shared if you get it in front of the right people: the most influential people within your niche. Your job is to determine who those people are. They might be bloggers, oft-quoted industry experts, taste-makers, authorities within your niche or campaigners with common purposes. Find the queen bees in each community – the main influencers within your customer base who know everyone and have built relationships within that community. Try creating a list of 10–20 influencers to start with. Then rank them in order of their 'social networking potential' (SNP), reach and influence – i.e. how frequently their name appears in Google searches, number of followers/fans, number of blog comments they get, their relevance and their Klout and Quantcast scores (which measure audience reach).

- **Examine the key influencers' profiles and get their attention by sparking a conversation.** On LinkedIn, do you have any shared connections and are there any connections of theirs whom you'd find it useful and valuable to connect with? Check out their Twitter profiles, are there any opinions or interests that you share or tweets that you can reply to – not in a sales-pitch-introduction way, but just to make that first connection and spark conversation? Read their blog posts and comment on relevant ones, addressing any synergies or commonalities. Connect their story and purpose to yours in some way. Tag influencers in your tweets about relevant content to entice them to follow and retweet you. Also aim to connect with them on LinkedIn. Participate actively in discussions they are having, as they are the currency of social media.

- **Seek the feedback of key influencers.** Send them a free sample of your product or service, saying that you would value their honest opinion if they have the time, then follow up with a phone call, brief email or an invitation to meet up. Give them something extra – some information that the general public don't know yet – to imbue trust and make them feel a part of your trusted tribe.

- **List those who are already frequent likers of your posts, retweeters of your tweets and so on.** They love what you do, so you can reward them by sending them free samples in exchange for their brand ambassadorship (i.e. that they promote you at regular intervals to their own networks).

- **Be generous and interesting.** Send opportunities, referrals and connections to people you aim to build relationships with. Seek out common ground and start conversations. Congratulate people; show an interest. Remember it's not all about you, it's about them, so don't simply tweet/post about your products; share useful links, tips, photos, inspirational quotes and video links.

- **Demonstrate your value.** Rather than say 'Founder of XYZ Company', write about what you do for people and why. Use your mission statement, elevator pitch or strapline if possible. If you are a bestselling author, say so. If you are a childcare consultant and aim to make mums' lives easier when choosing childcare, say so. They may not have heard of XYZ company, so it makes sense to highlight your skills (and it makes you easier to find when people are searching for childcare).

- **Leave a digital footprint leading back to your website.** Provide links to your site in a 'signature' whenever you comment in online communities and groups, industry blogs and review sites.

- **Set up content swaps with other people targeting your audience.** For instance, guest blog and comment on other people's blogs but also invite others to supply you with content. Retweet messages you believe in and ask others to do the same. You gain validation of your content and build relationships with fellow content authors.

- **Follow journalists, bloggers and magazines on Twitter.** Respond to case study requests. You can try searching for the commonly used hashtag #journorequest, which journalists often use when looking for experts or quotes.

- **Use social media search tools to enhance your productivity and effectiveness.** Use the advanced search functions on LinkedIn and Twitter (https://twitter.com/search) to find people to connect with based on location, keywords, product names, what people are interested in and how many years' experience they have in certain fields.

- **Consider setting a small weekly budget and paying to promote your posts.** Facebook is now a form of highly targeted, low-cost, paid advertising, and you can promote offers and drive targeted prospects towards your website or fulfil an action you'd like them to take. Facebook uses an 'edge rank' algorithm to determine what is shown in people's newsfeeds, based on how many comments and 'likes' particular posts get, the affinity you have with the recipients and the duration of engagement. They change this constantly and in mid-2014 shifted the focus away from business pages, which are getting far less free engagement. The only way people will see your posts is if they opt in to get notifications from you or if you pay to promote your posts.

- **Plan your social media posts.** Don't think about what you want to tell people, think about what they want to know, then plan your posts accordingly. Keep them short: keep tweets around 100 characters to allow people to retweet and comment and keep posts relevant.

TWITTER DOS AND DON'TS FROM JACQUELINE GOLD

- **'Do be authentic and true to yourself,'** says Jacqueline Gold. 'It's the only way that you will find common ground with your followers.'

- **'Do get involved in the conversations your customers are having to build on synergies.** We do this very well on social media – that's how we were able to build on the *Fifty Shades of Grey* opportunity,' explains Jacqueline, who tapped into what her customers were saying about the erotic toys mentioned in the popular books.

- **'Don't bombard people with business products and don't talk at them,'** advises Jacqueline. 'You have to talk about you as an individual and your lifestyle. They want to know that you are a real person, what your values are and what matters to you. You need to understand the different channels of your business, whether it's the individual behind the business or the product side; both need different voices (and profiles).'

- **'Don't ignore complaints,'** Jacqueline suggests. 'Twitter is the new garden fence, which means you will get people saying how wonderful your product is and you will also get the odd complaint. Tell people you're really sorry to hear that and will get on to that first thing tomorrow morning. It's important people see that the company cares.'

TOP TIPS TO BOOST ENGAGEMENT ON TWITTER

- **Define your objectives** – i.e. the actions that you aim to encourage. This might be driving traffic to your website (otherwise known as DR, direct response, tweets), sales via compelling time-limited offers, sign-ups to your mailing list, downloads of your content or apps, more followers, retweets or favourites.

- **Test engagement.** Try out different tweets at different times and measure the results. Which tweets met your objectives the most?

- **Tweet effectively.** Start with a question (e.g. 'Want your child to eat more veg?'), then provide a solution, call to action and link (e.g. 'We've compiled the 10 best recipes. Check them out here: [insert web link]').

- **Use hashtags wisely** depending on your objectives. For example, use them minimally if you are trying to drive more traffic to your site/generate more sign-ups, so as not to distract from the link itself. However, if your aim is to get more followers, you could start your own relevant hashtags, such as #feedkidshealthily or #healthyfood to spread the word, or tap into trending relevant hashtags for the same purpose.

- **Use compelling words** if your main aim is to boost sales. Words such as 'free', 'sale', 'code', 'bonus', 'limited' and 'exclusive' make offers more compelling.

- **Create Twitter-specific promotions.** For example, 'The first 30 followers to RT this tweet win a free feeding bowl' or 'Just 2 days left to use your coupon code TWITTER for 50 per cent flash sale items [insert web link].'

- **Create Twitter-specific competitions,** such as: 'Today's #HealthySnack contest has begun. Join in with your snack idea tweets for a chance to win [insert web link]'. Don't forget to announce the winners and use their Twitter handles, the contest hashtag (#HealthySnack) and thanks with a link to the winning tweet/recipe on your site.

- **Try the 'flock to unlock' strategy,** where your followers are invited to gain an offer or freebie only once it has been shared/retweeted a set amount of times. For example, 'Tomorrow we're announcing our biggest offer yet. Check back at noon tomorrow for details.' At noon the following day, tweet 'Get 70% off baby clothes for 24 hours only. #BubbaFlashSale. RT to spread the word. Coupon code unlocked after 100 RTs.'

- **Use Twitter analytical tools to measure your response rates.** Try https://ads.twitter.com, Hootsuite.com, SocialFlow.com, Topsy.com, Wayin.com, Brandwatch.com or Sysomos.com. Also track your competitors to see what they are doing and what campaigns are working best/not working so well.

HOW TO ATTRACT AND RETAIN LOYAL CUSTOMERS

❝❞
IT IS HIGH TIME THE IDEAL OF SUCCESS SHOULD BE REPLACED WITH THE IDEA OF SERVICE.

Albert Einstein

Networking enables you to find and build new relationships and strengthen existing ones. There are many other methods to building existing relationships. Indeed, looking after your existing customers is critical to building and sustaining a healthy business. Some brands are so intent on looking for the next big idea or new customer that they forget to look after the ranges that they have already launched and the customers who have already bought them. These need nurturing too and you can never be complacent.

The hardest part of marketing is attracting a new customer and persuading them to buy your product. But once they have bought your product, they become your customer and, if you do things right, you can harness the power of that customer to grow your business. They will come back again and again to buy from you, and they'll tell their friends about you; they might even supply you with one of the most powerful pieces of marketing collateral – a testimonial and/or case study. That's a whole lot of value from one satisfied customer. But that's the key – the customer must be satisfied, nay delighted, in order for any of this to happen. Everyone is looking for new business but never forget to look after existing customers.

Today's sophisticated consumers *expect* to be satisfied. If you can go the extra mile and be extraordinarily good, you'll delight them and, in doing so, get the most from them. And the good news is, repeat business and referred business costs you nothing; once you've spent your marketing budget on attracting them, once they are your customer, as long as you follow the customer satisfaction rules, you won't need to spend more on retaining them. Ultimately, delighted customers will increase your revenue, shorten your sales cycle and reduce your marketing spend. They'll become an extension of your sales team by liking, following, socially sharing, providing testimonials, referrals and reviews. To leverage social channels and the power of your customer, all you need to do is simply:

- Amaze them by providing an awesome product that they love, which solves their problem and meets their unmet needs.

- Be brilliant at customer service aftercare and make the whole experience of buying from you enjoyable.

- Provide customers with the tools to promote your services, from the opportunity to review or share details of their purchase to a referral programme or invitation to their friends with a discount for them.

- Go the extra mile for those 20 per cent of customers who are your best customers, for it is likely that 80 per cent of your sales will come from them – either directly, or from recommendations they make.

People power is effectual. By providing something amazing and/or free, you can build an enthusiastic community that spreads the word like wildfire. Customers today have the power to drive other customers towards or away from you because they have many platforms on which to talk about your products and your aftercare. They can create a positive buzz or a negative buzz.

As Amazon's Jeff Bezos says, 'If you make customers unhappy in the physical world, they might each tell six friends. If you make customers unhappy on the Internet, they can each tell 6,000.' And he should know. The American Customer Satisfaction Index recently revealed Amazon. com as champ in customer satisfaction.

ANNABEL'S KITCHEN CABINET

A WORD-OF-MOUTH SUCCESS: LIZ EARLE

'Our customers are our best advertisement – word of mouth is more valuable than any campaign,' says Liz Earle, co-founder of Liz Earle Beauty Co.

In fact, this word of mouth came about thanks to the outstanding products and the passionate purpose which went into creating them, along with a top-notch focus on customer service. This has led the company to its growth from four initial products sold by mail order into a multi-million-pound brand where products are bought at a rate of more than one per minute in 82 countries across the globe.

After forging a successful career as a beauty journalist, author and broadcaster, writing more than 30 books on the topics of health and beauty, Liz first moved into manufacturing when she was given nutritional advice to treat her eczema. She had tried everything to cure her skin condition but the simple advice to try evening primrose oil was a revelation for her; she realised it was possible to help control our skin through what we put on it and what we put in our bodies.

Meanwhile, Liz's friend, Kim Buckland, an ex-marketing executive for John Frieda, had spotted a gap in the skincare market for something straightforward, effective and well-priced. She suggested that the pair bring together Liz's knowledge and experience and Kim's marketing nous to create a luxurious yet affordable range which harnessed the power of nature.

Having had a lifelong passion for plants and the natural world, Liz Earle set about sourcing natural ingredients and botanical extracts to create beauty products with an ethical purpose.

They launched in 1995 with just four items, but their fantastic products and strong customer service led to customers and team members alike becoming passionate about it themselves and spreading the word. 'We also put customer service first from day one and, by doing so, quickly built up a network of happy customers who recommended us to friends and family,' says Liz.

Liz Earle's customers became an extended sales force. 'We were fortunate being in the skincare business that our products were constantly on show – we had lots of happy customers walking around with radiant, healthy-looking complexions who were naturally being asked what their secret was!' explains Liz.

They chose not to advertise in the early days: 'Partly because we couldn't afford it, but also because we believed that the powerful dynamic of word of mouth spoke far more profoundly, especially to women,' says Liz. 'Rather than spending our early limited budgets on advertising campaigns, we decided to pour money into the highest-quality ingredients and great packaging, while ensuring our range remained affordable.'

Liz advises: 'If you chase customer satisfaction rather than profit, your customers will be happy to recommend you, whatever business you're in, so put yourself in their shoes at all times and treat them as you'd like to be treated yourself.'

This focus on customer service and creating an excellent product paid off. In 2001, the duo opened a shop in Ryde on the Isle of Wight, which became the brand's HQ. The following year it launched online and, following thousands of requests from customers for a London shop, Liz and Kim opened a flagship store in Chelsea and expanded overseas.

Subsequently Liz has been able to enjoy the fruits of her success. After the brand's acquisition, she remains an ambassador for the products she created, while launching a new business she is equally passionate about from her West Country farm: Liz Earle Wellbeing.

HOW TO AMAZE YOUR CUSTOMERS

Ultimately, your customers pay your wages so make your customer service shine. Despite this reasonably easy way to differentiate yourself from other businesses, so many businesses fail on the customer service points. Here's how you can come out on top by valuing your customers.

- **Make your business a customer-centric one.** Everything should stem from them. Constantly consider how you can make your customers happier, more successful and less stressed. How can you improve their lives or make their lives easier? Focus on that and serving their needs rather than on how you can improve your company. Amazon's Jeff Bezos has always brought an empty chair into meetings, which is occupied by 'the most important person in the room' – the customer. 'We're not competitor-obsessed, we're customer-obsessed,' he says. 'We start with what the customer needs and we work backwards.'

- **Be brilliant.** Create outstanding products which people want to talk about and the press wants to write about.

- **Create a memorable and enjoyable experience.** 'Customers today have so much more to choose from, so you have to ask yourself, why will they choose me over others?' says Jacqueline Gold.

- **Exceed expectations and keep promises.** 'It's very simple to gain customer loyalty,' says Jennifer Irvine, founder of The Pure Package. 'You just do what you have told them you're going to do, so you fulfil the promise you made in the first place.' Jennifer also gives her customers extra goodies in their packages as an added bonus.

- **Ask your customers what special customer-service extras they'd like to see.** What could you do in order to deliver extraordinary customer service? By implementing those ideas you not only impress them with the outstanding service but with the fact that you've listened to their suggestions.

- **Add your own special touches to treat people as you'd wish to be treated.** Send a get-well message or card to a customer who's been complaining about an ailment to check they're okay; hire a car-cleaning firm to valet your customers' cars while they're in a meeting at your office or hand-write thank-you cards and pop them in with your invoice, along with a wrapped chocolate or similar small token of appreciation.

- **Respect your customers' time and respond fast to enquiries.** Don't leave them on hold while you try to find an answer. Arrange to call them back within the next 10 minutes so they can get on with their day. Set delivery measures such as answering emails within 7 hours and returning calls within 30 minutes.

- **Know how you'll deal with customer complaints.** Be transparent and honest. Apologise in a heartfelt way. Plan ahead so that you know how to deal with customer complaints or bad reviews. Show respect and say thank you, always. Learn from mistakes to improve your decisions moving forward. If a customer requests a refund, give them a refund and an extra gift. Not just a voucher to spend with you, but something they are not expecting that will make them consider trying another product at some time. By handling complaints well you can turn a dissatisfied customer into a loyal one. And, as Jennifer Irvine advises, 'Even if a customer is very nice when they complain, you still need to take it as seriously as an angry customer.'

- **Go the extra mile for customers and reward team members who do so.** Exceed expectations; deliver early; make them feel valued. For example, The Ritz-Carlton asks all staff to submit examples of other staff members going beyond the call of duty to help or delight a customer. The best story, known as a 'wow story', is chosen and distributed to all of the Ritz-Carlton hotels across the world and read out at pre-shift staff meetings. This is a great way to focus conversations on examples of outstanding behaviour and customer service instead of directing staff on how to behave. An added incentive to staff is there: a small cash reward if their story is chosen and a competition for the top 10 wow stories at the end of the year.

- **Gain feedback on how to improve.** Invite customers to score your different touchpoints of service and work on improving each area, even those areas you score highly on.

- **Be available.** Invest in an answerphone or redirect calls to your mobile.

- **Smile.** A friendly attitude and warm genuine smile can leave a lasting impression. And it costs you nothing.

- **Record every contact you make with them,** along with all their contact information and responses. Note down objections, feedback, what they've bought and when, plus why they've bought and where they heard of you.

- **Request referrals.** If you don't ask you don't get, so ask. Request referrals from friends, family, the local post-office owner, members of networks, your bank manager, accountant, club members and, once you have some, your customers.

- **Reward people for referring.** When you contact your customers to request feedback, also ask them for a testimonial or if they'd like to feature on your website as a case study, or if they could forward a special offer or introductory gift coupon on to three of their friends. You could reward those who do that with money off their next order.

- **Set up an affiliate scheme.** This means you pay a commission to those sales that come from your affiliates.

- **Value your customers.** Use their names, remembering their preferences, listening to them and following up.

- **Involve your customers in your customer-service programme.** For example, Kiddicare.com went one step further and recruited customers to become customer-product champions in return for loyalty points. So, customers who have reviewed a product positively will be asked to answer pre-sales questions asked by other potential customers.

DEVELOPING COLLABORATIVE ALLIANCES

SUCCESS IN THE MODERN WORLD DEPENDS ON THE REAL CONNECTIONS YOU HAVE.

Reid Hoffman, founder & CEO of LinkedOn

The Internet and the rise in digital media and social networks has effectively made the world smaller. It has provided small-business owners with the chance to connect with people from all over the world, and this has opened up market opportunities as we can find synergies with other businesses and source partners who can fill gaps in our own skillsets. Together, connected, we can pool resources, share insight, share audiences and share revenues and, ultimately, pursue new routes to markets and fast-track our success.

Alliances are of vital importance in today's open and collaborative world. They enable and fuel growth. You can create an eco-system that is based on reciprocal win-win collaboration and share the upside of what you each bring to the table, and you can do this while spreading both the risk and the cost. But how do you go about finding and establishing strategic partnerships with the right kind of companies? And which kind of partnership should you endeavour to pursue?

When you're building your business it's best to build relationships based on mutual benefit rather than cash exchanges. Once you know who you want to reach and what you want to achieve, the trick is to find out what your value is that you can offer potential brand partners. It's got to be a win-win for everybody; it can't be a one-way benefit. They've got to gain something from you and vice versa. Then you've got to invest time in creating and sustaining that relationship with your brand partner, being open and honest about what each of you shall gain. By taking this approach I have managed to create some very interesting relationships with some very interesting people, from a leading Middle Eastern airline to Marks & Spencer.

Here are eight steps to collaborating effectively:

01. Consider first what objective, or number of objectives, you are striving to achieve through a collaborative approach. For example, you may wish to prove your dedication to a certain purpose and enhance credibility by working with a charity on an event, or donating a percentage of profits to them. Or you may wish to gain PR by being able to announce that you are working with a high-profile company on a specific project. Perhaps you are seeking to enter a market, or extend reach in a market, by finding a collaborative partner who already has a significantly large audience in that field. Or maybe you'd like to join forces with a range of like-minded businesses to give you each a competitive edge over larger corporations. You might be looking for ways where you can help each other to work smarter and faster.

02. Consider what you have to offer in return for your partnership. How can you each be the bridge towards each other's objectives? What can you offer to each other? And how can you complement each other's proposition? For example, if you are partnering with a charity, you both might benefit from PR exposure, but they'd benefit from your donation and you'd benefit from showcasing your purpose. Or you might be able to enter into a partnership with a TV company who could give you airtime or a magazine with a large readership; in exchange you could provide content and competition prizes. Alternatively, you might be able to provide a product for a partner but under their own brand name. Consider how you can develop relationships which create long-term value.

03. Seek the win-win. Focus on the mutual gains. You both need to succeed rather than the balance being tipped in favour of one or the other. As James Caan says, 'All parties need to feel that they have a good deal so that they are incentivised and motivated enough.' There needs to be good reason for collaboration in order for you to bolt your product on to someone else's, rather than simply referring business to each other. For example, with my collaboration with Disney, Annabel Karmel had integrity and authority and Disney had the child appeal.

04. Seek out brands that share the same customer base as you but aren't competing and then study them. Can you find out what their objectives and vision for the future are? Have they blogged about it? Are they mentioned in their annual report? Are there potential gaps in their revenue streams which you could help them to fill? Do you have a shared vision or purpose? Are they your kind of people? As Jennifer Irvine advises: 'Only collaborate with brands that you personally really believe in and like.'

05. Decide what kind of partnership you'd like to enter into. For example, you may want a formal joint venture, which is an actual business established by two or more organisations to share cost and pool resources and skills; or you could have a simple partnership where you cross-promote to each other's customer base, refer business to each other or enter into a revenue-share agreement.

06. Ask top customers or connections who know your business to match-make you with potential partners or approach them directly.

07. Manage expectations from the outset and show empathy. Ensure that everyone knows what they are expected to bring to the table in terms of effort, resources, assets, skills and so on and that they understand each other's point of view. 'You don't want to resent the person you are collaborating with,' says Jennifer Irvine. 'It's important to set down ground rules so you find out if you are both going to mention each other in your newsletters, or what precisely you will do for each other, and be clear about expectations.'

EXAMPLES OF COLLABORATIVE MUMS IN BUSINESS

- At **Annabel Karmel** we have set up brand-building partnerships with Disney, Butlins, Haven Holidays, InterContinental, Tesco Baby Club, The Co-operative and BBC Good Food, each of which targets mums/families and/or have a focus on food or parenting. They benefit instantly from working with us because we're trusted by mums. And we benefit from partnering with brands which already have a large targeted audience that we can tap into. Mums in business without that trusted track record can build it up like I did by working with experts. For example, I worked with Margaret Lawson from Great Ormond Street Hospital for my first book. Experts may endorse your product if you send it to them or collaborate with you on it, which gives you that first bit of credibility.

- **Ann Summers** has collaborated with Shop Direct. 'That collaboration is very successful,' says Jacqueline Gold. 'We have a double-page spread in the catalogue and it's one of our four routes to market, through a wholesale relationship.'

- **Made.com** is all about collaborating with designers. The company has collaborated with Studio Putman, one of the biggest names in Parisian design, to create its 'Contrast' collection; with fashion designer Philip Colbert to create a pop-art inspired 'Rodnik Band' collection and a host of new and established names in design. Chloe Macintosh uses her high-level collaborative partners as her conscience, to keep her on track.

- Jennifer Irvine of **The Pure Package** has collaborated with a variety of like-minded companies. 'We tend to collaborate with people who have similar clients to us – people who care about their health. So we work a lot with Elemis, Bliss, Matt Roberts, the Soho House group and the golf club Wentworth.'

- **Caroline Castigliano** first kick-started her bridalwear business by collaborating with famous designer Jasper Conran on a range of wedding dresses. 'That collaboration was 100 per cent the best thing I ever did,' she says. 'By having his name attached to mine it was a great starting point for me to then go off and do it on my own, having met so many great contacts, having learnt so much and witnessed how, once you have the foundation of the corset right, everything else flows; plus the press that we got as a result of our partnership was phenomenal.' Caroline continues to seek mutually beneficial partnerships, putting on 'Designer Days' with her stockists, and events to engage current and future brides, and also involves other industry leaders. 'One event we ran was at The Dorchester hotel. 'We paid for the champagne tea and sold tickets, The Dorchester provided the room, we invited people and advertised the event to potential brides. We put on a low-key fashion show, with models walking among tables; we got Wild at Heart to do flowers, Bobbi Brown on make-up and Bruce Russell on wedding planning. In total, we had eight partners and each of us sat at one of the tables with the guests, we then moved tables every fifteen minutes so we got to speak to everyone. The clients loved it. I'm quite into partnering with people,' she says.

ANNABEL'S KITCHEN CABINET

THE IMPORTANCE OF COLLABORATIVE CONNECTION: LYNNE FRANKS

'Business today is all about partnership and collaboration,' says Lynne Franks, founder of the SEED Network and Lynne Franks PR.

Lynne started her entrepreneurial journey when she founded her own PR company, Lynne Franks PR, in 1970, from her kitchen table at the age of 21. Her first client, Katharine Hamnett, paid a weekly retainer and Lynne grew that business from her kitchen table into a business worth millions, with clients ranging from Annie Lennox and Lenny Henry to Coca-Cola and Amnesty International.

Lynne has always made the most of her networks. 'When I created London Fashion Week I got the tent sponsored by other clients of mine, whether it was Swatch or Harrods, so I just created this flow of interconnectedness between my own clients and other brands and NGOs,' explains Lynne. 'In the 1970s we created something called "Lloyds Bank Fashion Challenge", which was on BBC television. Lloyds Bank were a client. We then got Vivienne Westwood, who was also a client, to come and be a judge. So business was about bringing lots of exciting things together and proving that, even then, you could do a lot more in partnership and collaboration than alone.'

Liz sold her PR firm in 1988 and went on to become a spokesperson on ethical business practices, women's rights, spiritual values and conscious living. In 2001 she launched the SEED Network, an on- and offline community of women entrepreneurs, followed by a range of workshops and enterprise programmes in partnership with Business Link and the DTI.

She has since set up further partnerships where there is a win-win for everyone involved, for example partnering with Regus to open a chain of women's business lounges and hubs. 'I had intended to do it all myself,' recalls Lynne. 'I'd raised the money and had found a place, but I thought, "This isn't the way to do it, why don't I go into partnership with people who know what they're doing?"' Within a week, Lynne met the owner of Regus, Mark Dixon, at a lunch thrown by Richard Desmond. She suggested the idea to Mark, and he gave her his business card. 'I persistently called him until he suggested I talked to a woman who worked with him to work something out. She was lovely and we did,' smiles Lynne.

'When it comes to collaboration, you need to see your strengths and weaknesses and decide what you are looking for in a partner to complement these,' says Lynne. 'I think the best way to find someone is word of mouth, referrals.'

Lynne's work at SEED is 'all about women's peer groups and circles'. Over the past 15 years Lynne has established women's leadership networks inside a number of companies from McDonald's to Tesco. 'We have to just be there supporting each other, that's what it's all about.'

08
MASTER
JUGGLIN

THE
G ACT

DEALING WITH THE DUAL DEMANDS OF BEING A MUM AND BUSINESS OWNER

In between the children's naps, running a busy toddler group, testing out my recipes and raising a family, I was able to complete my very first book.

Within three months of *The Complete Baby and Toddler Meal Planner* coming out, in 1991, the book sold out. This was despite virtually no publicity. I had one article in *Practical Parenting* and that was it. The book's success was based on one mother talking to another, sharing the straightforward advice with their own networks.

I had no idea then how it would change my life. It launched my entire career; not only is it the second bestselling hardback non-fiction book of all time in the UK, but it's still my bestselling title and remains at the core of everything I have done since. That first idea became the platform on which I built everything else. I had not sat down and written out a 10-year plan. It grew organically and, as a mother juggling bringing up my children with my writing work, it needed to.

I initially chose to write books because, apart from being passionate about cooking, I wanted to spend time with my children. Being a mum and being at home was so important to me. Writing became a passion that enabled me to take my children to playgroups and Tumble Tots, be there on sports days, help them with music lessons and cook dinner for them of an evening. Every time they were napping during the day or sleeping at night-time, I would get to work on cooking up recipes, researching and writing my book.

Children need you when they get older too. It's really important you are there for them. Older children don't tend to come and say they want to talk to you; instead they might just wander into your home office when you are in the middle of writing an important email. Yet that is precisely when you need to stop what you are doing and focus on them. It's really important not to lose touch with what is going on in their lives. You don't stop being a good mum just because you have a career.

I have the utmost respect for mothers who are solely devoted to looking after their children and family. If you don't work or run a business, there's still a huge multi-tasking job to be done, which requires oodles of patience. Being a mum in business is just another piece in the great multi-tasking puzzle, and we do our best to balance the dual demands of motherhood with those of running our own business.

'Women are very good at juggling many different hats,' nods Jacqueline Gold, CEO of Ann Summers. 'You have to be organised in order to cope – you can't survive otherwise. I have charts and lists for everything; everything is foolproof. I have spares of everything around my house. Being a mother enables you to suddenly tune into your organisational skills.'

THE BENEFITS OF BEING A MUMPRENEUR

As a juggling mother in business, there's plenty to be thankful for. The upsides of being a mum in business are:

01. YOU CAN INSPIRE YOUR CHILDREN BY RUNNING YOUR OWN BUSINESS

You can be a great role model for them. They get to see you develop something that you are passionate about; they can join you in the office and learn an important lesson about female independence. Indeed, one of the most vital roles as a parent is to help shape children to become comfortably independent. Starting your own business is a wonderfully inspirational example of fostering and epitomising independence. When they see you enjoying what you do, and working hard to achieve your goals, it inspires them. All my children have spent time working with me. My son, Nicholas, was an assistant producer on my TV series *Annabel's Kitchen*. My older daughter, Lara, has worked with the team on new-product launches and often helps out in the office, and my youngest daughter, Scarlett, is a whizz at social media.

'I absolutely love being a working mum,' says Jacqueline Gold. 'I hope that, as a successful businesswoman, I have a positive impact on my daughter. If there was one gift I could give my daughter it would be self-esteem and I feel well placed to do that. I want her to look at me and think, ''I can be whatever I want to be.'''

Liz Jackson of Great Guns Marketing has also found that her business has inspired her daughter. 'Maddy understands what I do,' says Liz. 'She is very aspirational. Even at six-and-a-half she knows I am the boss and wants to be that too. She is a very confident young girl and both [of my children] are sociable.'

'I think there's something about being a role model to my kids and doing a job that I like, that I get satisfaction from and that I enjoy,' says Carrie Longton, co-founder of Mumsnet. 'I think it's important to show your children that you make some choices in your life and make them work for you,' she adds.

Frequently your children will inspire you to start a certain business in the first place or lead you down a different avenue of business. That's what happened for me with my recipe books and food for fussy eaters. I would have never written my books if it wasn't for my children.

That's how The White Company came into being soon after Chrissie Rucker's son Tom was born, and how Climbing Trees Clothing came about, when mother-and-daughter team Cheryl Rickman and Brooke Suddaby couldn't find any girls' T-shirts with dinosaur and pirate motifs on for Cheryl's 'tomboy' daughter. The same is true for Lucy Jewson of Frugi, who started her business after struggling to find clothes to fit over the cloth nappies her son wore, and for Myleene Klass with her Baby K range, as she wanted to create clothes with a certain edge that she herself would buy for her daughters.

'My whole business has always been linked to my life,' smiles Chrissie Rucker.

02. YOU ARE IN CONTROL

You can choose to take the afternoon off to go to sports day and make up the time in the evening. 'Having the freedom to work my own schedule (even if that does inevitably mean more hours), is what I love most about being a self-employed mother,' says Liz Earle. 'Also having the choice of workplace – from bedroom to boardroom – wherever I have my laptop I can be productive.'

'I have the choice to prioritise my children over a client. It is my choice,' says Liz Jackson. 'I like that I have control over that.'

'The beauty of being your own boss,' says Chrissie Rucker 'is if you want to go home at 5 o'clock, you can. I always leave in good time to spend time with my children and put them to bed, then pick it up again if needed, once they are in bed. That flexibility to be mum from 3–8pm and business owner the rest of the time is a key attractor for mumpreneurs, so use it.

'The first five years are challenging but then you start to find your way – one that works for you,' Chrissie Rucker reassures. 'I feel so lucky, I now work three days a week, and I am absolutely there 100 per cent for my children at the weekends. There are times when it is exhausting, but gradually you learn how to make a bit of sanity time for yourself and most importantly quality time with the children.'

Sometimes you just need to take control by taking a leap of faith. As we explored in Chapter 1, as a mum starting your own business you need a large dose of belief in your business to make it happen. Often, you need to back yourself and pay for childcare in order to generate revenue. You need to believe that this business of yours is going to work in order to take that leap. That was the case for Fiona Clark, founder of Inspiredmums. co.uk, who had her first child as she was setting up her business.

'I retrained and then I got pregnant, so was finishing my training just before I gave birth,' explains Fiona. 'I had four months off when I had my baby but did a bit towards setting up the business during those four months. I then realised I needed to go to networking events and so on. It was about being brave, so I asked people I'd coached for free during my training if they could write me a referral and recommend me to other people,' says Fiona.

'Time was my biggest obstacle with a new baby to look after, so I had to consider how much I should pay for childcare while not having any clients yet. I needed enough childcare to generate the work, but I needed enough work to justify paying for it. So I had to be quite brave and back myself. I knew this wasn't going to happen if I didn't have any childcare, so I took that leap and invested in flexible childcare to get my business off the ground.'

Her children are now eight and five, and the youngest has just started school. 'Now I have wrap-around childcare, so I manage by being really efficient with my time,' says Fiona. 'I am very focused and often it feels like I'm doing about 10 hours' work in 6 hours. But, vitally, I am in control of those hours.'

As your business grows and becomes less dependent on you and you are more able to delegate, you can take more time away from the office and regain some of that work–life balance.

Some mothers work from 9am to 3pm and 8pm to 11pm (and beyond). Others work four days a week and have three days off; some work full-time with full-time childcare and make the most of weekends and holidays. Regardless of your circumstances, it's all about doing the best you can with what you have.

Alex Polizzi has a full-time nanny five days per week until either she or her husband get home. She is away from home at least three days a week, generally filming *The Fixer* or *The Hotel Inspector*. This may mean work–life balance on a day-to-day basis is rarely achieved but it also means she can take extended periods off work completely to spend with her children.

'The best thing about being self-employed is at Christmas I took three weeks off and this summer I will take seven weeks off,' says Alex. 'I make sure that I then play catch-up mummy.

'When I first had my daughter I thought I was such a bad mother,' she says. 'It's so slow-paced and so I was always trying to do something exciting on the computer. Nowadays the weekends are amazing – until they've gone to bed I just hang out with them all day.'

Myself, I love being a self-employed mum. It gives you more choice and that is empowering. I can make my own decisions and run with them. I can move quickly. When I was younger I could take time off to be with the children. I can choose the people I work with. When you're employed you may be forced into an office environment with people you don't want to be with. Self-employment rids you of those uncontrollable variables.

And yet, juggling those dual demands of entrepreneur and mother is demanding. It's difficult keeping all the balls in the air without dropping one occasionally.

And then, of course, there's the guilt.

A MOTHER'S GUILT

66 99
YOU ARE ONLY AS HAPPY AS
YOUR LEAST HAPPY CHILD.

Betsy Brown Braun

Betsy Brown Braun's quote is very true for me. When Natasha died my life stopped. It just reinforced the fact that children are the most precious part of our lives.

We all need to find our own guilt threshold. I needed to work from home while the children were young. I purposely chose writing as I could fit it around taking care of the children, but I always imagined that I would work full-time when they got older and I was laying down the foundation of a career in the early years, but pacing myself.

However, whenever you are working you think you should be with your children; and whenever you are with your children you think you should perhaps reply to that email or book that meeting. That's why working while they are at school or asleep is beneficial as there is less guilt.

It's within your power to let guilt overwhelm you or not. Perhaps we should not be too hard on ourselves though. We simply do the best we can do with what we have. In the end I found that it was possible to have the best of all possible worlds – and now my children have been able to come and spend time working with me in the company for work experience, and I have made lots of contacts that will help them in their careers.

As a mum, we're either working at bringing in money or working at being a mum, but we're always working and trying our best to please everyone, so we should give ourselves a break and just keep juggling.

'Being a working mum and not feeling guilty is challenging, there is no doubt about that,' says Jacqueline Gold. 'And it can take you a while to get in a pattern that works for you. There will be a period of going two steps forward and one step back but you'll find what works. I was very lucky because my daughter loved pre-school. I used to take off Fridays, and I think she would rather have been at school than with me, but I was doing that for me, to spend time with my daughter.'

'It's difficult to deal with the guilt,' says Myleene Klass. 'I've just learnt that guilt goes with the territory, but I pacify it by knowing that I am their sole provider and Ava is at school half the time I work. So when she's in bed I work. When she's home she has my time. But I work very late, sometimes until 3am.'

We all feel guilt, but children will adapt. And you will give them quality time when you have the time to give it. But you shouldn't beat yourself up about not being able to be with them all of the time. You work because you need to for financial or personal reasons, or simply because you feel that you won't be the best mum you can be if you don't put in some hours of work – we might need that for our sense of worth or sense of purpose (and so that we can have some grown-up conversation, have a laugh with colleagues and flex our skills).

If you are lucky, you can get the best of both worlds by working while they're at school and sleeping, and being 'mum' in the hours in between. Many mums in business relish this opportunity as they can work from 9am to 3pm, be mum from 3 to 7pm and then work again from 8 to 10pm or later (as is often the case). But that's hard work and the only time you switch off is when you are asleep.

Know that your children are very likely having a good day, with or without you. Whether they are at school, nursery, with a nanny (or grandma), at pre-school or with you, they'll be having a good day as they are with people who are taking care of them and focusing on them. And if your child cries when you leave, they often do so for a few minutes and then they are absolutely fine.

Focus on the positive aspects of working for yourself. 'You can't control everything that happens in your life but you can control what you feel and what you think, and I decided that feeling guilty was a waste of my energy and mental capacity,' says Fiona Clark. 'Focus instead on what the positive benefits of you working are, such as being a good role model by feeling fulfilled through working hard, and valuing the time you do have with your kids.'

Avoid going to that guilty place. Don't beat yourself up, because nobody benefits from that negativity; not you and certainly not your children.

'I don't feel any guilt at all,' says Alex Polizzi boldly. 'I am absolutely guilt-free. I was brought up by a mother who worked. My father died when I was nine and Mum is a different woman now to how she was in my childhood. Certainly with my family I had a lot to live up to. I was Lord Charles Forte's granddaughter and Rocco Forte's niece and Olga Polizzi's daughter, so I have always worked hard and always will. My husband is a bit cross with me as he would really love me not to work, but I think I would just be a miserable person if I didn't.'

10 RULES OF JUGGLING MOTHERHOOD WITH BUSINESS WITHOUT TOO MUCH GUILT

There are a variety of rules that these successful mothers abide by when it comes to juggling family with business.

01. PUT FAMILY FIRST. PRIORITISE FAMILY IN YOUR DIARY

Make the most of being your own boss by choosing to be there for the important stuff – being there when they really need you to maximise their smiles and minimise your regrets. 'I get the really important family dates, such as school plays and concerts, holidays, parents' evenings, into the diary at the beginning of the year and then schedule work events around them wherever possible,' says Liz Earle, who worked after the morning school run and again once the kids were in bed, alongside her business partner, Kim. 'That way family always comes first.'

'Decide what is non-negotiable,' agrees Jennifer Irvine, founder of The Pure Package. 'There are certain things I absolutely won't miss. I'm on the school Board of Governors so at the beginning of the school year I find out the school timetable to get the exact dates for school plays, assemblies and ballet performances. I don't miss any of them.'

'Like all working mothers I find it incredibly challenging to balance a career with raising my children,' adds Shelley Barrett of ModelCo. 'I make it a priority to sit down and have breakfast with my girls before the hectic day takes over. I also try not to overcommit too far in advance and keep my diary as free as possible.'

As for me, I spent a lot of time with my children when they played musical instruments. I had a musical background, so I could help them. They all learnt Suzuki violin from the age of four, and subsequently became talented violinists. I'd ensure I was present at every concert. They need to have an audience – otherwise who are they playing to? I also went to many of their lessons so I could help them with their practice. Schedule those moments into your diary so they take priority. Meetings can be moved or arranged around those prioritised family moments. If you do that, you'll feel less guilty as you are doing your best to think 'family first'.

02. BE PRESENT AND FOCUSED

When you are being mum, be mum and make the time with your family count. Similarly, when you are being a business owner, focus intently on pressing forward with business tasks.

'It's either work time or it's mummy time. When I'm mummy, I'm present and I switch off, which isn't always easy to do,' admits Fiona Clark. 'I subsequently try to have this rule about being present. So being present at work and not worrying about the kids during that time, and being a present mother while I'm with them. I try to separate the two, which is difficult when you get an email on your phone or a call after school pick-up. But we can only do our best.'

Make sure you are present and attentive when you are being mother. Put the answerphone on, don't check emails (unless doing so sneakily while in the kitchen making dinner), respond to questions, engage in conversation, do their homework with them, read, play and enjoy your children.

'I discipline my time with my daughter Scarlett like I do with work,' says Jacqueline Gold. 'When I get home at 6 o'clock, I have an hour before she goes to bed. I make sure that is all Scarlett's time, no matter how tired I am. It's very rare I stay out overnight and, at weekends, I make sure the time is packed with quality time. I don't want to be tidying the house, I want to be doing crafts or doing whatever Scarlett wants to do.'

'I make sure that the time we do spend together as a family is proper quality time,' says Frugi founder Lucy Jewson. 'We pack the weekends full of child-centric activities. We go kayaking together, out on our little putt-putt boat, swim in the sea with them, lots of dog walks and so on … that really does make our time together special.'

If you have access to free childcare (i.e. grandparents), so much the better. 'Don't assume you won't need any childcare if your baby is tiny and sleeping for half the day, because it won't be like that for long,' advises Fiona Clark. 'When they suddenly turn 10 months and they start putting their fingers in plugs you can't even go to the toilet without them doing something. You cannot run a business without support. If you can't afford childcare be creative and swap childcare hours with friends or ask favours of grandparents – whatever you can do to get your business going.'

03. BE EFFICIENT WITH HOW YOU USE YOUR TIME

'Having more than one role makes you more effective with your time,' says Jennifer Irvine. Myleene Klass agrees: 'I haven't got time to waste … I'm on the clock because I've got to go and pick up my kid from school.'

Here are some ways to improve your efficiency so you can fit more in your day:

- **Make the most of 'dead' time** – for example, working while you're on the train to a meeting or emailing while you're in the supermarket queue.

- **Work while the children are napping, at school or in bed.** 'I work almost every night,' says Alex Polizzi. 'Because there are not enough hours in the day … Also somehow mentally, once the children are in bed, I can start to focus again.'

- **Prioritise brutally.** Don't procrastinate and get on with tasks in bursts of focused time. According to *The Flourish Handbook*, you should: 'Focus by giving yourself blasts of allocated time for certain tasks. Focus on your prioritised tasks for at least 45–60 minutes at a time and get rid of other distractions while you genuinely focus on completing each of the three to five top-priority tasks on your list. Switch off your Skype and instant messaging, step away from Facebook and close your email or any other distractions during that set time. If you really must, once that 45–60 minutes is up, go and check your social media/email. Then get back into the zone and focus for another chunk of time. This really works.'

- **Use technology to keep you on track.** Fiona Clark uses reminders on her phone and Baukjen uses email to help her stay organised: 'I have one email where I put in all the to-dos, such as buying new wellies for the kids, doing a clear-out of one of the kids' wardrobes and so on, which I have in my work inbox. This means it's close and I can open it and update it during lunch.'

- **Focus on one task at a time rather than multi-tasking.** 'My grandfather [Lord Forte] gave me the best piece of advice I've ever received,' says Alex Polizzi. 'He told me, only ever try and do one thing at a time. Do it properly and don't leave it until you have completed the task. Only move on when it is finished. So, it's not a question of getting everything done, it's a question of getting one thing done. I am very focused on the task at hand. Focusing on doing one thing properly helps me in so many ways; it's a productive way to be.' So at work focus on doing one task properly and then, when you are back in mum mode again, focus on one task with your children. You can leave the multi-tasking to the periods in between (such as when you're getting everything ready for school; or when you're cooking the tea, while booking the dentist appointment and loading the dishwasher).

• **Put less on your to-do list.** Alex Polizzi advises: 'Don't put 20 things you have to do on a list – choose three or four that will help you to achieve your goals, and be really proud when you have done them. Write everything down but use a highlighter to choose the most value-added or most urgent/important tasks on that list, and be happy if you achieve those.'

04. PLAN METICULOUSLY BUT UNDERSTAND THAT YOU WILL HAVE DAYS WHERE THINGS DON'T GO TO PLAN

'Being a mum and running your own business is a pretty tough race to run; it is a marathon, not a sprint, and you have to be a very good planner in terms of setting goals,' says Liz Jackson.

'I try to plan everything,' says Thea Green of Nails Inc. 'It's vital to be very organised, so I write absolutely everything down. There's so much going on in my head so I like the mind dump where I write it all down to give myself a bit of relief. As a rule it works.'

Of course, in business, we have to expect the unexpected from time to time and there will be days where we are left pulling our hair out, exasperated, as something hasn't gone to plan. However, those days are usually in the minority.

'You have got to accept the demands of your business and that they may take primacy over the needs of your family sometimes, and vice versa; you can't feel guilty about that because it works both ways,' says Alex Polizzi. 'Sometimes a kid is sick or something dramatic is happening at home, or your parents are ill and then the business must wait for you. Running your own business gives you that flexibility. You have got to be confident about that. Other times your family just have to suck it up because you have a deadline or need to be somewhere.'

05. GIVE YOURSELF A BREAK

Just do the best that you can with what you have. Life is a compromise, so take pleasure in small things and focus on appreciating what you have rather than what you lack or on what you've done wrong.

'Go easy on yourself,' says Liz Earle. 'We can't always get it right all of the time. As long as most of it gets done and most people are happy most of the time, I would consider that to be a success.'

Fiona Clark agrees. 'Don't aim for perfection on any front. Good is good enough. Some mums who work part-time say to me they feel they are doing a bad job at home and doing a bad job at work, but good is good enough. For example, my child's school wants us to read with our eight-year-old every night for 10 minutes. But, if I'm not home until 7pm and he is too tired by then, I'd rather not have a screaming tantrum, just to be the perfect mum doing what I've been asked. We try to read three times a week, which is fine – as is his reading. It's important not to aim for perfection and to compromise instead.'

'There are only 24 hours in the day so naturally you can't be all things to all people all the time,' adds Dessi Bell, founder of Zaggora. 'Sometimes you are a better friend, sometimes a better mother, sometimes a better wife and daughter. I don't believe in trying to be perfect; no one is.'

06. DELEGATE. GET HELP WHEREVER YOU CAN AND ASK ADVICE

'I quickly learnt how to delegate,' says Liz Earle. 'I used to try to do everything myself, but soon realised that I simply couldn't. At Liz Earle Beauty Co. we gathered a team of consultants and part-time specialists that hugely helped to share the workload. On the home front, I learnt to accept all offers of help – a neighbour helping with the school run or walking the dog, or a friend picking up some shopping. I also encourage the children to help out with simple things like tidying their rooms, simple cooking, clearing the table and emptying the dishwasher as much as possible. You have to work as a team – and the children get satisfaction from being part of the workforce too (most of the time!).'

Jennifer Irvine agrees. 'Never apologise for having help with your family, children and work. What man has ever apologised for having a wife at home?'

Thomasina Miers, founder of Wahaca concurs: 'The most important part of being a working mother is to know when to accept help,' she says. 'I have never had a problem asking for advice so, since Tatiana was born, I have asked for help too. Women have to stick together, and give each other advice and assistance. Some women think they have to do everything by themselves but they really don't.'

'I have a cleaner so I don't have to clean at the weekends as that is family time,' nods Liz Jackson. 'That is something I would advise to mums starting their own company who get to the point when they can earn enough money to afford a cleaner. Don't try and do the housework. Outsource ironing, cleaning, food shopping – delegate all of those things so you can have some precious time at the weekends and in the evenings with your children.'

Husbands or partners need to understand that running your own business is a full-time job. Even if they too have a full-time job, you need to share the workload of running a home and bringing up a family – whether you share responsibilities or they take a more focal role.

Dessi Bell took two weeks off work when she had Byron and then her husband looked after him for several weeks. This meant that her husband was capable of looking after his son himself and really bonded with him. 'No one cares, so you should do whatever feels right to you,' says Dessi.

See pages 205–7 for more on getting support from your family and friends.

07. LEARN HOW TO SAY 'NO'

❝❞
SOMETIMES THE BEST WAY TO COMPLETE A PROJECT IS TO DROP IT.

Arianna Huffington

'You cannot be everything to everyone,' advises Lucy Jewson. 'At the start especially it's tempting to see everything as an opportunity, supply anyone who will pay you, but this trips you up in the end. Value your time and effort and think about whether it's an opportunity that has real longevity. Don't stray away from the core of what you do … it takes too much energy to do that!'

'It's hard to say no to opportunities when you are self-employed, but you need to consider the "be present" rule,' says Fiona Clark. 'For example, I agreed to deliver a workshop for 26 people on 4 January and it ruined my Christmas holiday as I had to prepare for it and it was on my mind throughout the holiday break. The workshop was on my first day back at work and the kids' first day back at school, and I thought, "Why did I say yes to this?" The timing was not right. So I have learnt from that and created new boundaries about saying "no" when it doesn't sit well with other priorities in my life.'

'Saying "no" is something women are particularly bad at,' says Alex Polizzi. 'It's just about being realistic about what I have on my plate and what I can and can't do … Instead of agonising about whether or not to do something, saying "no" has transformed my life,' adds Alex. 'Because instead of worrying about the fact that I said yes and the fact that I will have to let someone down, then having sleepless nights about it months beforehand, I now actually get the pain over with straight away, and just say "no".'

08. UNDERSTAND THAT SOMETHING HAS TO GIVE. HAVING IT ALL MAY NOT EXIST

'You have one life, and I want to have a satisfying career and be an amazing mother too,' says Alex Polizzi. 'However, the reality is no one can have a life like this and not let something slip. With me it's my social life, which is pretty much zero.'

Lucy Jewson agrees. 'I definitely don't have the time to catch up with friends like I'd like to. They all meet for coffee, do lunch, etc., and I just can't, so I miss that. The important ones understand though and always support me when I need them, and I'd like to think they always feel I am there when they need me too.'

09. DON'T NEGLECT THE PEOPLE THAT LOVE AND SUPPORT YOU

Don't forget that it's important to take time out for your loved ones – even if it means doing something they want to do and you don't. For example, Chloe Macintosh told me, 'I prefer small, independent films, which are more focused on the psychology of the characters, but I have three boys at home who are action junkies so I have to give in most of the time.'

If you have a husband or partner, plan to do things together. It doesn't have to be anything special or take very long. As long as you're relaxed, and listening to them, they'll be happy. Or it could be a good idea to have one evening (once the kids have gone to bed) when everything stops, just for them – a nice meal together, watching a favourite film. The main thing is to be relaxed. And when it comes to switching from work mode to family mode, 10–15 minutes to shower, change and zone out can help – those closest to you will pick up on your mood.

10. TAKE TIME OFF FOR YOURSELF

'Make sure that you schedule time off, because it is very easy to get so caught up in the next thing and the next thing,' advises Alex Polizzi. 'As you get older you just realise that the time is flying by and you are never going to get it back. I think you are very conscious of that when you have children. I have always been in a hurry and worked incredibly hard. When I was younger I worked all day and I danced all night. Now between work and kids, another week has gone, so it's important to schedule some time off, whether that's every single weekend or regular breaks.'

'I cherish my time with my girlfriends, the occasional G&T, walks with my scruffy little dog and cuddles with my children,' says Mumlin founder Katy Hymas. Lucy Jewson also enjoys walking her dog to and from work. 'That's a big thing for me as I've been rubbish at finding time for myself,' says Lucy.

I agree. My dogs are one of my greatest pleasures. I have a golden retriever, a Samoyed and an American cocker spaniel. They follow me around everywhere. When I had to live in Ireland for seven weeks recording my TV series *Annabel's Kitchen,* I took Hamilton, my Samoyed, with me. It was incredibly hard work recording 30 programmes back to back, and having him with me kept me sane. We would go for walks on the beach together, which cleared my head. Animals have this great way of relieving stress and they give you an incredible unconditional love.

ANNABEL'S KITCHEN CABINET

DEALING WITH DUALITIES: CHLOE MACINTOSH

Chloe Macintosh, co-founder of Made.com has spent most of her adult life juggling.

As a fourth-year 21-year-old student studying architecture in Paris, she came to the UK in 1996 on work experience when her tutor landed her a place on the Norman Foster training programme. 'I remember sitting in my office in this great big glass building by Battersea Bridge and thinking to myself, how am I going to make it look like I know what I am doing?' recalls Chloe.

'After two months they asked if I wanted to stay, which threw me a challenge. If I took the job, I would delay my studies and might never get a diploma, but if I didn't go for this opportunity, I might never get such a great offer again.' So Chloe told her tutors in Paris about this amazing opportunity within one of the best practices in the world to see if they could find a way for her to juggle working and studying.

'For the next two years I worked full-time at Foster's and continued to study for my diploma. I then went back to Paris in my holidays to pass my exams,' explains Chloe. 'I had this dual, slightly neurotic life, but it meant I graduated with two years' work experience.' Chloe went on to be the youngest ever associate architect at the firm.

Chloe stayed at Foster's for 10 years and then had her first son. She went back to work after five months and juggled being a mum with work, but it was when she fell pregnant again a year later that she began to reassess her job. 'I began to feel fatigue in a job which required so much travel. I was finding it harder to stay motivated, being on building sites in a very male-orientated environment.'

That's when Chloe took the decision to leave Norman Foster's and joined the team at Mydeco.com, and soon after the idea for Made. com emerged.

Since then she has had to juggle her dual role of being a mum and being her own boss. She gives credit for managing that duality to three things: refusing to be a perfectionist, having a supportive husband and focusing on the task at hand.

'A long time ago I decided that trying to do everything perfectly was the best way to fail. Juggling effectively is all about compromise. Everything in my life is about working out what is important: evaluating what I really care about, and what I thought I cared about but actually don't.

'A lot of my success is down to my husband because he takes 50 per cent of the load. We both work full-time, but we complement each other, so we share our duties at home. My marriage wouldn't work any other way. My experience is that men need to take some of the childcare on board. I can only manage because my husband wants to have an equal part in family life.

'Having that ability to focus is critical. I now achieve more in less time. I do that by visualising the day and what is going to happen, considering what time I need to be home, and I plan around that.' Chloe also makes sure she is completely focused when she is wearing her mum hat: 'When I'm with the kids, I take time to do things with them individually and I am completely with them, immersed.'

Chloe has a strong belief that what she is doing is right for her and her family. 'I believe that if I didn't work I would be a horrible wife and horrible mother. I would be unsatisfied and frustrated. I have an entrepreneurial nature and want to be an example for my children, which also means being financially independent while doing what makes you happy.' Chloe says that stems from being raised by a single mother who didn't have a career and raised her family with very little. 'I grew up in a one-bedroom flat with my sister and mother, who had three jobs throughout our upbringing. It made me very proud of what she achieved in this context, but it also means that I value my financial autonomy enormously. I'm trying to raise my children with this view of the world that everything is possible.'

GETTING SUPPORT FROM YOUR FAMILY

Running your own business is time-intensive and all-consuming. It requires time, effort and dedication. As such, it also needs support and buy-in from those around you, notably, your family. Think about the impact your dedication to your business will have on all the other members of your family; you need them to be supportive not resentful.

My mother has always been a huge support; she still tests my food. Simon, my ex-husband, also understood what I was trying to do when I started writing. He realised it was the expression of coming to terms with Natasha's death by doing something positive. He gave me some very good advice on my first publishing contract and supplied office space when I needed to expand from the kitchen table. I've made the most of the backing and encouragement my family has provided me with.

Support can come in many ways:

- Understanding that you need to focus during certain hours and being flexible enough to take up the slack in other areas – whether that's running the children to football or cooking tea if you have an afternoon phone call with a client.

- Encouraging you and being there to pat you on the back when you win deals and commiserate with you when you don't.

- Financial support. Family members can be a source of funding as well as potential employees; it is important to think through the implications and ramifications of both of these options, especially if the business starts to struggle. While backing from friends and family is the lowest-cost way to secure finance, the pressure of owing someone you love can be difficult, so it needs careful consideration.

- Skills support. Many women find that their partners can provide support through their own skillsets or contacts. For example, my partner Stephen is a great help to me with contracts and commercial dealings as he trained as a lawyer. You have to accept that you can't be an expert in everything (and I find contracts really mind-numbing!), so it's important to know when to take advice and find the right people to help you. Often those right people are standing right opposite you in your life.

'I was very lucky because my husband Chris was a chartered accountant and an entrepreneur,' says Caroline Castigliano. 'He was very influential about what the next move would be, what we did and how we did it. Obviously having him advising me on the finances and how we went about doing anything was hugely helpful.'

GOING INTO BUSINESS TOGETHER

Some mums even opt to make their life partner their work partner too. Apparently 75 per cent of all businesses are family businesses. You trust your family more than anyone, so this can be a great and supportive way to launch your own enterprise, with a shared vision.

Lucy Jewson set up organic children's clothing brand Frugi with her husband, Kurt. The couple have found there are various pros and cons to working together on their own business.

'Kurt and I have polar-opposite skills and that's always helped,' says Lucy. 'I look after what we call the "tomorrow dept" – design, money, marketing, sales – and Kurt looks after the "today dept" – customer service and warehouse, basically getting orders out the door and keeping customers happy. We are even on different floors – he's downstairs, I'm upstairs … I think that degree of separation is quite helpful in a marriage,' Lucy smiles.

'Certainly, the pros are that you are in it together and you understand completely each other's stresses and strains. You really feel like you are building something and are on a journey together,' adds Lucy. 'However, the cons are that you never escape it.'

Alex Polizzi owns Millers Bespoke Bakery with her husband Marcus and advises family businesses as part of her series, *The Fixer*. If you do go into business with your family (either by joining an existing family business or starting up your own), she has some great advice to follow.

'I have worked with my uncle, my sister, my mother and my husband. I think in all of those the nicest thing and the worst thing is you tend to know each other's failings as well as your best qualities. You can be honest and loyal too, but there are factors to consider,' says Alex. These are:

01. **'Never expect less from a family member than you would from any other employee.** I am dealing with a family at the moment on *The Fixer* and I can hardly bear it because they let their children be so lazy. I said if the mother can get someone else to do a better job for the same money then why wouldn't she? I don't get it, and that is the way that family businesses fail.'

02. **'Have well-defined roles and be clear about each person's role and what their responsibilities are.** I tend to give that advice a lot. The other thing is, in family business, because you have all grown up together, it is quite often true that lots of members of the family are all good at the same thing … I know my cousins, all of whom are going to go into the hotel business, were all more or less at the service side of it. They made a conscious decision to get some experience in marketing, and one had to get experience in accounting. I think if

you don't have that experience within the family you must buy in; you must not just ignore it.'

03. **'Try not to take the negative side of business home.** Marcus and I have learnt to do it. Both of us are quite fiery, so we do a lot of screaming and shouting at each other but we try not to do that in our home environment.' There can also be crossover if you have risked your home to fund your business. 'Try not to put the house up against your business,' advises Alex. 'Try to protect that family asset, or it can be a cause for so much rage.'

The danger is that if you are not careful, business can dominate your relationship, so it's important to release the pressure where you can. For example, as your business grows it's good to get advice on strategy from someone who has had a lot of experience in your sector.

MUMMY'S LITTLE HELPER

For many mothers in business, their children are an integral part of their working life.

My children have been involved in my business from day one. They have been the inspiration for my books and business, and guinea pigs for my recipes (to the point that when they grew older they'd chorus, 'Mummy, please can you not experiment with food on our friends when they come over?') They've also been models for my books, and when I did a TV series called *The Gurgling Gourmet* with Hilary Jones, Scarlett featured on it as a six-month-old baby. Before she got a job in marketing at Liberty department store, my daughter Lara did work experience in the office; she even helped transcribe many of the interviews for this very book (thank you, Lara). My son Nicholas and I (the little boy who inspired me to write my first book) worked together on the *Annabel's Kitchen* TV show, on which he was an assistant producer. What was funny was that some people would be quite scared of telling me something, such as not to wear this or that, or to do something in a different way, so he'd say, 'The director doesn't want to tell you, so I'm telling you.' You get that whole level of honesty from your family.

HOW TO FLOURISH AS AN ENTREPRENEUR AND MUM

01. INCLUDE YOUR FAMILY IN YOUR SMALL-BUSINESS JOURNEY

Talk to your family about how things are going. They don't need to know all the ins and outs, but share successes as well as problems – you may be pleasantly surprised at the range of their own business experience. I talk about work a lot and I tell mine what we've done today. I enjoy doing that. They should never be kept at arm's reach; they should be included.

As well as being kept in the loop about where you will be on certain days, your family should understand your vision and be kept informed about where you are now and where you aim to get to. Talk with your family at the dinner table or on car journeys, for example, about the decisions you are pondering and the opportunities you are pursuing. Share your excitement and your fears. An inclusive environment will help them to understand why you are putting so much effort into this venture and will help you by sharing your ideas and thoughts with them. You may even get some useful feedback from them. Also, if you include your family, they are also more likely to support you through the tough times.

That's certainly the case for Thea Green, whose husband is also an entrepreneur. 'We are great when we have had horrible days,' she says. 'We find the comedy in it, and support each other through the crises.'

Talking about your business and involving them can also be a good education for your children. It was for Alex Polizzi: 'As a family we had a very traditional Italian upbringing. We were all around the lunch table every Sunday and all the adults ever talked about was business. We children were supposed to be seen and not heard, but I was listening, and took it all in.'

However, while being inclusive and sharing the ups and downs with your family is a positive thing to do, don't forget that you shouldn't take work stresses and arguments home. Your work shouldn't adversely affect your family relationships, as Alex Polizzi advises above (see pages 206–7). A clear line should be drawn, so the money worries or big obstacles don't need to be mentioned around the dinner table. Especially if you work with your husband or another family member.

02. SET CLEAR GUIDELINES AND BOUNDARIES

Family and friends need to know that during such and such hours you will be focusing on your work and will therefore require no distractions during that time. You may find that friends and family phone you or turn up on your doorstep, because you work from home and they assume it's therefore fine to get in touch because you are there, rather than 'at work'. Be clear that you are at work, it's just that work may now be at home. This doesn't mean you are free. Set boundaries regarding your workspace and also your working hours. Do this from the outset. Use a 'mum at work' sign and keep people in the loop.

03. USE YOUR DEDICATION, PERSISTENCE AND 'CAN-DO' ATTITUDE AS INSPIRATION FOR YOUR CHILDREN

'My family have a very big can-do attitude so I was very much brought up in a family that supported me starting my own business,' says Liz Jackson, whose father works alongside her. 'The Henry Ford notion of "If you think you can or think you can't – you're right" was something they held dear, so I always believed I could achieve.'

ANNABEL'S KITCHEN CABINET

TWIN BABIES AND BUSINESSES: KATY HYMAS

Juggling a business with parenthood isn't easy, but imagine doing so when you're a single mum with twins. That's what Katy Hymas did. After working as an advertising agency account executive, Katy set up her own PR company, Cherry Pie PR, in 2008. Four years later Katy had twins and co-wrote a book called *Twins*, a juggling act in itself. However, she was about to add a new business to the mix.

Frazzled Katy had grown fed up using grubby, unattractive muslins to protect her clothes while burping her babies. 'They looked horrid, were invariably on the wrong shoulder, in the wrong place and frequently fell on the floor,' said Katy. She was surprised that no alternatives were available, and had her light-bulb moment. She realised that a U-shaped piece of cloth would be both a more stylish and practical way to protect your clothes when burping your baby – and Mumlin was born. Now Katy had a book to promote, a PR business to run, a new product to design and launch and twins to take care of. That's more than two hands full! So how has she taken her business to fruition, won awards and achieved success … without running back to the safety net of a job or hiding under her twins' beds?

'My working day wouldn't fit any conventional schedule or adhere to union rules of maximum hours. I stay up late, get up early, take phone calls while making tea and hastily finish emails before sprinting to nursery, and of course there are no holidays! Once you become a mum you are never off duty, and the same is true once you launch a business. But I wouldn't change any of it. I go to sleep thinking about all of my babies and wake up wanting bigger and better for them all.

'I am certain friends I don't see often enough would say I prioritise my career over them, perhaps questioning how I have time to write books but not make it to the wine bar for a catch-up – but logistically it is impossible for me to venture far from Twin HQ! Squeezing my career ambitions into what little space is left around all things single mum is a survival strategy, not a sacrifice.'

Katy admits that she does feel guilty, but she accepts that is 'part and parcel of motherhood and entrepreneurship'. She explains: 'Guilt is an integral part of motherhood and I think you question and doubt almost every decision you make along the way, regardless of what career/child choices you make.' She adds, 'My children come first and the business babies slot in around them, but that doesn't mean I think I always get the balance right. I expect things to get dropped occasionally; it's the law of averages!'

09
BUILD
GROW
BUSIN

“ ”

**ONLY THOSE WHO WILL
RISK GOING TOO FAR CAN
POSSIBLY FIND OUT JUST
HOW FAR ONE CAN GO.**

T. S. Eliot

AND
YOUR
ESS

Expanding your business brings with it a whole range of other issues – employing staff, moving to larger premises, securing finance, and all the responsibilities and admin that entails. At the same time you must not let the additional paperwork and management take you away from what you are good at.

To ensure that you remain focused, you need to hire well, seek help from a mentor and/or executive team member and/or get the help of an investor who can provide strategic advice and contacts as well as cash. That said, the process of raising finance can be time-intensive, so you need to be in a position where your business can continue to make money while you focus some of your attention on securing the capital you need to fund growth. In theory, the best time to raise money is when you are making money, not when you haven't yet made any or are losing it.

To minimise the growing pains that small businesses can encounter, you need to grow in the right direction, at the right speed and with the right support. And that's what we'll be examining in this chapter.

GROW IN THE RIGHT DIRECTION AT THE RIGHT SPEED

Growing a business enables a future for its survival, but it can also jeopardise its current existence. You have to think through the implications of expanding. Here are four key points you need to think about:

- **Consider scalability. How scalable is your product or service?** If you invested your profits into buying more stock or hiring more staff, could you sell more?

- **Do your homework. How can you get advice and know which advice to follow?** As you begin to build your business out from your original core area, you cannot stay a one-woman band or you will spread yourself too thin. But this is the time when your instincts about advice from consultants have to be at their most fine-tuned. They don't share the same passion you do: you are just another client.

- **Be patient.** If an idea you think is good for expanding the business doesn't work now, don't dismiss it completely. Its time will come. I only had to wait 20 years. Similarly, you don't need to expand too quickly, for example to new territories. As ModelCo's Shelley Barrett says, 'Expanding internationally sounds glamorous but be careful not to expand too quickly. It is far more strategic to conquer one market at a time.'

- **Stay agile.** The joy of a small company – as mine still is – is that you can move fast. If we like an idea we do it: we don't need the apparatus of months of approval systems. We are all in it together. Try not to lose that spirit of camaraderie as you grow.

Of course, there are different stages of growth. From moving out of the home office into a more appropriate space, to taking on freelancers and employees, to growing your brand overseas and/or online, to diversifying your range to include other lines and scaling up.

For me, I knew it was time to move from the dining table to an office because I wanted to feel that I was moving forward – after all, I was. I also wanted my dining table back! We couldn't have anybody over for dinner as I'd taken over the dining room for two-and-a-half years. I think my husband got fed up and I had earned enough through royalties, so I paid to take over an office within his office space. That was my first step towards growing and building a team and expanding further still. And what a journey it has been!

Justine Roberts of Mumsnet ran the business from her home for the first eight years before making the transition to Mumsnet Towers. She knew it was the right time to grow and move out of her home office when the business started to make money. 'Mumsnet really didn't make any money for the first five or so years. It was only then that I could see a revenue model working that could sustain the overhead,' explains Justine. 'By 2008 we were just beginning to be of sufficient scale to generate significant advertising revenue, and so the time was right.'

FROM SCRATCH COOKING TO SUPERMARKET FOOD AND BEYOND

My business has been all down to organic growth – each development naturally leading on to the next. I wanted to explore the gap in the market for food for toddlers. Chilled pre-prepared meals were available for adults, but there was nothing of a good quality or that tasted good for ages one to four. I spent 18 months developing a range that was as good as my homemade recipes, then worked at pitching my range to retailers. Once we got Sainsbury's on board the chilled toddler meal range grew from strength to strength, eventually going into over 400 stores. Five years later we received brand exclusivity as their only branded supplier of chilled toddler meals. This year the range is also being listed in more than 500 Tesco stores. We are also launching a big range in Australia.

A natural progression from my toddler meals was to look at how I could re-create my delicious baby puree recipes as ready-made food. We got a listing in Tesco in August 2011 and shortly after we launched in Sainsbury's, Waitrose and The Co-operative.

Despite various ups and downs (we'll explore failure in Chapter 10), I continued to build my company. One thing leads to another in business, and one evening, after a TV appearance on *BBC Breakfast*, I received an email from Paul Campbell, who ran Clapham House Group (which included Gourmet Burger Kitchen, Tootsies and The Real Greek). He wanted me to develop his children's menus. I was already working in food service in a small way, designing children's menus for Harvey Nichols and Villandry. However, what I really wanted to do was design a range of children's meals for food service, which I could sell in a frozen format while ensuring a top-quality meal. It is difficult giving out recipes and putting your name to them and then relying on someone else to keep up your standards. Expanding into food service meant I wouldn't need to do that.

I found a company, Brakes, that offered a great distribution network. If I had not already had the Clapham House Group as a customer I don't think Brakes would have taken me on, but I brought the business with me, which was music to their ears. Within a few months we had designed a fantastic range of meals and launched them in Tootsies.

Shortly afterwards, Merlin, who runs Legoland, Alton Towers and Thorpe Park, rang to ask if we could meet for a tasting. Subsequently, our meals were placed into all their theme parks too. We also began working with Bourne Leisure, owners of Haven and Butlins. We were supplying around 1 million children's meals through food service.

From that first diversification into chilled food in retail, I had successfully grown the business and diversified further into food service, supplying chains like Wetherspoon, Mitchells & Butlers, Orchid pubs and BHS. And success in these areas enabled me to take on more staff and grow my team. I've also expanded into markets beyond the UK, including Dubai, Abu Dhabi, Hong Kong, Kuwait, South Korea and Australia. Each of these opportunities grew naturally, working with local partners to ensure I had the best understanding of these markets.

This kind of progression all goes back to believing in what you do. I honestly believe that the food we produce is the best-quality available in the supermarkets, and that nothing tastes like it – nothing. That is not marketing hype. I genuinely believe it and so do my customers. If I think I can do something better than what is already on the market, I am going to do it. I would not let the products into the marketplace otherwise. That belief and passion for what the food tastes like and the nutritional quality of it continues to fuel me, to give me the energy to tackle often daunting challenges of entering a highly competitive market and taking on giant businesses.

BEWARE GROWING PAINS

Many entrepreneurs underestimate the time investment required to grow a business. Growing pains come in many variations – from lack of cash flow or bursting at the seams, to being so consumed by the business and working in it that you cannot think strategically and move onwards and upwards.

Caroline Castigliano grew her business to 15 stores but ended up having to reduce the number of stores to two. She points out, 'One of the mistakes I made in business was to spend a significant amount of time growing a retail group of small shops, rather than developing the brand on a wholesale level, where I get much more efficiency on the time I put in. I found that, over the years, I was adding more stores and spending the entire time trying to manage them remotely. In hindsight, each additional store only paid for the increase in overhead I had to put on to assist managing the business. As you get bigger, you need support functions, accounts, customer service, HR and so on, and these add additional cost.

'I ended up with a group of small stores with large overheads by proportion and I spent my life on the phone sorting issues. Be they HR, customer services, production, marketing or financial, there were always problems somewhere and the one thing I love, designing for people, had become the one thing I did for the least amount of time. When you develop a niche business and you want to grow, you need ambassadors for your brand to run your shops; this sounds easy to put in place, but in reality it isn't.'

HIRING A TALENTED TEAM

❝❞

TALENT IS THE NUMBER-ONE PRIORITY FOR A CEO. YOU THINK IT'S ABOUT VISION AND STRATEGY, BUT YOU HAVE TO GET THE RIGHT PEOPLE FIRST.

Andrea Jung, former Avon CEO

To grow or sustain your business at a level you are comfortable with, you need to focus your time and energy on what you do best, on the areas where you bring the greatest value. At first, you wear all the hats and do all the tasks; from doing your own PR and sales calls to all the financial admin, customer relationships, distribution and so on. But there's only so much juggling you can do before it all gets too much. Something either has to give or you need to find support to help you to survive, thrive and grow.

If you ask any successful business owner what have been the key drivers to help them achieve their success, as well as having an outstanding product and a strong brand, they will unanimously say, 'having a great team'. Indeed, just as small businesses are the lifeblood of the economy, so people are the lifeblood of those businesses. People enable success. They are your greatest asset because they make things happen and deliver immense value, but sourcing and retaining those people is not an easy task. Unfortunately people can also hinder success. Those who are ineffective can create huge problems. They can sap morale and resources, and be expensive and time-consuming. So it's important to get your hiring right.

The pressure of doing so can put fledgling business owners off recruiting at all, but you can't do everything yourself forever. Yes, it is hard to let go of control, because you like to do things in a certain way, and other people may do them differently. But if you don't let go, you'll never be able to build your business. Of course, taking that step to recruiting people can be difficult. You may be wondering:

01. Can I afford to pay other people?

02. How will I know who's right for the job?

03. Will I be able to manage and motivate them? I can tell my children what to do, but other grown-ups?

Everyone has those concerns but, when you reach a certain stage and are over-stretching yourself to the extent that your customer service or productivity is suffering, it's time to take that leap. And you'll be glad that you did.

SUCCESSFUL SCALING UP

In order to scale up effectively you need to have the right people performing the right tasks. You need to cover the following areas:

- **Back-office tasks** – such as IT, administration, legal, HR and so on.

- **Developing the business and bringing in revenue** – performing tasks that result in invoicing a client or charging a customer in some way. This could include sales and delivery, but also operations in terms of product development, manufacture, marketing, copywriting, advert design and so on.

- **Strategy and what's happening next year** – working on areas that won't have an impact on this year's revenue but will enable future growth. For example, establishing joint ventures or partnerships, research and development (R&D), establishing new markets, setting up new outlets, launching new products, finding new distributors and so on.

It is important to figure out which gaps need filling. You need to consider which areas need attention that you simply cannot devote enough time to yourself. 'As an entrepreneur you need to recognise your strengths and weaknesses, especially the weaknesses, and plug those gaps,' advises Thomasina Miers, founder of Wahaca. 'Get people who are good at what you are not good at,' she says.

The key to successful scaling up is often about 'capacity planning'. This involves getting the ratios right around how many people you will need to take on in order to scale up effectively. I once heard a story about a man with a £1 million business that was refused a £50,000 overdraft to hire three more people as they couldn't see how that would impact his business. After getting some expert advice on 'capacity ratios' he realised that he actually needed another 12–15 staff, so he returned to the bank with a proper business plan. Two weeks later the bank loaned him £220,000 with no guarantee, as they'd previously requested. Three years later after successfully scaling up, he sold the business for £50 million. He needed those people to get him there and, had he not taken them on, he'd still be where he was. But, crucially, he also needed to work out his 'capacity ratio' to know how many people he needed to put that plan into action.

Most businesses tend to grow by simply adding a few more people during busy times. They add one, then another one and add one more. Eventually the senior team realises the business used to make more money when it was smaller. You need precisely the right percentages for your size of business to maximise profit and growth. Too much excessive back-office infrastructure and you won't make enough profit. Too few people generating revenue for this year and you'll run out of cash.

Recessions can drag people away from future growth activity and towards back-office activities. To survive and scale up, you need to focus mostly on the activities that generate revenue today, this year, with some focus on next year and away from the fire-fighting back-office administration tasks. As a business owner, once you have a solid back-office infrastructure in place, you should move away from dealing with customer issues, invoicing and other administration tasks and focus on finding new opportunities for the future, securing and converting leads and deals.

If it's just you, then you need to split your time accordingly. You need to make sure that you are focusing enough time on both current and future revenue generation and back-office admin, leaning towards the former rather than the latter (as you can hire people to deal with the back-office admin or to help you with the sales side, dependent on your needs at any given time).

HOW TO FIND THE RIGHT PEOPLE

'The best piece of business advice I've ever been given is to employ a great team,' says Thea Green, founder of Nails Inc. 'Great people pay for themselves much faster. There were many frustrating years when I didn't want to employ a finance director on an FD's salary because I didn't think they would have enough to do,' says Thea. 'However, I have learnt that if I employ the right person on whatever salary, if they are as good as their salary, they always pay for themselves. For example, in the first month they might have a quick sales win, or they may do something you hadn't thought of yet, save money here or make money there. Those people are the ones who don't just do what you tell them to do, they give added value.'

However, it's not always that easy to get the right people. 'We've all employed terrible people, and always will,' says Liz Jackson, of Great Guns Marketing. 'That's the trouble; you can do all the profiling tests in the world, it can still go wrong.' It's an unfortunate fact that, if you employ enough people, sooner or later you could be faced with a member of staff who breaks your trust.

'When an employee accuses you of something you haven't done, it's really tough,' says Liz. 'But sometimes you end up paying them just to get rid of them. The fact of the matter is that 99 per cent of your employees will be consistently amazing, but 1 per cent may put you through hell.'

In my experience, the vast majority of employees are intrinsically honest and reliable, which makes it a real challenge to deal with the very few who are not. Yet, any small-business owner will tell you that you should resolve to learn from every experience – however testing.

I too have faced challenges with recruitment. In 2014, I went through a distressing time in order to prove that an employee I had previously hired, and subsequently dismissed after 4 months, had invented the most outrageous lies about me. I had built a successful business with 25 years' experience and expertise, and here was someone trying to destroy it.

Out of the blue, several months after the termination of his contract, this former employee alleged sexual harassment – one of the only grounds on which he could legally claim anything from me as he had been on a probationary period. He was demanding £50,000, and I regarded this as some kind of attempt to extort money from me.

I vigorously defended the allegations from the outset as having no merit, but was distraught to find out that this individual's claims had been leaked to the press prior to the tribunal date. It was my birthday, and I was faced with these salacious lies right ahead of me in black and white. I felt completely violated.

This made me even more determined to fight to clear my name. Yet, on the morning of the tribunal, the accuser's lawyer immediately requested to settle, so I agreed reluctantly to settle for £3,000 – essentially nuisance money for him to go away and to avoid further stress and costly legal fees. However I ended up paying him nothing …

The former employee unreservedly retracted all of the allegations, and shortly after this, I was contacted by a number of individuals who knew this man very well and had seen the articles in the press. It came to light that he was a serial litigator. He'd had at least seven jobs in the last 10 years and brought legal claims against three employers, including a claim for £50,000 from a small private company that made furniture for disabled children.

There was no way I was standing for this. I made the bold decision to tear up the confidentiality agreement. *The Sunday Telegraph* carried out a full investigation, and the evidence secured enabled me to clear my name unequivocally. This also provided me with an opportunity to speak out to help protect other employers facing similar challenges.

As a spokesperson for the Confederation of British Industry said: 'For large employers, the high costs and reputational damage resulting from lengthy or vexatious claims mean that many choose to settle even where they are in the right. And for smaller employers, employment tribunal cases present a threat to their very existence.'

It had cost me £60,000 in total to defend myself and there was a call for a reform of the employment tribunal system over the cost and time of such spurious cases.

But herein lies the issue: details of cases which are settled are wiped after one year, while cases which go to judgement are erased after six years. So how do you know the true identity of the person you are employing? And how do you know if they've erased or omitted previous places of employment from their CV? It's a tough one.

I've been campaigning for a central register to be made available to companies or their lawyers should they be taken to a tribunal. This would show if the individual putting the case forward has previously sued other companies and on what grounds. This would help protect unsuspecting employers from being held to ransom, as the credibility of their accuser would be seriously questioned.

Thankfully, the incident above was an extreme case of dishonesty. But it highlights a key challenge around recruiting people to join you on your mission. How do you know they are who they say they are and have done what they claim to have done? The simple truth is you don't. People present the best version of themselves at interview stage and will tell you what you want to hear. I've always considered myself to be a good judge of character, which is why this event was even more shocking and upsetting to me. However, I hope that what I've gained from this experience and the tips I've gathered from leading ladies in this book will go some way to helping you to hire well.

Thankfully, the law states that there should be a probationary period so that employers can see if a person is right for the job and vice versa: the employee can see if they like the job and want to continue working for you. In this case I was impressed at interview stage but my instinct that he wasn't right for the role kicked in during the probationary period.

Fortunately, apart from this one 'bad egg', I've been very lucky with my team. Every other individual I have chosen to work for me has proved to be amazing at their job, trustworthy and the right fit.

Sometimes you find an employee who is so outstanding you want them to work with you forever. For example, Sarah, who manages all of our PR and marketing, is incredible, just amazing; she's like four people rolled into one. I have such a fantastic team and such a warm atmosphere in the office – it's like a family and there's a great team spirit. I love coming to the office; everyone does. And when people come here for meetings they like it too.

So how do you find the right people? Here is a set of tips to help you recruit right for your business.

- **Attract like-minded people who share your vision.** Make your company one with a strong set of values and clear mission or purpose (see chapters 1 and 6) which people therefore want to work for. For example, Lucy Jewson of Frugi has found that her company's ethical values around using organic cotton attracts good like-minded people with the same set of values as her.

- **Have a good understanding of what each role requires.** If you have done the role yourself, as is likely as a sole trader, you'll know how to do (and how not to do) the job. 'When I first started the business I used to do all the deliveries myself,' says Jennifer Irvine, founder of The Pure Package. 'So I know what I am looking for in a person. I am looking for someone who is reliable and who is very happy in their own space and respectful of what we do. I also know what I am seeking in each role from doing it myself. For some people we hire we are looking for speed, and we'll see how many cashew nuts they can bag in a set time period, or, for marketing roles, I'm looking for efficiency and for the ability to prioritise,' says Jennifer.

- **Get clear about the gaps you need to fill.** Figure out which gaps need to be plugged both in terms of areas where skills, experience and knowledge are weaker, but also in terms of where opportunities or challenges are larger and where you need the most help. For example, you might think you need to hire an administrator because you detest admin and it's time-consuming, but you may be better hiring a person who could provide you with leverage: a sales person for example. Between you both, you'd get the administration done, or you could outsource the admin or hire a virtual PA rather than a staff member. Says Bev James of The Coaching Academy, 'People make mistakes by hiring people who they like and who are mirror images of themselves. For example, if you have two people who are more reserved in nature and they like product development, they will spend the majority of the time concentrating on product development and avoid going out and selling. Without selling, you don't have a business.' Wendy Shand, founder of Totstotravel.co.uk, agrees: 'I hire people who have a different skillset to me, preferably much stronger than I am. It's tempting to hire people who you see yourself in, but actually I need to be surrounded by people who are not identikits of myself.'

- **Use a variety of recruitment methods to attract the right people.**
  Try LinkedIn, Webrecruit.co.uk, Gumtree, recruitment companies, word of mouth and putting details on your company website. Use your networking and existing contacts too. Sometimes you don't know where your next good hire may come from. Take Sam Roddick, founder of Coco de Mer, for instance; she ended up hiring a customer to redesign her website after he'd complained about it. 'I received an email which said, "Dear Sam, I love your company, these are all the things I love about it, but I hate your website. It is a disappointment." I wrote back, "Dear Nick, if you think it could be improved why don't we meet up and you can tell me how?" I found out he was a web designer, so I challenged him to improve it, and he did.'

- **Look at your network of friends, family and their own networks.**
  The ideal person may be within that group of people. For instance, I needed someone to help with the finances, but I didn't really have a big enough business to hire someone full-time. But my (then) husband had someone called Jackie who looked after his accounts. So she worked two days a week for me and three days a week for him.

- **Use a variety of tools to assess your candidates' personalities and uncover what is motivating them to apply for this role.** Try different methods of finding the right personality fit to join your team. For example, you could use various models of scientific profiling. A friend of mine does graphology (handwriting analysis), which I've tried out on my friends but not employees yet. However, it's so accurate on friends – they can't believe that the person who has done the graphology doesn't know them – so I think it's a good idea. You might try using psychometrics or DISC personality profiling and strengths-based assessments, but you should have yourself tested too.

- **Focus on attitude and cultural fit, not just skills.** Hire to fit within your team. 'When you do your job description, look at what behaviours you want, not just the skill,' advises Bev James. 'What is desirable and what is essential? Be realistic. I spend a lot of time in the first place figuring out what I want and whether that is idealistic or realistic. Sometimes you look at the job description and they say you need to work as part of a team, be good at detail and be outgoing, and you think is it realistic to gain an employee with all those skills? I actually work out for the job I am advertising what kind of profile would match that job. I don't base the decision solely on the profile, but it helps me in getting the right kind of people,' explains Bev. 'Attitude is always more important than expertise,' says Jacqueline Gold, CEO of Ann Summers. 'While skills are important, you can always train those; you can't train or change the attitude.'

- **Include your team in the interview process.** 'At the second interview … I invite candidates to spend five to ten minutes with each of the team,' explains Bev James. 'If one of the team members doesn't like them I won't take them on; the team's opinions are important to me.' It's certainly worth inviting the candidate to spend some time with you in the office and/or to come to an event with you. Have your staff members spend some time with them and take them out to lunch. Your staff members can ask less formal questions about their previous jobs and motivations and judge how well the person would fit within the team. As long as you trust your existing staff not to make judgements based on their own agendas, staff can be great at recruiting well-suited new staff in this way.

- **Take your time to find the right person.** Endure the interview process no matter how long it takes. 'In the early days, I've made mistakes hiring staff,' admits Bev James. 'You can have interview fatigue, and think that no one particularly stands out but that one is probably better than the rest, so you hire them. I would never do that now. I would now start from scratch over and over until I get the right person.'

- **Consider what might make people leave your business** and be sure to find out during the interview process what their motivation (and de-motivation) factors are. It could be that you want them to stay doing the same job forever without promotion or that you expect them to always strive to be the best they can be. It could be that the rate of change is off-putting. 'We have a fairly robust recruitment process now where we really investigate how people deal with change, as the only constant at Frugi is change,' says Lucy Jewson. 'If you are growing as fast as we are, things change constantly. You are quite literally twice the size of business every couple of years, with new people joining all the time, team structures and responsibilities changing … that certainly isn't everyone's cup of tea. It IS exciting though.'

- **Test people's knowledge with practical tasks and questions that test their skills.** I often set interviewees a task for the second interview, for example coming up with ideas for how they would launch a lunchbox range, how they would promote it and how they would sell it into a retailer. People who've not prepared for the interview don't know who your competitors are; don't know which supermarkets you're in. If they haven't bothered to prepare for the interview, they won't prepare for other meetings either, so they're not the right person. Jennifer Irvine holds trial days for job applicants to see if they fit. 'I come up with a series of tasks just to see how they deal with an issue and deal with the problem.'

- **Have a long probation period** – because problems may not manifest for a while. I now do a six-month probation period and Liz Jackson does a nine-month probationary period. Caroline Castigliano says, 'Employment law in this country makes it very difficult to let go of people you have made a mistake with … I wish I'd hired people on a longer probationary period.'

- **If a hire goes bad, act fast.** Obviously you want to keep good staff for as long as possible. However, occasionally you have to terminate someone's employment contract because they have not turned out to be right for the role, they are not coping with the job, or – in certain cases – they have misled you to believe that they could take on the role when they couldn't. Within six months you should have a fair idea of whether they are happy and effective in their job and how well they fit (or don't fit) into your business culture. To avoid problems, get independent advice on what your obligations are and what you can do, and follow the correct consultation procedures. You should know precisely why you are terminating the employment and be direct about this. Make sure you keep detailed records of everything and file all email communications. You should only say what you are willing to repeat in public; everything in emails or texts can be disclosed later so avoid saying anything that could lead to difficulties. For advice on these issues, call the employer helpline at ACAS, and consult an HR specialist if you are struggling.

ANNABEL'S KITCHEN CABINET

SURROUNDING HERSELF WITH THE RIGHT PEOPLE: CHRISSIE RUCKER

Chrissie Rucker credits a large part of The White Company's success down to the help and the creation of a supportive team. Her story is testament to letting others in to enable such growth, and, crucially, of finding the right people at the right time for the right stage of business growth.

'When the team is right it is a joy, it becomes stressful when you don't have the right people doing the right jobs at the right time,' says Chrissie. 'Having a fantastic team behind you gives you the confidence to set exciting goals and growth plans,' she adds.

'I was so lucky having Nick [her then boyfriend, now husband]; his shirt mail-order company was always two years ahead of mine. A lot of the growing pains I went through, he had gone through before me. So I couldn't have had a better mentor at home. I also took on my first NED, and I was never afraid to ask people for advice. I very quickly learnt what I was good at and what I was useless at. So my goal was to surround myself with people who had strengths where I had weaknesses.'

What started as a mail-order range of designer-quality affordable essentials for the linen cupboard has become a full range of lifestyle products available in over 50 stores across the UK. So what made Chrissie decide to go from mail order to retail?

'More and more customers wanted to come and see the stock,' replies Chrissie. 'Many were happy to buy over the phone but those new to shopping by mail order wanted to come and see the product and feel the quality. We had a little showroom in Fulham but as the company grew it became unmanageable. So we opened our first shop in Symons Street, which was three doors from where our lifestyle store is now. It was tiny … 1,000 square feet, whereas today we have 8,000 square feet. We then gradually opened one to three shops a year.'

But Chrissie couldn't have opened those shops without help. 'It started off just being me,' says Chrissie. 'But, by the end of year one, there were three of us, and by the end of year five, ten of us. It was very gradual, but effective,' says Chrissie.

'Because the business was all direct in the begining, i.e. done over the phone or by post, we didn't need that many people. So the team at that time were primarily in the warehouse and manning the phones,' explains Chrissie.

In 2000 Chrissie launched The White Company website and moved to bigger premises and staff doubled in size. The following year was a pivotal one. In 2001 Chrissie hired her first MD and the company opened its first store in Symons Street, Sloane Square. 'My first MD joined when we were turning over £9 million. He brought fantastic financial control, planning and operational skills to the business which meant I could concentrate on the product and marketing at that time,' she says.

'Although the business was successful, six years later it became clear we needed much more help with retail. Our second managing director joined bringing many years of retail and operations experience and that's when we really started to expand.'

The company has continued to expand steadily and the ranges have diversified enormously. Various awards have followed, including Chrissie being given the Everywoman Ambassador Award and an MBE for services to retail. Today, the team size has reached over 1,200, turnover is in excess of £150 million, there are 53 UK stores, franchises in Dubai, a US website and they have moved into a much larger warehouse. Chrissie has now recruited a CEO with both extensive UK and international experience.

'At each stage of the journey I have been lucky enough to find a great leader for the business, who has always brought the leadership qualities, skills and experience needed for that particular stage of growth. Going forward we plan to also start really tackling international now.

'I have a wonderful chairman, Tony Campbell, who has guided and mentored me over the last seven years,' adds Chrissie. 'Whenever I have been in a muddle, or had very difficult decisions to make he has always given me wonderful, sound advice and a very valuable outside perspective.

'My mission is always to try and build a passionate, dynamic team who really support each other and who are instrumental in creating the company's next vision and plan,' says Chrissie. Evidently, it is choosing the right people with the right expertise for the right stages of growth which has propelled The White Company to where it is today and where it will go in the future.

EXTRA SUPPORT FROM MENTORS AND OTHER RESOURCES

Aside from hiring staff and freelancers, there are various ways you can find additional support to help grow your business. You can seek advice from your peers on forums, use resources to help you to boost your business or find a mentor to act as a sounding board and keep you focused.

There's a lot of support out there. You really don't need to do it all on your own. From Enterprise Nation to StartUp Britain – you can watch videos containing advice, learn from experts and access tools to help you reduce costs and increase sales. You can even group together with other small-business owners to 'group buy' to gain the benefit of volume discounts. Check out sites such as Huddlebuy.co.uk.

If you are looking to manufacture as part of your business, a great resource is the Manufacturing Advisory Service (MAS) – an impartial and practical business support service for manufacturing businesses in England, helping them improve and grow. Through MAS you could even access a grant of between £300–£3,000 towards your next project. We secured a grant for product development, which was simple to apply for and made it more affordable for us to get our project moving.

As well as finding support and asking for advice and help on an ad hoc basis, there will come a time when you need more assistance to help you drive your vision forward. When you start your own business it can be invaluable to learn from someone who has been there and done that. Maybe they have already run their own business or are knowledgeable about a certain area or industry?

'A mentor can act as a sounding board and ask you the right questions to give you that all-important clarity, focus and structure,' says Lisa Barber, who mentors businesswomen via her business Roots & Wings. 'From boosting confidence and enhancing performance and positivity to helping entrepreneurs secure finance and attract more clients, a mentor can be an essential asset to a growing company.'

When I decided to enter the food retail market, I decided to seek some extra support from someone who was also a business owner, someone who understands the weight and responsibility of making certain choices. So I took on Philip O'Connor in a mentorship and consultancy capacity. He has worked with Kerry Foods for 20 years and I really trust his judgement. He always gives me good advice. Sometimes you can be too close to your business, but he sees things strategically. It's great to have somebody who's worked in the industry for many years, who has good contacts and can identify with and relate to the problems and obstacles I face. He comes to really important meetings with me and I call him if I need advice. I think it's important to get help, whether that's from a mentor, coach or executive.

Liz Jackson agrees. She sees having a mentor as a way to help you save time by getting help to focus and prioritise. 'A great mentor gives you support and some accountability for the decisions you are making,' she says.

Wendy Shand also values the role of mentors. 'I spend a lot of time meeting people who know more than I do,' she says.

Sometimes your friends who have business acumen may act as your mentor, and vice versa. That has been the case for Jennifer Irvine. 'Every Sunday, rain or shine, my friend Sharon (who runs a marketing firm) and I go for a long cycle ride and we chat about everything,' says Jennifer. 'From strategy to staff, to how we are working out bonuses for the team this year. We bounce everything off each other. You don't have to have a mentor who is senior to you that is just going to advise you on work-related topics, but a woman who you can talk to as a friend – that's just as important as a strategic mentor.'

Sometimes you might choose to hire a mentor, coach or consultant, or your executive team may act as mentors. Chloe Macintosh has ensured that she has created a board with a range of expertise. The Made.com board is made up of individual investors who each have a stake in the company and come with their own level of expertise. See pages 242–3 for more on her story.

“”

WHENEVER I AM ASKED WHAT IS THE MISSING LINK BETWEEN A PROMISING BUSINESSPERSON AND A SUCCESSFUL ONE, MENTORING COMES TO MIND.

Sir Richard Branson

HOW TO FIND THE RIGHT MENTOR

By definition, mentors have often done what you are trying to do before you did it. To find the right mentor, you need to figure out which gap you need them to fill. 'If you had a mentor, identify what it is you would want to learn from them,' says Bev James. 'Find people who have what you'd like to learn within or outside your own network.' While you can go online to find a business mentor, Bev prefers to be more strategic when sourcing a mentor. 'I prefer to find someone that is doing what I want to do really well, but is not in competition with me,' she says.

As well as supporting you and acting as a sounding board, mentors can bring value. So do you need a mentor who has industry knowledge and contacts to fill the gap that exists in your business? Or perhaps you need someone who can fill the gaps in your business acumen – someone who has already built a business the next size up from yours? Just make sure the gap they can fill is still relevant, as they may have done things over a decade ago that are no longer valid.

HOW TO GET THE BEST FROM A MENTOR

In order to make such a relationship work for you so that your mentor can effectively support and champion you from the sidelines, you need to follow a few rules. Lisa Barber suggests the following:

- **Be open to mentoring.** 'The relationship will only thrive if you are open to the idea,' Lisa advises.

- **'Take ownership,'** she suggests. 'The mentor's role is to facilitate your development, not do it for you … So come to the conversation with a good idea of what you would like to focus on, give an update on progress and developments since the previous contact, and propose an agenda for the session.'

- **'Be open and direct with your mentor,'** adds Lisa. 'Share hopes, concerns, strengths, triggers and goals openly. Giving specific examples of how you have benefitted from the relationship provides the mentor with insight into how additional value can be added. Discuss expectations and ask direct questions about what you most want to know. Set up the conversation in a way that provides the most relevance, opportunity for learning and value for you.'

FINANCING GROWTH

There may come a time when you realise that you can't manage on your own and you need extra funding to help you grow the business. For 20 years I funded my business myself, using my book royalties and other earnings to build up the food production side. If you had asked me last year what I would do with several million pounds I don't think I would have known, but this year it's very clear what I need to do to fast-track the growth of the company. I need to speculate to accumulate and consider giving away equity (i.e. shares in my company) in exchange for funding.

Those taking investment will often say that it's better to own a smaller chunk of something huge than a huge chunk of something small. While I agree, there is a lot more to taking on investment than that. You need to consider issues of control, scalability and exit.

Many businesses aim to grow organically, by reinvesting as much profit as possible back into the business to finance the growth. 'The money that comes in you should reinvest to the business, it's a mistake to take money out too soon,' advises Jennifer Irvine, founder of The Pure Package, who admits she was lucky that she had a working husband, as she was able to reinvest over and over to grow the business. 'When my clients paid me money I was able to buy a bigger oven and bigger fridges and invest in the company that way,' she says.

However, if you are either a) already doing that and wish to grow at a faster rate, or b) can't invest all the profits back into the business as it's your main source of income, then a combination of debt and equity finance will probably suit you best. If you borrow money you'll need to factor in having enough cash flow to pay the debt back; whereas, with equity finance, you'll be giving away a slice of your business in exchange for an injection of cash, contacts and market knowledge.

'Growth is expensive,' says Liz Jackson. 'While growing is a wonderful thing, it sucks up all your resources.' Liz used a combination of The Prince's Trust, small-business loan-guarantee-scheme finance, self-funding and invoice financing to fund the growth of her company.

FORMS OF INVESTMENT FOR GROWTH

We have already covered the basic sources of financing on pages 95–100. These methods can be just as beneficial for financing growth as for the initial start-up stage, so refer back to these pages to review the various options.

There are also some forms of financing that are more relevant for businesses that are already established, including getting private equity from venture capitalists or business angels, generating cash through your client base or selling your invoices to a factoring company. These are covered below.

Private equity from venture capitalists or business angels

Although we've briefly touched on this form of financing on pages 97–8, it is more suited for financing growth rather than for early-stage business. With private equity, you secure investment from a third party in return for a share of equity in your company (i.e. a percentage of ownership of your business). These third-party investors are generally either private investors known as business angels (who invest typically between £10,000 and £500,000) or venture-capitalist firms or trusts, who tend to invest no less than £1 million. How much investment you can secure will depend on how profitable, successful and valuable your business already is.

The more money invested, the more sizeable the chunk of equity required, so a business that is already generating £1 million in profit, and is therefore worth a few million, would give away far less for £500,000 investment than a small business with a £250,000 profit.

Venture-capitalist firms are best suited to fast-growth companies who are aiming towards exiting the business and giving their investors and themselves a healthy return on investment (ROI) when the business is sold. Venture capitalists tend to want significant equity in exchange for larger sums.

The benefits of securing a private-equity investor include the fact that those investors often bring more than just cash to the table. They can introduce you to the right people to help you implement your strategy and can ultimately help you to achieve your vision and get you where you want to be.

Says James Caan: 'One of the things I like about angel-investor groups is that, having built and sold businesses before, they now have capital they want to invest, which is what I call "smart capital", because they bring expertise with their capital.'

Such smart capital doesn't come cheap, though, as investors will expect you to meet targets, plus you will be giving away some control, depending on the amount of equity you give away. The higher the risk, the more equity an investor would want.

To find business angels you can look on LinkedIn and also try Angels Den (angelsden.com) and other matching services. However, be warned that angel networks do charge upfront fees and 'finder's fee percentages' of any capital raised in exchange for their giving you access to high-net-worth individuals. Visit UK Business Angels Association (ukbusinessangelsassociation.org.uk) to find business-angel networks in your area and register to pitch at events in front of 50–100 investors. This gives you a higher chance of finding the right investor for you than pitching to individual angels. Ask people in your supply chain, including your accountants, for recommendations, and search trade publications for interviews with those who have invested in your sector.

Venture capitalists are generally listed on BVCA.co.uk, the British Private Equity and Venture Capital Association website, where member firms are listed. It's wise to seek investment from those who specialise in investing in companies within your industry.

Using your own client base to generate cash

That's what Jennifer Irvine did. Once Jennifer had established her Pure Package business, she needed cash to fund further growth. She didn't really want to borrow from banks or venture capitalists, so she looked at her clients and took a different, yet effective, approach. 'At the time, my clients were paying me 10 days in advance, around £300,' she explains. 'So, instead of paying me 10 days in advance, I gave them a discount if they paid 30 days or 90 days in advance, and they took to it. Suddenly my clients were paying me £3,000 rather than £300 and I raised a huge amount of money doing that.'

As a result, Jenny was able to move to fantastic premises in New Covent Garden Market, close to both their customers and suppliers. 'So, within six months of launch I'd gone from a fridge freezer at home to a 1,000-foot fridge, while retaining control and avoiding debt.'

Alternatively, you could even ask your customers for an amount each in exchange for equity, so you give your customers shares in your business – crowdfunding through your customer crowd.

Or, as I did, you could talk to your suppliers or manufacturers to see if they can invest in you by not invoicing you until you've made some sales – advancing you some orders before taking payment. This is what I did with the factory I used for my chilled range for children.

Asset-based lending via invoice finance or factoring

Factoring involves selling your invoices to a factoring company. You get cash quickly, and don't have to collect the debt, however, you lose some of the value of the invoice. The factoring company gets the debt and has to collect it. They make a profit by paying you less cash than the face value of the invoice. You can use factoring to get money quickly, avoid the hassle of collecting bad debt or smooth your cash flow.

With many large firms imposing 90- or 120-day terms when you are having to pay your suppliers on 20–30-day payment terms, this can cripple cash flow. However, many traditional invoice discounting and factoring firms will lock you in with long-term exclusive agreements and request that you hand all of your invoices over to them to finance, so you can't just pick some of them to be financed. You can end up paying to use the service even when you're not using it. Also, the debtor is informed that the invoice has been sold on to a third party so you lose charge of your credit control.

Platform Black offers a more flexible, 'pay as you go' service that does not tie people in. It brings companies wishing to raise money against some or all of their outstanding invoices together with investors who are ready to advance the funds, so that small to medium-sized enterprises can essentially get tomorrow's invoices paid today by selling them online. There are no arrangement fees or lock-ins.

The best thing to do is to look for companies supported by the Asset Based Finance Association (ABFA).

DEMONSTRATING DEMAND AND ROOM TO GROW

In order to win further investment and convey your value, you will need to demonstrate that you have customers already and, ideally, that you are in a growth sector. If you are looking to gain investment via equity finance, you will also need to value your business by demonstrating its potential.

'*The* definition of potential is growth,' says serial investor James Caan. 'If you can demonstrate growth in a tangible way then you will maximise your investment.'

For example, securing custom in another country proves that there is demand. And if that market is sizeable, you are also demonstrating there is potential to grow. James explains: 'If I expanded into Dubai and I got an order there and that order may be worth half a million, but the market is worth 10 million, I would include that in my business valuation in order to get capital. I would say, "Dubai likes me, I have had an order".' He adds, 'That's how Gü [the chocolate dessert brand] got 30 times earnings when they sold the business because they had expanded into different markets and they got their product on to Virgin planes. They hadn't really built a business but they demonstrated that there was demand in France, and they had half a million in revenue, so the buyer looked at the potential in growth. So the key word here is growth.'

EXPANDING OVERSEAS

Taking your business international can be very profitable, however, James Caan suggests that you only ever expand overseas if you have fulfilled potential here in the UK, as it can be a costly exercise.

'Only expand internationally if you have maximised on your current market,' he advises. 'Why would you want to go to overseas markets where you don't know the legislation, you don't know corporate governance, you don't know taxation, the laws and pricing? It'll take 10 times more work in an overseas market than it would in your domestic market, where you still have a good share of the market [to expand into],' adds James.

'In most cases people expand because they expand, not for a logical reason,' he says. 'As somebody who has had businesses in 30 countries around the world, I realised I did it for putting flags on the map not because there was a commercial reason to do it. If I had my time again, would I expand internationally? I wouldn't. Simply because I have experienced the amount of time, effort, energy and risk it involves. On balance, the costs of doing business abroad are much higher than doing business in your domestic market. Therefore, only when you absolutely believe you have maximised on your domestic market should you expand internationally, [and only] if it adds value and potential.'

I expanded internationally when it was the right time for my business. I was already well-known in the UAE with my recipe books and had made lots of successful trips – undertaking media tours, book signings, speaker events and developing menus for hotels and a leading Middle Eastern airline – so extending my supermarket food ranges into that market was a natural progression for me. We started to export to Dubai and Abu Dhabi in 2013, and then we expanded within the UAE and Kuwait, supplying Carrefour and other large retail chains. We also now supply to Hong Kong and South Korea.

Australia is another key market for my brand, where my books and app are already very successful. In 2014 we began work with a leading Australian food manufacturer to create a bespoke range of Annabel Karmel lines. Working with a local partner is good as there are no set-up costs and they produce and hold the stock. The risk is also limited as we work on a royalty basis. And the local manufacturer has existing relationships with key retailers in the region, which is really important in getting a foot in the door. This year we are launching a whole range of products in Coles and Woolworths, the two biggest retailers in Australia.

Securing the right help is so important when getting your business off the ground, especially if you have limited knowledge of the particular market you want to go into.

If you are looking to export overseas, it is definitely worthwhile looking into the UK Trade and Investment's 'Passport to Export' service. This programme provides training, planning and support for small and medium-sized enterprises wanting to grow their business in new territories. For more information, visit: www.gov.uk.

ANNABEL'S KITCHEN CABINET

INTERNATIONAL EXPANSION: DESSI BELL

Growth overseas for Dessi Bell's activewear brand Zaggora has been huge, with 85 per cent of their custom coming from territories outside the UK. America in particular is a huge market for them. So how did Dessi take a brand into 126 countries?

'This is the power of social media,' says Dessi. 'Women have friends all over the world. The fact that we had such a large social following really helped us here. Selling to the US is great as it is over five times the size of the UK market.'

Growing at this rate internationally has been a huge learning curve about selling into different markets.

'I've learnt that you have to have your logistics right,' says Dessi. 'You might be delivering fabulously to 99.9 per cent of your customers, but those two people who had their delivery delayed in India and Australia will persistently go on Facebook and disproportionately sway the impression of new people that your service is bad.'

As such, attention to detail when you expand is vital.

Despite such rapid growth, Dessi still has a reasonably small team of 10 people, which helps with staying agile. She has learnt that in order to grow successfully you need to focus on the customer and on their satisfaction above all else. 'Growing too fast is as bad or even worse than growing too slow,' she says. 'You have to have your ducks in a row, because if you disappoint your customers you have to rebuild your business from a defensive position. We have had our fair share of that. We were so focused on top-line growth, delivering the most amount of revenue in the quickest amount of time possible, we thought we'd bring in all these people in all these countries, but you don't realise what needs to happen underneath to make that happen. You must take care of your customers. That's vital to focus on. From what I have learnt the answer has to be – am I going to be able to serve my next customer as well as I served the last one? If yes, then let's grow. If not, then we consider, what do we need to do to make sure that happens before we grow?'

TESTING THE WATERS

Having a strategy for expansion is one thing, but how can you determine whether there is international demand and a potential for growth overseas?

Jacqueline Gold has harnessed the power of the Internet and digital technology to fuel Ann Summers' international growth via an eBay store. 'We have launched overseas via eBay and, while it is actually the smallest side of our business, it's also growing the fastest.'

'eBay was the quickest and cheapest way to launch overseas, because it already had a platform,' explains Jacqueline. 'One of the difficult things of doing it yourself is working out which countries to start with. The great thing is that eBay already had that set up … It was our opportunity to dip our toe in the water and see in which countries the success might be. As a result of our partnership we are now selling online in Australia and the US as well as four European countries,' adds Jacqueline. 'We are essentially using eBay to test the market and potential for growth.'

Ann Summers is scaling up and out and is using multiple methods of distribution, but its core proposition and product range remains focused. Some businesses, however, choose to diversify in order to grow.

DIVERSIFICATION, INNOVATION AND SCALING UP AND OUT

So which is right? In order to grow and boost revenues and company value, should you diversify or focus? A diversification strategy can drive growth. Sir Richard Branson's Virgin brand is testament to that. Imagine the scene – a girl on a train talks animatedly to a friend on her mobile phone. She looks out of the window and watches a plane coming in to land. What's remarkable about this scene is that the mobile phone, train and plane are all bearers of the Virgin brand. Disparate? Yes. But connected too. They are connected by Branson's ethos to disrupt industries and do things better.

Other ways to diversify, other than launching new products under the main 'umbrella' brand name, are to create new products or projects, under different names, but which appeal to the same markets (and can therefore benefit by promoting to the same core audience). These projects will all be connected in some way, whether that's audience or purpose. Such entities could be joint ventures or operated under the same roof; either way there are lots of options to diversify in order to grow.

Generally, diversification comes as a direct result of responding to and seizing an opportunity that arises. This is a natural progression. Customers who run businesses within a certain market may ask you for your help, or you may find customers within a specific niche ask if you can add a specific service to your range. You may find that one product or service feeds another. For example, my recipe books enable parents to cook from scratch for their growing family, but if they don't have the time to cook, they can rely on my supermarket range; and while they're on holiday, they can order my food from various hotels and leisure resorts. Each complements the other. They serve the same market with the same needs – to give their children wholesome tasty food, whether it's prepared from the kitchen cupboard or bought from the baby or chiller aisle.

Just as I diversified into food service, selling my food to businesses targeting the same market as myself, so you too may be able to diversify from selling direct to consumers to selling to other businesses who sell to those same niche groups of customers.

Some businesses choose to diversify if they operate a seasonal business. So someone providing chocolate ice cream or catering to summer events, such as weddings or fairs, may choose to diversify to avoid the peaks and troughs – perhaps providing hot chocolate during the winter months. Ski holiday specialists may venture into the villa holiday market to bring in sales during the slower summer months.

The downside of entering into a diversification strategy is use of your time. By devoting time to a new project or product, you are taking your attention and focus away from your core area of business. Whatever you diversify into, the core business should be stable first. Otherwise you dilute the success of each.

Ideally, you should only diversify once you have sufficient infrastructure in place and have hired people to deal with the three key areas of back office, current revenue and future revenue for that core business/product, *before* you start to diversify. Or, if you remain a sole trader, before you diversify you must find ways to split your time accordingly and consider outsourcing certain tasks to freelancers in order to give each project the time and attention it deserves.

You need to ensure that your customers will still be cared for and that you have either automated processes or allocated people/time slots to deal with sales and marketing. Because, ultimately, success and growth in business continues to be primarily about meeting (and exceeding) customer expectations. Once you have all of this in place, only then should you venture into new areas. If you get it right, diversification could be an engine for growth; if you get it wrong, diversification could be a costly distraction.

Some of my 'Kitchen Cabinet' contributors have found great success through diversification.

- **Myleene Klass is the queen of diversification:** her enterprises sell everything from baby clothes to bedding to beauty products in her bid for 'world domination and the school run'. But diversifying has served her well. 'There are lots of facets to us mums. When things have not worked out in certain areas, they'll work in others and it's the diversity that has now kept me afloat,' says Myleene. 'I'm laughed at for being a jack-of-all-trades, or a Jacqueline-of-all-trades, as I call myself. But they're all still connected and that's what you need to look at. Are the areas you are diversifying in connected? Do they fit well alongside each other?' Certainly Myleene's work tends to focus on three key areas: music, fashion and children, with her Save the Children work complementing her enterprises which serve mums.

- **Jacqueline Gold has adopted a multi-channel approach to grow Ann Summers.** Annsummers.com launched in 1999 so that the business would not be reliant on their stores and parties. 'Companies are going to be left behind if they have not grasped the technology aspect, whether it is tablets in store or Click and Collect. You definitely need a presence online, whether it is transactional or not.' In order to de-risk the business and scale up successfully, Jacqueline suggests that you should take the multi-channel approach step-by-step. 'You have to start somewhere; don't start with all channels at once,' Jacqueline advises. 'Choose the best channel that works for you. So if you decide to start in retail, establish that first then move online.'

- **Jennifer Irvine diversified by launching a complementary new business after spotting an opportunity.** She decided to launch a little sister to The Pure Package called Balance Box in 2013. 'The reason I decided to launch the Balance Box was because I fully understood the customers and their needs, and I wanted to introduce something that was more accessible with a nationwide delivery programme,' explains Jennifer. 'The Pure Package is really for just London or around London, as we have to do these really fresh daily deliveries and we couldn't find a nationwide carrier. But also, if The Pure Package client is going to a restaurant they will usually call us and say, "I am having lunch today at the Ivy, what should I eat?" So we call the Ivy, and we suggest what the client eats from the menu. They want to stick to their programme. I rethought the entire concept, re-designed all the packaging and took our most popular programmes and turned them into the Balance Box, which is delivered twice a week instead of every day. It is still very high standard but it is not as personalised.'

HOW TO GROW YOUR BUSINESS: TIPS FROM THE TOP

- **Understand what you want from your business.** If retaining control of your business and pursuing your purpose is more important to you than money, securing investment won't be as high a priority as if your intention is to grow your business and sell it for the maximum possible value. If the latter is true, you would prioritise seeking partners and investment to enable you to get there faster.

- **'Grow according to your resources,'** advises Liz Earle. 'This way, you build a financially secure business that protects the brand and its employees.' Liz grew the Liz Earle Beauty Co. from mail-order distribution to QVC, then having their own flagship stores, selling online through e-commerce, and then expanding into high-street retail through John Lewis and Boots. 'For us in the early days, the business grew naturally and organically. We never took a bank loan or used credit – we simply ploughed the revenue that we made back into the business to build it slowly and build it strong. This dictated our rate of growth, which was actually not that fast, but very solid and built on firm foundations,' explains Liz.

- **Know how fast you want to grow and how much risk you are prepared to take (or not take).** If you want to avoid the risks involved in rapid growth, be patient and opt for a more measured organic growth. Liz Earle says, 'I have always believed in crawl, walk, run – basically don't rush anything and take your time to make sure that everything you do is right for everyone involved … Don't feel pressurised into doing something just because someone's saying it has to be now. My former business partner Kim Buckland taught me that sometimes you have to take a deep breath and say, "Well, if it has to be now, it has to be no."'

- **Understand that, when growing a business, change is the only constant.** 'Growing a business was hairy,' says Thomasina Miers of Wahaca. 'I recently read a headline in the *FT* that 30 per cent of a business is the idea and the rest is its application. As you move from one to two and then more restaurants, issues of control and quality come into play. Despite the difficulties – we found years two and three of the business very challenging – it was hugely inspiring to have created it from nothing, something that continues to evolve. We warn our incoming employees that the business is always changing, that we never sit still.'

- **'Get as much advice as you can from people that have been there, done that before,'** advises Lucy Jewson, whose company, Frugi, has grown at between 37 and 47 per cent each year. 'You'll get a lot of differing opinions, but listen to them all and then find your own truth – what feels right for you and what you want out of your business.'

- **Spend wisely and have very good management accounts.** 'It's really important to have realistic growth targets and well-worked-out overheads,' says Lucy Jewson. 'Every time you want to do something else – recruit a new person, invest in more IT, etc. – run that through the accounts first; don't let anything be a shock. Control those finances. Analyse return on investment on everything you can, as often as you can … stop things that don't work straight away. If you don't know the numbers, you can't run a business.'

- **Plan carefully.** 'Have good bottom-up plans,' advises Lucy. 'Which are the prospects that are going to give you growth? Plot the potential of each and every one. If one doesn't work out, where do you need to make that up from? … In our industry our lead time from putting pen to paper to create a design to actually receiving it in the warehouse is 18 months. That means that we have to be accurately forecasted 18–24 months ahead.'

- **'Know your market,'** advises Myleene Klass. 'You know the time is right to diversify as a result of researching your core audience and seeing a genuine way you can [solve a problem or otherwise] contribute.'

- **Understand the differences and similarities between different countries.** 'Certain things just do not translate on an international scale, both culturally and climate-wise,' says Myleene. 'For example, I have to simultaneously design my range for summer in the UAE and winter in Russia, which brings its own challenges. Saying that, I sell more snowsuits/pramsuits in the UAE than any other country [and this is] down to their air-con settings and what they require from my clothes.' Just as an awareness of differences between countries into which you expand is critical, so is understanding similarities, as this can give you some welcome common ground. Chloe Macintosh of Made.com says, 'Having launched in France I thought what everyone wanted would be quite different for the different countries. However, I realised quite quickly that there were more points of similarity across the countries than I thought.' She explains, 'The space they are in in life defines them as a customer, so their same age group, habits or lifestyle. As a result we focus on what's the same and not on what's different.'

ANNABEL'S KITCHEN CABINET

MADE FOR GROWTH: CHLOE MACINTOSH

Made.com is testament to the fact that an influential investor coupled with a disruptive idea can be a powerful combination to fast-track growth. Having launched in 2010, the company has expanded into Europe and turns over many millions. In early 2013 Made.com launched in France, which was the next logical place to stamp their geographical footprint. The company is well on its way to achieving the dreams of its founders.

The story of Made.com stems from putting a great team together to work on an innovative business model with financial backing and support from an influential investor. That investor was Brent Hoberman, who co-founded lastminute.com with Martha Lane Fox before moving on to other ventures such as Mydeco.com, where he had hired Chloe Macintosh. Chloe and Brent were keen to get a 'direct from the factory to consumer' business model off the ground and reached out to Ning Li, who had also had the idea, and who crucially had experience of investment banking and sourcing products directly from factories to the table. He only moved to London to start Made.com with Chloe as a result of the backing from Brent. He brought the third co-founder, a friend from business school, Julien Callede, with him to bring operational nous to the business.

Brent became the financial backer and chairman, and together the four of them raised £2.5 million for the UK launch. The credibility of Brent, the track record of Ning and the innovative disruptive business model (see pages 57–8) helped them to raise the cash.

Their collaborative model – of working with designers and manufacturers, and allowing customers to choose which products are actually made – has worked. But none of this would have been possible without the credibility of each founding member. 'People invest in people; you have to remember that it is a team and that team is the value,' says Chloe.

That team has grown as the company expands overseas and the business even has a showroom on the ninth floor of their office building.

Meanwhile, Chloe has had to spend time reorganising the business while keeping up momentum. She has also ensured that their core promise – the ability to fulfil the growth of orders – is retained.

'We've had to ensure that our expansion doesn't create issues for our customers,' she says. 'In order to do that the Made.com team have had to work closely with their partners to ensure that they have the capacity to grow alongside them.'

Within just eight months of launching in France, French sales represented a very large percentage of the group's revenue. Chloe has been visiting France to connect with her old network and, as a result of the encouraging French launch, the company launched in Italy and, most recently, the Netherlands too.

'Although we are only online it proves that selling all over the world can be quite straightforward. We need to continue to choose the right fulfilment partners and ensure that our new overseas customers have the best experience from browsing the site to receiving their furniture,' says Chloe.

'Made.com is very scalable as it has just one point of sale and can grow with the customer base,' she adds. 'We can therefore pick up on the activity as it hits the site and react accordingly.'

In working in this collaborative way first and scaling up and out across the Channel into Europe, country by country, Made.com is a great example of furnishing well-managed international growth.

10

PERSIST, YOUR IN AND EM YOUR FA

" " " "

**CHALLENGES FORCE
YOU TO JUST GET ON
WITH IT; THEY MAKE
A FIGHTER OUT OF
YOU; THEY GIVE YOU A
HUNGER TO GET ON AND
DO IT, WHEN EVERYONE
IS SAYING YOU CAN'T.**

Chloe Macintosh, Made.com

TRUST
STINCTS
BRACE
ILURES

BELIEVE AND YOU'LL ACHIEVE

Running your own business is a roller-coaster ride of ups and downs. Optimism, determination and resilience are frequently required in equal measure.

'So many people fall when they get a few disappointments or knock-backs, and it's especially hard working on your own without a team to spur you on, but you have to take the knocks – realise something just wasn't meant to be or keep on going knowing that there are plenty more opportunities out there,' says Fiona Clark, founder of Inspiredmums. co.uk. 'When things don't work out, I think to myself, I'll just take any learnings I can and move on.'

That's the attitude you need to take with you in business: that resilience around rejection and persistence to keep going, pivot where necessary and keep at it. When I know I have a good idea, I will stick with it. I will not let it go. From the outset I had the intention, at some point in the future, of producing my own baby food to complement the recipes in my books. It took an extremely long time to reach that point – the best part of 20 years – but I never lost sight of that ambition; I never let go of the idea.

Persistence will be valuable throughout your business activities. For example, following up sales opportunities and potential contacts requires positive perseverance – it's very easy to become discouraged when people keep saying no. But, if you believe in your idea and have done sufficient research to back up your own belief with viable data, you should persist.

I learnt the value of persistence with my first book. When I first told people I was planning to write a book of recipes for babies and toddlers, the reaction I often got was, 'Why would you want to do that? Don't you know it's impossible to get a book published?' And they were nearly right … I kept getting rejected, time and time again.

Once I'd written the book I initially set out to find a literary agent. I found a book which listed agents and sent letters to those that looked most suitable. Not one of them wanted to represent me. After all, no book on feeding babies had ever been a commercial success, and nobody could see the gap in the market in the same way I had been able to, from working with the playgroup. My passion to make this happen drove me to try on my own, so I decided to find a publisher myself, without the help of an agent. I visited bookshops and looked at all the other cookery books in the market to see which publisher would be suitable. Random House and Dorling Kindersley stuck out. And so, despite knowing absolutely nothing about publishing, I bundled up my manuscript in an envelope and sent it off to 20 or so different publishing houses.

Some didn't reply but one by one I received letters from the others, all of them rejecting the idea. I sat at my dining table glancing over the pile of 15 rejection letters in front of me and wondering if I'd ever get this book out, but still feeling incredibly passionate that it would be published somehow. I wouldn't let up, and I told everyone I knew about it.

Fortunately, some time later, as I mentioned in Chapter 7, a tennis partner of mine introduced me to a small dynamic book packager. They understood what I was trying to achieve and worked with me on shaping my initial version and getting it right for the marketplace. They agreed to take my book to the Frankfurt Book Fair, where they sold it to US publisher Simon & Schuster, who ordered 25,000 copies. Having the backing of a major US publisher helped; together with the packager, I went back to Ebury, an imprint of Random House. At the time it was run by Gail Rebuck, who is now chair of Penguin Random House UK. Recognising, as a mum, that the book was interesting and filling a niche in the market, she agreed to take me on.

It sold out within the first three months of its print run. There was one downside to all of this: because I had to go through the book packager, I earned low royalties, despite my book being a bestseller. After a good number of years of strong sales and low returns, I went to my book packager to buy back the rights, but of course they'd already sold them to Ebury and publishers all over the world. But Ebury, seeing that I had already had great success with them for many years, realised that it was unfair I was earning very little, so they bought out the book from my packager, which allowed me to get a much better royalty – and my relationship with Ebury blossomed.

Without that passionate persistence, I'd have given up at the third or fourth rejection letter. I was determined to get the book out into the world and make it work, whatever it took. In business, we need that passion to fuel us forwards. It's what keeps us going during tough times.

Even when the book was doing well, nobody believed in it as much as I did. Despite amazing sales for the first book, Random House weren't sure about doing another, so I went to BBC Books to publish my second book, which also just went on selling and selling and selling. On the back of that success, Random House decided we should do another book after all. Yet I couldn't get my books into America with Random House. I felt that America was important, so I started publishing with both Dorling Kindersley in the US and Random House in the UK. I would go on gruelling US tours, travelling to eight cities in two weeks – Atlanta, Minneapolis, Denver, Dallas … Almost every day I would get on a plane, but I knew it was really important to get out there and publicise my books.

The effort I had put in paid off and, instead of me travelling all around the US, Dorling Kindersley would organise satellite media tours from New York, so I would do face-to-face interviews there and then, from the same studio, and link up with TV stations from around the US. It was busy, as I would have about 25 media link-ups in any one day, but a far more economical use of my time. However, I wouldn't have been so popular with the media if I hadn't put in the groundwork to begin with.

I have published 12 books in the US with Dorling Kindersley since 1999, and I also signed with Atria Books – a successful imprint of Simon & Schuster – and have published 12 books with them. I've been told that very few UK authors make it in the US market, but I found that, with persistence and a good product in a niche market, you can get there.

That belief in what I was doing led me to be published all over the world. In fact, my books are published in 25 different languages.

ANNABEL'S KITCHEN CABINET

OVERCOMING OBSTACLES WITH PERSISTENCE: JACQUELINE GOLD

In 1999 Jacqueline Gold proposed to set up an Ann Summers store in Dublin but the city council weren't keen. So Jacqueline invited them to the UK and head office to demonstrate that they were a normal business and that 'there weren't women in PVC thigh-high boots walking around'.

However, the council weren't convinced and told her that they couldn't be held responsible for what might happen if she went ahead with the opening.

However, rather than give up, Jacqueline persisted by going on Ireland's *The Late Late Show* to dispel the myths. When a city council audience member criticised the retailer, women in the audience stood up to defend her. 'How dare you tell us where we can and can't shop?' said one woman. The media subsequently shifted their opinion and gave Jacqueline positive press. A writ was served on that first day of opening, but 10,000 customers flocked in, demonstrating demand for the store. The court battle was won and, these days, the shop is on the tourist bus route and is one of her top-performing stores.

Jacqueline also faced the obstacle of job centres refusing to allow Ann Summers to advertise. She took the government to court as a result and won. 'I am hugely proud of that moment,' Jacqueline says.

'The way I overcame those obstacles is from the passion I have felt for my business,' she says. 'All I have ever wanted to do is empower women in the bedroom and there was a perception that I was going to corrupt everybody. I have always stuck by my mission of empowerment … I will always overcome the challenges; I am relentless when it comes to my passions,' declares Jacqueline.

That inspirational persistence has paid off, as Jacqueline has taken the company from a turnover of £83,000 in her first year to the £145 million-pound empire it is today. She is also achieving her mission of empowering women – not only in the bedroom but in business too – with her weekly WOW campaign on Twitter.

RESILIENCE AND PERSISTENCE AGAINST ALL ODDS

IF I'VE LEARNT ANYTHING, YOU ROLL WITH THE PUNCHES. I'VE TAKEN MORE PUNCHES THAN ROCKY.

Myleene Klass

Most people face challenges when they set up their own businesses – from raising funds or finding customers to hiring staff or sourcing suppliers. However, it is a common trait among successful entrepreneurs that they don't let any obstacles get them down.

'There are lots of things that people see as obstacles, but you need to have the right frame of mind and turn them around – see them as opportunities,' says Jennifer Irvine of The Pure Package. 'When you have a business that you love and you have clients who you love, you feel an obligation to keep going for them.'

'Out of every experience, good or bad, you learn from it,' advises Chrissie Rucker, founder of The White Company. 'It's important to keep looking forward, learn from the past but always move forward positively.'

Chrissie herself experienced her fair share of adversity. 'In our first year, our main factory's roof came off and it flooded and ruined our whole stock,' she recalls. 'There were all sorts of things that went wrong along the journey, we ran out of money, but then I won a small-business competition and a further £5,000 pounds, which meant that we could pay for six months' rent. Everything progressed at the right time.' Each time she faced a setback, Chrissie dusted herself off and carried on. Now her company, The White Company, turns over hundreds of millions of pounds and has over 50 stores.

Liz Jackson of Great Guns Marketing has been similarly determined not to let obstacles get in her way. Her sight had been deteriorating for many years, having been diagnosed with a severe eye disorder as a child, but she finally lost her sight entirely in the same year she set up her award-winning business. 'It was a bit of a shock but I'd got so much to do … I didn't have the choice to sit around and mope. So I had to just employ someone to help me pretty quickly and get on with life,' says Liz.

'Yes, it was a challenge,' she admits. But Liz has managed to see the positive side of her circumstances. 'I think it was quite a good thing,' she says. 'A lot of entrepreneurs who start a company run themselves ragged trying to do everything, from HR, accounts, salary and so on – everything that they are pretty rubbish at – when actually, if they had outsourced from day one, that would have freed up their time to do the things that they are good at on the client side, building relationships and so on. I was forced to outsource right from the beginning, which was a good discipline for me. At that stage it was a telemarketing business so no one on the end of the phone knows you are blind. It probably enhanced my listening skills, and it was probably a blessing.'

In business, as in life, there will be pitfalls, obstacles, challenges and dramas. That's the way it is. You need to be prepared to find a way around stone walls, to take the detour and persist.

HOW TO PERSIST AGAINST ALL ODDS

- **Look at your strengths and find the detour.** When I launched my baby purees I had difficulties securing retailers, despite having a better product than the existing ones. So I took a different route in to achieve my goal. As a trusted expert for babies, I was approached to become Tesco Baby Club's baby expert. They recognised the value in being able to offer my expertise and knowledge to their shoppers, so I provided my services in return for ensuring my organic baby purees were listed. It made sense for Tesco mums to be able to read my advice, cook my recipes and then purchase my baby food in store. What I have built is trust and credibility, which I can leverage to build my brand.

- **Find the silver lining.** Perhaps you've not secured the deal you wanted or have struggled to find the right supplier. Look for the good in that situation. Perhaps, like Liz, a situation has forced you to outsource or delegate, which enables you to focus on what you're good at and grow your business; or maybe not getting that client (who was not quite right) gave you the freedom and the grit to go out and find the right client for you.

- **Just keep on keeping on.** We initially found it incredibly tough to get into one particular retailer. I discovered that a competitor's partner was based there, although we'll never know if that had anything to do with it. Whatever the reason, we remained persistent, and we continued to pitch to them. I asked them what they had to lose and they agreed to trial us. You have to be in it for the long haul when it comes to persuading retailers to stock you.

- **Find an alternative customer for your products that you believe in.** I knew there was no place for a frozen children's food range in the supermarkets, despite the fact that frozen can be just as good quality as – if not better than – chilled. So when an opportunity arose for me to supply frozen food to restaurants I jumped on it. More and more clients came on board until we were soon producing a million children's meals annually. Finding that alternative by seizing an opportunity got me into food service, which is now a large part of our business. I have also, as a direct result of what I've learnt through food service, launched a pilot menu for schools without kitchens as a not-for-profit initiative. This is wonderful as it means I'm helping children to have nutritious food that they love to eat at lunchtime. All of these alternative routes to market have come as a result of persisting and finding new paths to take when the first path didn't bear fruit.

- **'Be in it for the long game,'** advises Lucy Jewson of Frugi. 'Make friends with the stockist over time. They may not have room for you this minute, but don't let that put you off. You can be persistent without being pushy, so send them something original every so often to help them remember you. You never know, next time they are rejigging their brand offer, you might just be at the front of their minds … Your offer might not fit right now but, as you grow successfully, some of those bigger buyers will start to sit up and take notice. Keep them informed,' she advises. 'And do everything you can to make relationships with the critical people. Don't forget they move around.'

LEARN TO LISTEN TO YOUR GUT INSTINCT (OR YOUR MOTHER'S INTUITION)

It is easy to feel that you must always rely on and trust the advice of other people who happen to have more experience and greater qualifications than you do. Over the years I have learnt that I can trust my own instincts, my own antennae, as much as I can trust the 'experts'. Your gut feeling is usually right.

That same sixth sense told me something was not right with my daughter Natasha, even though the first doctor I had taken her to told me not to worry. The medical experts also told me not to have another baby too soon after Natasha died. But I knew I needed to have another child so I could return to being an active mother, rather than a grieving one, as soon as possible. Nicholas was born the following year. It proved to me you have to be brave and stick your neck out.

In business, if every decision was so obvious and easy to do, everybody would be out there doing the same thing. For example, I decided to fund and develop my own Annabel Karmel app, simply because there were no real experts out there providing simple recipes for babies and toddlers on the go – the medium was still so young. You have to take risks, but ensure that they are calculated risks. Being a risk-taker does not mean being reckless. For me, the risk to venture into something relatively unknown paid off, as the Annabel Karmel app is now regularly in the top-grossing food and drink apps.

I first gained the confidence to launch my own range of children's food when I learnt about the retail sector by acting as an expert to retail giants Marks & Spencer and Boots. M&S had wanted to launch a range of children's food and, completely out of the blue, asked me to be their food consultant. I spent nearly two years talking to focus groups and it was a complete education in building a food range from scratch: thinking about who the consumer was, working out the nutritionals and the recipe choice, understanding packaging and the importance of pricing.

Three years later Boots asked me to work with them on a baby range that would be jointly branded Annabel Karmel and Boots. They wanted me to decide which products I thought would work in their stores. I designed a range called 'Make It Easy', which included both equipment and baby foods, and would be sold on the shelf alongside my books.

This experience was invaluable. Under the aegis of two major retailing companies, I was given the opportunity to listen, learn and become my own expert – at someone else's expense. And it was during this time that I learnt to tune in and listen to my own instinct. I was proved right on many occasions, despite not being an expert in retail.

The key is not to reject all expert advice lock, stock and barrel – that would be sheer madness – but to learn when to believe and trust, and when to question and challenge that advice if it feels off-kilter, if your instinct says it should be questioned. Remember, professional advisers and consultants tend to rely on systems – that's why they are consultants and not entrepreneurs. Find the ones who are prepared to discard the system and think outside the box with you. If you want your business to work, it's up to you, no one else. If I had listened to everyone who said it wasn't possible, I wouldn't have a brand.

'Women tend to have this instinctive need to seek validation on new ideas and opportunities from other people,' says Jacqueline Gold. 'Women should be encouraged to trust their gut instinct. Yes, listen to the experts, but you are making those decisions and it's a good thing to listen to your gut.'

Myleene Klass agrees: 'If I had listened to everyone else's advice, I'd still be sitting as a session musician, not even broadening my horizons. I wanted to create my own mini Klass empire. I want it for my girls and I want it for myself. People try to give me a lot of advice because they think they know how to run your business. However, if they knew that much they'd be doing it … I base my decisions on my own informed choices based on instinct and knowledge.'

'Be confident and trust your own instincts,' adds Liz Jackson. 'People can give you all the advice in the world and a lot of it is rubbish, so you need to trust your own judgements. Be careful who you trust and who you listen to.'

'Go after what you want and stay focused,' advises Liz. 'Keep tunnel vision to a certain extent; do not get side-tracked from what you want to achieve.'

In business you need to follow your instincts in order to set trends, rather than follow them, so that you can be different and better than the rest. By the time you know that trend it's too late. Make your own trend. Follow your heart. I like to be innovative, to create something different. My book was definitely different, as was my advice. I remember in America they said giving meat at six months was wrong. However, the American Pediatric Society now agrees that meat should be provided at six months. I was ahead of my time in that respect because I combined my instinct and feedback with research – I made informed decisions based on a combination of knowledge and instinct.

Listen to yourself, to your inner instinct, more than you listen to others (unless you have no knowledge of a sector and they are true experts). Take advice, hear it, but do so alongside tuning in to your own gut instinct.

BE PREPARED TO PIVOT

Persistence brings focus. I have so many ideas that I can go off on a tangent and someone else has to bring me back. That's good – it keeps the ideas flowing – but I also have to prioritise and make sure that the bills and salaries are paid. Being persistent requires a delicate balancing act: you must stay committed to your original passion and vision, but avoid becoming so inflexible that you are not prepared to change your ideas for the better. So, while you should persist and focus, you can also persist but pivot, if needs be.

'Know what you want to achieve. Be focused in achieving it and work hard, but ultimately be realistic and prepared to bend and adapt to what the market wants,' advises Myleene Klass. 'If you have a bona fide incredible idea, yet no one is interested, it won't get off the ground. Supply and demand is what you have to acknowledge and, while determination is admirable, know also when you're flogging a dead horse, then move on or tweak your ideas.'

THE IMPORTANCE OF FAILURE: USING HINDSIGHT TO CREATE FORESIGHT

66 99
FAILURE IS SIMPLY THE OPPORTUNITY TO BEGIN AGAIN, THIS TIME MORE INTELLIGENTLY.

Henry Ford

We all make mistakes, and yet no one really talks about them. For some, failure is deemed as feedback and mistakes are viewed merely as learning tools, providing insight to enable more informed choices as we progress. Others utterly fear failure. They beat themselves up over each mistake, from the botched job interview to the failed relationship; from the bad business decision to the bungled dinner-party dish.

For the former, who accept failure, downfalls have the upside of providing a lesson they simply wouldn't have had the opportunity to learn had they not made the mistake in the first place. Learning lessons the hard way can be a better (albeit more painful) way of learning. Because those lessons stick.

For the latter, regretful choices create a self-perpetuating loop of dismay, where failure is feared and avoided at any cost. This can lead to risk-aversion and guilt, which, according to psychologists and scientists alike, are not conducive to a successful life or career.

In essence, the more we try and the more we fail, the more we learn and are likely to succeed. Learning from your failures enables you to know and to grow, to equip yourself more readily for what lies ahead. The only real failure is failing to learn from mistakes and repeating them down the line. This recognition of failure as a valuable tool in your business armoury will ultimately help you to accomplish your goals faster. In that sense, mistakes are good and failure is useful.

66 99
IF YOU LEARN FROM DEFEAT, YOU HAVEN'T REALLY LOST.

Zig Ziglar

Somebody once told me that they had started a business which, initially, had not gone well. They had borrowed money from the bank, and when they went back to the bank for the next meeting, they were quite depressed, imagining that the bank would never loan to them again. So they were flabbergasted when the manager said they would lend them more money. His rationale was, 'You've failed once so we don't think you are going to fail again. We think you are going to have learnt from the experience, and that this time you will succeed.'

Most of what I have learnt about business has been as a result of tackling problems and challenges, especially learning from the mistakes we all make. It's a fantastic education. Indeed, if you look through history, it is often those people who have been marginalised, belittled or have experienced adversity, repeated rejection or frequent failure who will look outside the box and persist. In doing so they will often become more successful than the majority of people (e.g. J. K. Rowling, Einstein, Freud and various Nobel Prize winners).

The same can be said for businesses which fail occasionally. Apple's Newton PDA product failed, and yet the lessons learnt from that failure created the operating system for the first iPods, iPhone and iPad. They failed, they learnt, they innovated, they succeeded.

'I'll go home and cry on the kitchen table,' says Myleene of making mistakes. '*Why has this gone wrong?* I'll ask myself. And then, I'll pull myself back together and figure out how I can learn from this and what I can do differently. The failures have led to the successes; the failures have been the making of me.'

However, we are generally programmed to ignore the lessons mistakes teach us. The status quo is to ignore failures that don't fit with our existing view of the world or our experiences. Subsequently, unless we actively choose to, we rarely learn from our mistakes. The dorsolateral prefrontal cortex, or DLPFC, behind the forehead suppresses 'unwanted representations', getting rid of thoughts that don't gel with our preconceptions. As such, we need to use other parts of our brain to reinterpret failures in order to uncover the right way to do something.

It's important to write down and reflect on what went wrong. As well as being cathartic, this will allow you to review it more analytically and gain valuable feedback. Every outcome therefore has value – even the outcome you didn't want.

𝕮𝕮𝕵𝕵
WOMEN ARE CURIOUS AND ARE SURVIVORS IN ALL SORTS OF WAYS. WE'LL TRY A NEW THING IF SOMETHING DOESN'T GO RIGHT ONE WAY.

Judy Lever, co-founder of Blooming Marvellous

According to statistics, 20 per cent of businesses fail in their first year, 50 per cent within the first three years. That can be alarming for people starting up. And yet what is not reported is how many of those business owners then go on to achieve success in a second business. Most successful entrepreneurs have bounced back from failures – read any of their life stories and you'll find it's a common theme.

LESSONS LEARNT FROM MISTAKES

Always try to consider how a recent failure or mistake opens up the doors for a different opportunity, or a way to reshape or improve something you've been working on, just as these leading ladies have done.

- **Jennifer Irvine of The Pure Package learnt to get everything in writing.** She explains: 'Some of the best things that have happened have been from someone saying I'll do this for you, but you don't have anything to back it up with. One mistake I made was to pay a lot of money for a website that someone had built for me … I wanted to change servers, and, all of a sudden, they sent me this new bill for something that they'd previously said would be included in the initial price. They changed the rules, and I ended up paying a £2,000 ransom to get away.' She adds, 'So there's a downside to handshake agreements and false promises, and subsequently I'm much more into getting things in writing nowadays. I don't need a contract with everybody, but I will send a follow-up two-sentence email so the key agreement is in writing. So it will say "Lovely to have met you today, I'm glad that we have agreed for x, y and z to be done by such-and-such a date."'

- **Myleene Klass learnt to do her homework when designing products for different countries.** 'Here's my classic fail,' says Myleene. 'I was standing up pitching my amazing pyjamas for Baby K. "You're going to love these," I said. "They can go into any country … here are the fairy pyjamas, these ones are owls and these ones have got stars on them." Within one second I was wiped down to the ground. "We can't buy anything that's to do with the occult," said the UAE and China. I can't use purple in Greece, I can't use white in India, I can't use red in certain countries, I can't use fairies, I can't use wizards, I can't use stars that have the wrong amount of points, I can't use owls as they are seen as the harbinger of death,' explains Myleene. 'I learnt that the hard way, standing there holding the item that is so offensive to them. I also had a picture of a cute dog on a T-shirt and the UAE said absolutely not again as dogs are not allowed in the house.' However, Myleene learnt from that, and from a closed door she found the open window: 'I said I promise I'll fix it because I don't want to lose this, and so I made pyjamas with a bear in sunglasses, which became my bestseller.'

- **Thea Green of Nails Inc. learnt to prioritise service over expensive extras.** 'Initially I was so in love with the brand and the creative side, I overspent on things that were not essential to the business, and in fact were wasteful: from branded coffee cups and plates, to a more expensive coffee machine than anyone would ever need. I learnt how unimportant the frills were and how much more important it was that the girls in the nail bars were going to do a good job – be polite, eloquent, talk to their customers – and that the product for the new launch was on display on Monday, not arriving on Friday and being left unpacked.'

- **Jacqueline Gold learnt to recognise when something isn't working and have the courage to stop it.** Having invested £1 million in a magazine called *Bite*, Jacqueline realised it wasn't working after a year and pulled the plug. Jacqueline explains, 'It lost a lot of money but as soon as I thought, "This definitely isn't working," I ended the project. Many people are emotive in their decision-making, and recognising and admitting that something is failing can be the hardest thing to do. We were passionate about the idea but had no expertise in publishing. The creative people got a bit carried away and the magazine was a little before its time. It ended up being put on the top shelf due to perception, but it shouldn't have been placed there. It was a woman's magazine. *Cosmopolitan* was changing its strapline in response to what we were doing, but it wasn't worth throwing more money at something which wasn't working.'

- **Alex Polizzi learnt not to put all of your eggs into one basket** when Millers Bespoke Bakery lost a key customer. 'We had one customer who accounted for 25 per cent of our business, but then four years ago they chose to go elsewhere and there was nothing we could do about it. It was a terrible moment, as we lost 25 per cent of our revenue in one fell swoop. It took us two years to build it back up to the same volume. Yet it taught us that we should never be so heavily weighted on just one customer.'

- **Liz Jackson of Great Guns Marketing learnt not to underestimate the time it takes to go off on tangents.** 'Franchising was my biggest mistake,' admits Liz. 'I decided to invest a lot of money and go down the franchising route yet I really underestimated the skillset that I had as the owner. It was very difficult to recruit people and train them while going out to clients and delivering a good service. Entrepreneurs generally get the deal then deliver the deal, but balancing both things plus all the other stuff is very hard.' Consequently, Liz decided instead to have hubs instead of franchises so that companies from all over the country could see the telemarketing people face-to-face. 'They can therefore drop in whenever they need to. So we became the marketing and sales departments for various "partners",' says Liz.

- **Liz Earle has learnt which business relationships are worth nurturing and focusing on** from how people have dealt with problems. 'Often when things go wrong it's an opportunity to test the strength of a relationship – perhaps with an employee or with a supplier,' says Liz. 'It's easy to have good relationships when things are going well, but I always judge its strength and depth by how someone responds to a problem – especially in the case of a supplier. I've learnt that the best business relationships are those nurtured over time, with people who truly care about doing a great job for the long term – and not just those who offer a quick fix, lowest price or fastest short-term delivery. In my experience, those who undercut or over-promise tend not to be there for your business in the longer run.'

- **Sam Roddick learnt that opportunities should be seized and people should be let in if they can help you achieve your goals.** 'With the benefit of hindsight, I think I would have taken more of the opportunities that were offered to me at the very beginning, when Coco de Mer was a huge marketing success and people wanted to buy into the company and grow it,' says Sam. 'I didn't seize them, because I didn't want to lose control, but my journey would have been easier and less stressful if I'd harnessed those opportunities and let people in.'

- **Katy Hymas learnt to consider all methods of connecting with people instead of choosing the most expensive route.** 'The only decision I would change with hindsight would be exhibiting Mumlin at a trade show,' says Katy. 'It was expensive and time-consuming and did not yield any notable responses or leads. I learnt that if you want to meet with five key industry buyers then it is more economical to target them individually than spend a large sum of money hoping they will come to your stand. The exhibitors had inflated expectations of who would attend and how rewarding the footfall would be.'

- **James Caan learnt to stick to what he knows best.** 'I invested in a sandwich shop called Benjys,' explains James. 'It was quite a large chain with 120 stores and it employed 600 people, had a substantial turnover and I invested quite a lot of money in that business to take a controlling stake, but I lost all my money. The biggest mistake I learnt from that is I went into a market I knew absolutely nothing about. I wasn't an expert in the food sector, I wasn't an expert on retailing. I had gone into a market because everybody else was in the market. Sometimes you do things because other people are successful; it doesn't mean you would be successful.' James adds, 'I didn't bring anything to the table – no expertise, no knowledge, no relationship and no contacts. That is why I do well because I am in a business I know and I understand.'

- **Made.com co-founder Chloe Macintosh learnt about the importance of transparency from the outset.** 'Initially we were afraid to be transparent about the fact that we were a small business and how we operated, as we thought it was a bit too "out there". This meant that people didn't fully understand the reasons behind the longer wait time, so it took a bit longer to pinpoint the correct way to communicate,' says Chloe. 'We also learnt about the importance of strong packaging and turning complaints into something positive,' she adds. 'Two customers complained about the packaging not being strong enough; a very senior *Evening Standard* journalist was one of those customers. So I ended up doing the delivery myself and going the extra mile. I remember driving the desk to hers thinking, "Gosh, the learnings!" I learnt then that the most important part, that 10 per cent – when the item is delivered, that's the part the customer sees, so it has to be prioritised, and we learnt from that.'

- **Caroline Castigliano learnt the importance of seizing.** She made the mistake of not selling her early fitness-product company, Survival Kit, when she had the chance. 'It was one of the most stupid things I have ever done. A sports shoe company had tried to buy the company and I should have sold it immediately. It was a brilliant name, and it cost me a fortune in legal costs to protect the name. But at the time of the offer it was my life, and my ego got in the way of a business decision. Two years later, all I wanted was to be back home with my mum and friends in the UK as my dad passed away. The opportunity to sell the company had gone – recession was setting in and I just had to start again.'

- **Caroline also learnt to have systems in place where everything is signed for.** This lesson was learnt after a customer sent a photograph of her dress, after the wedding, with an enormous brown iron mark on the back of it. 'She claimed that the dress had been given to her like this, but she had been so busy in the run-up to her wedding that she didn't call and tell us, and had no option but to wear the dress to her wedding! When asked to provide pictures of the dress with the stain on view at the wedding she was unable to do so … The customer then tried to get a refund.' says Caroline. 'Now everything a client has asked for, has to be signed for. And before they leave they have to inspect and take ownership of the dress.'

- **Caroline also notes that, with bridal fashion, you can sell your mistakes on if the price is good.** 'If a range doesn't work, I can sell it to stockists at a third of the price and move the dresses on. As bridal does not go in and out of fashion quickly, you can always sell a dress if it is priced right. This gives you your "dead money" back,' she says.

CRJJ

BUSINESS AND LIFE ARE ONE LONG LEARNING CURVE AND WE LEARN SO MUCH FROM OUR MISTAKES.

Jacqueline Gold, Ann Summers

MY OWN LESSONS LEARNT

When I worked with Marks & Spencer as a consultant I had the opportunity to learn what worked but also what failed: the sales figures made that quite clear. Some of the food we tried in the range failed because it was too exotic. One product I created was a chicken fajita which you put together yourself. The food tasted amazing but it never sold as well as spaghetti bolognaise. That was frontline experience which taught me never to assume that taste will win out.

I also wrongly assumed that the retort process (heating products to lengthen the shelf life) was what made baby food taste awful; that assumption led me to delay bringing out my own baby food. When I did come to producing my own, I decided to produce a chilled range. But I had forgotten the key piece of advice my food consultants had given me: wastage. We were selling well, but the wastage was enormously high because of the short shelf life. I would have to pay several thousand pounds a week to support the wastage levels. I learnt then that expert advice can be worth listening to, especially on areas where you have no knowledge.

I pulled the range, but had lots of letters from people saying they really liked the food. That's when I decided to put it through retort. That was a roller-coaster ride, the packaging didn't have a nozzle at first, so parents couldn't reseal the food. Then the manufacturers who made the nozzle we switched to went into administration. Fortunately, somebody bought the company and all was well, but there have been many hurdles along the way, which have taught me to always have a plan B and to pay attention to the detail.

I learnt another salutary lesson in 2009 when the BBC's *Panorama* ran a programme claiming that the level of salt in my children's food was too high. I agreed to appear on the programme because I felt so passionate about what I was doing and wanted to explain that the level of salt in this particular food sample came from one tiny piece of cheese and that the age basis they were judging it on was also skewed. I thought the interview went well, but it was edited in a way that did not look good. That experience taught me that in a similar situation you should simply send in a statement, because in an interview your words can always be manipulated. I thought it was the end of my business at the time. Although sales did not go down, I was in tears. Three years later another piece of research on children's food in restaurants came out proving that my food had the lowest salt level. It comes full circle.

These kind of failures, obstacles and setbacks are part and parcel of being in business. Don't deny them, hide from them or be frightened by them. They should make you stronger, more savvy, more determined.

❝❞

IT IS IMPOSSIBLE TO LIVE WITHOUT FAILING AT SOMETHING, UNLESS YOU LIVE SO CAUTIOUSLY THAT YOU MIGHT AS WELL NOT HAVE LIVED AT ALL – IN WHICH CASE YOU FAIL BY DEFAULT.

J. K. Rowling

ANNABEL'S KITCHEN CABINET

PERSISTENCE PAYS OFF: GAIL REBUCK

Gail Rebuck was the woman who saw something in me and my book. She was working at Random House when they bought the rights to it. These days she is the chair of Penguin Random House UK and was recently made a life peer.

Gail has always had a persistent attitude to achieving her goals. She was keen not to go into the family business like her brother had aged 16, and her parents found her academic nature puzzling. 'They couldn't see the point of me going to university,' says Gail. 'I was always a great reader and used to go to the library every Saturday. I would read assiduously all week. I wanted to go along a different pathway so I went to the University of Sussex and read Intellectual History in the School of European Studies, which was the history of ideas.'

Following university Gail made her first forays into entrepreneurship. 'I travelled up north to buy antiques and would sell them down south. We opened a stall in Antiquarius in the King's Road called Déjà Vu, but I was sitting there one day and thought, "Is this it? There must be more of a purpose to life," so I left.'

However, job-seeking Gail was told she was underqualified so she did a six-week secretarial course. 'I went back to interviews, but I was then told I was overqualified as they thought I would be bored as a secretary because I had a degree.

'Some time later a production director for a children's book packager took me on as an assistant, which I was so pleased about, although I was completely hopeless, as I hated typing.' However, that experience sowed the seed for Gail's dream career and, once she'd made that decision, she would determinedly persist to achieve that aim.

'I decided I wanted to be an editor, so I camped outside a particular employment agent's door and eventually she took pity on me and sent me to an organisation called The Barry Group,' recalls Gail. 'They needed somebody to run Robert Nicholson Publications, which were London guidebooks – so I was not only the editor but running a list of books. I thought it was very grand and stayed there for three years. The managing director of that group was headhunted by the Hamlyn Group and he asked if I would go along too and set up a non-fiction paperback imprint. I was there for about four years.'

It was here that Gail took her second step into running her own business. 'I was approached by another publisher who had decided to launch a new publishing house. Five of us, all passionate about books, joined forces to set up Century Books in 1982. We all had to put money in, so I had to re-mortgage my flat,' explains Gail.

'We sold Century Hutchinson (as it became) to Random House in 1989, and as I was on the board in those days, I was quite involved in the process,' says Gail. 'I gave birth the day the sale went through. Women took very little maternity leave in those days and I was back at my desk within six weeks.'

In 1991 Gail became CEO of Random House. She was the first female CEO of a large publishing house, surpassing her original ambition to become an editor, primarily down to her persistence.

'The main personal quality needed to run a business, irrespective of what you are doing, is resilience, as starting off is really tough. What I would look for is passion and persistence; otherwise there is no fuel to propel you.'

"ENJOY FRUITS YOUR L

THE
OF
ABOUR

THE END GAME: WHEN AND WHY TO SELL YOUR BUSINESS

When you set up a business there must be a goal. An important part of the journey of building a business is what will happen at the end, how you will sell or pass on the business. You should always start with the end in mind; your vision is your destination – it's where you intend to end up in 5, 10 or 25 years or more.

Of course, you don't have to build a business to sell it on or to pass it down the family. It may be a means to work for yourself until you retire. However, if you do have an exit in mind, you will need a strategy in place because it can take a good few years from thinking of selling up to actually passing the business over.

Selling your business is all about timing. Just as the best time to raise investment is when you don't need to (i.e. when you are doing well), so too is the best time to sell your business – when you have maximum potential and are looking your best, not when you have to sell due to declining performance in downturned markets. If you are approached about selling due to strong performance in a buoyant market, you don't want to miss the boat.

Says James Caan, 'For me, the time to sell a business is when you can get a price that you wouldn't pay. Every business I have sold I have generally sold at a price that I thought was more than I would pay, which, by default, means it must be worth selling.'

Your business must be ready, buyers must be buying and the marketplace must be hungry. You'll struggle to sell your business if the marketplace isn't ready to buy.

For instance, you may find that selling your business to a larger company in the same space could be the best way to enable the business to expand internationally, while also giving you an exit so you can enjoy the fruits of your labour. Liz Earle knew when the time was right to sell Liz Earle Beauty Co. to beauty giant Avon. 'The management team, my co-founder, CEO and all other stakeholders felt that it was time to grow the Liz Earle Beauty brand and fly the Great British beauty flag around the world, and that this could be best achieved by handing over the reins to a much larger organisation with broader shoulders and international business experience.

'The company still operates as a fully standalone brand, firmly located on the shores of the beautiful Isle of Wight, and our original founding principles of exceptional quality and customer service continue the same as always,' explains Liz. 'Now, as a consultant, I'm proud to still play a part in the brand that carries my name.'

The essential element is timing. There are many businesses which have been sold for a lot of money, and the following year they have been worthless because of new market entrants or similar. The owners could have waited another 12 months hoping for a better deal and would have been disappointed.

The time to sell a business is not necessarily when you have 'made it'. It is a question of the book value of the business – not what you are making now, but what you might be making in three years' time. In some circumstances it is a good idea to bring in a strategic investor by selling part of your business and guaranteeing they will have the opportunity to buy the balance of your business, which encourages both of you to work together in partnership to build the company and groom it for sale.

You need to be exit-ready, whether you have a suitor in mind who may acquire you (a business) or a successor in mind (a family member); you need to ensure that the business will be able to function independently of you. Owner-dependent businesses are unlikely to attract a significant capital value on a sale. Furthermore, the business will need to stand up to detailed due diligence by a potential acquirer, demonstrate growth prospects and potential, have realistic financial projections and a clear plan of action for what will happen to the assets, staff and yourself once the business is sold.

Ultimately, though, exit is the last chance to be rewarded for all of your efforts, to bring your vision to fruition, to enjoy those fruits of your labour. As such it will be one of the most important financial transactions you will make. This chapter will therefore help you to consider all that you need to in order to maximise value and sell your business at the right time to the right people at the right price.

ASSESS YOUR WINDOW OF OPPORTUNITY

To work out if the timing is right to sell your business, you need to assess the following:

- **Study the market dynamics.** Are there plenty of acquisitions and mergers taking place within your industry? Is it a buyer's or seller's market?

- **Consider the scope for growth and potential within the market.** Is the market growing, declining or static? If the market is growing and you are approaching the peak of the cycle (but importantly with plenty more room for significant growth), that's the best time to sell your business.

- **Assess your input.** Are you still adding value to the business or is it time to let go and pass on the reins? How dependent is the business on your input and what steps can you take to reduce that level of dependency?

PREPARE YOUR EXIT STRATEGY

Adequate preparation for exit is critical. You need to be profitable and valuable but you also need to tidy up loose ends and optimise value. According to research by Coutts, business owners rarely allow long enough and it can take at least a year to sell a business, from marketing the business for sale to the final deal being signed, and up to three years from the decision to sell to a sale actually happening. The more planning involved, the less likely that a deal will collapse. Here are the steps you should take:

- **Gather paperwork.** Due diligence will be done by potential buyers, so if you can pull all paperwork together – from leases and staff/customer contracts to case studies, testimonials and financial data – and put it into a virtual data store, such as Dropbox or Google Drive, you'll be ready to share the necessary data quickly whenever it is required.

- **Figure out what you want from the sale.** Financial freedom? Long-term security for the company's existing staff and continuity of the business? A rapid exit? To pay as little tax as possible? This will help when you have advisers on board to help you achieve those aims. James Caan says, 'When I sold my first business, Alexander Mann, I spent months deliberating because there were so many other variables, whether you should or shouldn't. Today, if somebody came along and offered to buy Hamilton Bradshaw, I would never sell it, irrespective of the price, because I love what I do.' He adds, 'For me, now, money is not the issue, but 10 years ago selling my business for a good price afforded me with the opportunity, when I sold, to have financial freedom. That meant I had the choice whether I would ever have to work or not. I went to Harvard Business School, I travelled, I set up a foundation. Selling my business enabled me to do those things.'

- **Gather knowledge about potential suitors and their strategic objectives so that you can groom the business to suit them.** How could acquiring your business help them to achieve their strategic goals? Could they enter new markets or territories? Are they competitors who could do well to access your database of customers? Unlock the value. Equally, unlock the value that they will bring with them to the business and why they are a good fit.

- **Create a plan to groom the business for sale and optimise value.** Ensure that you have a strong management team in place, good staff-retention levels, a strong brand with positive PR, plus efficient systems and operations, clear manuals and plans and robust processes. Make sure you can demonstrate scalability and growing profitability too (see pages 214–15 and 218–19). There's a lot of value in a scalable business, and scalability is all about streamlining to reduce the cost of sales as the business grows, while continuing to generate repeat revenue from customers. How can you sell existing products to existing and new customers, and new products to existing customers and new customers?

- **Create another plan to define how the business will run effectively, continue to trade well and hit targets during the exit process.** If you take your eyes off the ball in order to court suitors and sell the business, you could end up missing key performance indicators and sales targets, which would concern buyers. If you miss targets during the exit process, acquirers will lose confidence. So there should be continuity in trading performance. Plan accordingly to ensure that targets can be met during this period. Additionally you will need to balance investment and expenditure well during this time to ensure that the business looks as healthy as possible.

- **Decide how you will market your business for sale.** It's generally agreed that public announcements of a business being 'for sale' creates uncertainty. It's much better if potential acquirers can be discreetly contacted on your behalf by a corporate financial adviser. If anyone has invested in your company already, speak first to them as they may wish to buy the entire business, or they may have an idea of potential suitors.

SELLING TO THE RIGHT BUYER AT THE RIGHT PRICE

Selling a business is not like selling a house. It takes much longer. You need to build relationships with potential buyers. One way to do this is by courting them as investors first and then seeing if they'd actually like to buy the whole company rather than invest.

It is generally better to sell to a strategic buyer (someone who will value you highly because buying your business will help them to achieve their own strategic goals and boost their own business) rather than a financial buyer, who is merely buying the business to generate a return on investment.

Before you start talking to potential acquirers you should have a good idea of what you'd like to get for the business and have a baseline price in mind. Discuss with a corporate adviser the potential for achieving that amount. You'll need to be rational rather than emotional when it comes to selling the business, yet, equally, if your baseline is achievable but isn't met, be prepared to walk away or negotiate.

FIVE TOP TIPS ON GETTING THE RIGHT PRICE

01. **Invite offers rather than informing buyers what price you are seeking.** Potential buyers will see a suggested price as a ceiling price (i.e. the highest) rather than your minimum and won't offer you anything more. They should reveal their hand first by putting a stake in the ground.

02. **Be completely transparent and honest from the outset when defining risks and weaknesses.** They will come out in the end via due diligence anyway, and it is far better to reveal risks, threats and weaknesses first and define how you would deal with them rather than hiding them. Revealing the state of your rundown warehouse or poor management team too late during discussions could result in a price reduction. Saying 'and by the way, we've secured such and such an order' once you've entered into discussions is far better than announcing 'and by the way, we've lost such and such an order.' The latter could cause a deal to fall apart, while the former would raise perceptions from the buyer's perspective. Furthermore, weaknesses can flag up how the buyer has a greater opportunity to add value and improve the business, which can make it an even more attractive proposition; this is often a key criteria for strategic buyers. They may have expertise in bringing in top management executives or already own ideal warehouses. Also remember, acquirers tend to begin negotiations with their lowest price, while you will begin with your ceiling price so you want to do all you can to ensure that negotiations head upwards rather than downwards.

03. **Include future value in your valuation.** What your company is worth today is what you'll be offered. However, if you can prove genuine potential, the price can be based on tomorrow's value too. See page 101 for more on this.

04. **Focus on the win-win for all parties.** While you should push for the best price, greed could lose you the deal. There has to be something in it for everyone so both buyer and seller feel they are getting a fair deal.

05. **Know beforehand what should happen after the sale.** Most acquirers will expect the owner to stay on during a significant

handover period. You need to be clear about what your future role will be and what they expect it to be and, if you both agree a successor should take the lead, if that successor will be chosen internally. Do you have someone in mind and are they ready? Or will the buyer need to fill that role? Clarity before the sale regarding where everybody will end up after the sale is important.

EXIT THE DRAGON: JAMES CAAN'S TOP THREE TIPS ON SELLING YOUR BUSINESS

01. Bring in the experts. 'Engage with a corporate finance boutique such as Bluebox (who I recently invested in). Most businesses, when they decide they want to raise money or exit, are not ready,' says James. 'I think it's absolutely crucial that two years before you plan to sell, you should engage with a corporate finance business, so they can advise you and help groom your business. They will know the buyer community a lot better than you, because that is what they do for a living.'

02. Spruce the business up. 'If you are going to sell your house, would you sell it in a tired condition, where the paint was flaking off the walls? Or would you tart it up a bit to present it? If you are going to sell a business where the website is a bit out of date, the premises are a bit tired, the brochures are not that good, your financial information is a bit poor, you will get the lowest rate,' advises James.

03. Create a 90-day plan that outlines what should happen after the sale. 'When somebody buys a business they will have some very clear ideas about what they are going to do,' says James. 'Will they change the pricing or the location? There is a whole raft of things a buyer may be planning for when they acquire the business, so I think it is really critical to ensure that the first 90 days are very transparent, that you and the buyer mutually agree the various elements to avoid surprises.'

ANNABEL'S KITCHEN CABINET

AN ATTRACTIVE ACQUISITION: SAM RODDICK

When you start a business, your main aim is to generate enough money to live on and to encourage as many people as possible to become your customers. Having lots of customers could make you very successful and wealthy if your profit margins are good, or your business could be less profitable but someone buys your company for lots of money, making you very successful and wealthy. Therefore, whether your profit margins are high or low, attracting a strong and loyal customer base is the key.

Take Sam Roddick, for example. Sam had spotted a gap in the market for ethical erotica. Although there were other erotic shops, the existing alternatives were not providing products which were ethical, artisan, handmade or which had an ethos behind them. So Sam pioneered a brand new way of doing things. Her company, Coco de Mer, stood out as different, and that's why it appealed to its niche audience. And, while the margins were low due to the expensive hand-crafted stock, the strong ethos and purpose of the business resulted in a large following with two stores in London, one in New York and another in LA, which her sister ran. This popularity meant that, despite tight profit margins, Sam was able to sell the business 10 years after she founded it to online sex-toy retailer Lovehoney.

'I wanted to sell the business when my mum [Dame Anita Roddick] died,' recalls Sam. 'I wanted to go more into being a creative, but everyone said to me, "Don't make a decision when you're grieving." So I kept it and I was so emotionally attached to Coco de Mer, it was extraordinarily difficult to let go. I found it a painful process, but I got somebody in to help sell the company. They found and approached Lovehoney, who were buying portfolio companies like mine,' explains Sam.

Sam was aware of her company's value and growth potential for the buyer. 'The Coco de Mer brand was valuable so I was selling the potential of the business,' says Sam. 'Lovehoney wanted the kudos of owning the brand, plus the luxury element. There is a huge potential in that market which they have kept going and tapped into.

'Once they had incorporated all of the running costs into their larger company, that's when they started to look at what their sales would be, as they would be taking a huge amount of the overhead out,' explains Sam. 'Their added value came from their ability to buy a much larger amount of stock on certain items that would then increase their margins. They had that scalability in place, which made the acquisition attractive.'

Three years on from selling Coco de Mer and Sam admits that she does miss elements of running her own business. 'I miss my customers,' says Sam. 'I loved my customers as they gave me the best education, and opening up Coco de Mer showed me what a merchant I was. I was a lover of retail; I loved the interaction, I loved what I heard – and I heard global sex secrets on my shop floor about what they desire and how they feel. I also miss the laughs we had,' adds Sam.

However, Sam doesn't miss the business itself. That's because she was clear about why she was selling and what she was going to do afterwards. 'In my view, emotionally you have got to move on,' she advises. 'You have to change your identity and have something else to do that you are passionate about.' Sam is now putting all of her energies into new projects, including continuing to make beautiful things and communicate her ideas visually around sex and sexuality. With these goals as her mission, Sam is creating a range of photographic art pieces for an art exhibition.

Ultimately, if you build a business which is more than just a company selling products, if you build a movement on a mission with crystal-clear ethical values built in, you can sell that culture and that belief system and the kudos that is built up – because you have created a valuable brand that bigger companies will be knocking on your door to acquire. Not only that, you'll leave the world in a better state than when you first started your business – and that can only be a good thing.

CONCL

**WHY WOMEN ARE
AWESOME AT RUNNING
THEIR OWN BUSINESSES**

" "

**IT IS IMPORTANT
FOR WOMEN THAT
MOTHERHOOD
IS VALUED IN ITS
OWN RIGHT BUT
EQUALLY TRUE THAT
HAVING CHILDREN
SHOULDN'T
NECESSARILY BE THE
FULL STOP AT THE
END OF A CV.**

Annabel Karmel

USION

Often women don't realise quite how amazingly enterprising they are, which can prevent them from launching forth to set up their own business. It's not that we are fearful of taking risks, more that we often don't believe in ourselves enough to take that first step. And yet look at all the other amazing things we do – giving birth, bringing up children, juggling umpteen tasks, being great friends and so on. I hope that this book has demonstrated that *you* have all the right ingredients to start up your own business – that it's helped you realise your own strengths, to evaluate your own skillset and realise that you can do this. You have all the skills you need and, if you have the passion and drive to make it happen, have clarity around your 'why' and have soaked up the knowledge across these pages from all of these super-successful women, you are more than equipped to set up and run your own successful enterprise.

Still, here's a gentle reminder about why women are awesome at running their own businesses – and that includes YOU!

01. WOMEN ARE INFORMED RISK-TAKERS

❝❞

IN SETTING UP IN BUSINESS, YOU NEED TO TAKE A RISK AND INVEST YOUR BELIEF INTO YOURSELF.

Sam Roddick

In business you cannot be risk-averse. That said, you should always consider eventualities and have a plan B where possible. Recent research by American accountancy firm Rothstein Kass has said that women are great at taking more informed risks because of how they question and manage them. The report claims that being 'risk-thoughtful' in this way is leading to female-led companies outperforming their male-led counterparts. And consequently financiers have started to invest more in companies that are led by women.

Kelly Easterling, who carried out the research, told *The Times*, 'They go in and, rather than shooting for the hills and trying to get enormous returns, they have a more specific process of how they get their return. When they make the choice to exit and enter investment, they think it through more than their male counterpart. Women do take risks but they do a spectacular job of managing risk better than men. They have a different way of looking at risk and questioning things.'

Sarah Pennells, founder of SavvyWoman.co.uk, a money website aimed at women, agrees. 'It is too simplistic to say women are more cautious when it comes to investing than men,' she said. 'For women it is a higher prioritisation of risk and how to manage it.'

02. WOMEN ARE HIGHLY SKILLED MULTI-TASKERS WITH TRANSFERABLE SKILLS

It's well-known that mums are good at multi-tasking, but did you know that mums juggle twice as many tasks as company bosses before breakfast? A study by Warburtons revealed that the mad rush to get children washed, dressed and fed in time for school makes for a frantic 'breakfast rush hour' for mums, making their mornings busier than most senior business people's. As shown in Chapter 2, the skills women learn as mums equip them incredibly well for the world of business.

Most mums had quite different jobs before they had kids, and employers are really missing a trick. The WiBBLE.us SWOT campaign (which campaigns for better financial support for self-employed women and more flexibility for employed mums) points out: 'While some employers provide a range of options, from enabling department heads to return to work part-time with two out of three days working from home or providing remote working and job-share opportunities, others are not so keen to provide flexible working solutions for talented people who happen to be mums ... This is a key reason why so many highly talented mums are looking for alternatives and venturing into the world of self-employment.'

Starting your own business enables you to turn your talents into turnover for your own enterprise and still be there for your children. It's a great opportunity to have it all – but it takes dedication and a lot of hard work. But that's okay because ...

03. WOMEN ARE GRAFTERS

'Where employers go wrong is that they underestimate how hard mums will work,' says Myleene Klass. 'They don't realise that they will get it done so efficiently and still be home in time for bed and bath.' She adds, 'I learnt that hard work will get you everywhere. I have never professed to be the most talented, most inventive, most enlightened person out there but I have the work ethic of a carthorse. I will work 20-hour days without blinking because I know that is what is required to make my Klass empire work. It's as simple as that.'

'Working so hard at the beginning when we started proved that I had backbone,' says Alex Polizzi of the hours she put in weighing ingredients and baking with her husband for their bakery business. 'Yes, I was born with a silver spoon in my mouth; I am very privileged. But I have worked my butt off, and I work my butt off even more now, as I have to do my business *and* look after my children, *and* still be a half-decent wife.'

04. WOMEN ARE WONDERFUL COLLABORATORS – OPEN TO JOINING FORCES WITH OTHERS

'I think women tend to work more collaboratively,' says Liz Jackson of Great Guns Marketing. 'I think we are great team players. We tend to be more humble. I was speaking to a school the other week and I was saying the world really is our oyster; this glass ceiling doesn't really exist. I think if we are talented we just need to showcase our talent, not hide it under a bushel.'

05. WOMEN ARE STRONG AND RESILIENT

We go through childbirth, sometimes traumatic ones. We have an ability to bounce back. Giving birth taught me that I have an inner resource. I'm only tiny but I've got this strength and I am quite determined. I've yet to meet a woman who hasn't got an inner strength, whether they realise it or not. When you have setbacks in life, it makes you stronger.

06. WOMEN TALK A LOT!

It seems obvious, but we talk a lot – women are good at this. Women tend to be programmed to share and be more open than men. We talk about our feelings, our circumstances, our thoughts. We talk through our decisions and we ask for help more readily. We seek advice and happily give it too. This makes us more open to networking, whether face-to-face or online. This can be helpful when sharing your business story, gathering support and making important decisions.

So harness the power of being a woman, of being a mum – you are well positioned to be brilliant at running your own business. I wish you all the luck in the world.

Annabel

USEFUL RESOURCES

START-UP ADVICE

www.bgateway.com/starting-up
www.dummies.com/how-to/content/small-business-glossary0.html
www.enterprisenation.com
www.nationalenterprisenetwork.co.uk
www.startupbritain.org
www.startupdonut.co.uk
www.startups.co.uk

ONLINE NETWORKS FOR WOMEN IN BUSINESS

http://femaleentrepreneurassociation.com
http://inspiredmums.co.uk
http://leanin.org
www.motivatingmum.co.uk
www.mumpreneursnetworkingclub.co.uk
www.mumpreneuruk.com
www.mumsclub.co.uk
www.prowess.org.uk
www.talentedladiesclub.com
http://theathenanetwork.co.uk
www.thewomensorganisation.org.uk
www.wearethecity.com
www.wibble.us
http://wibn.co.uk
www.womenunlimitedworldwide.com
www.workingmums.co.uk

OUTSOURCING

www.99designs.co.uk
www.crowdspring.com
www.elance.com
www.fiverr.com
www.freelancer.co.uk
www.getafreelancer.com
www.graphicleftovers.com
www.graphicriver.net
www.odesk.com
www.peopleperhour.com
www.smallbusinesslogos.co.uk

MARKET RESEARCH

www.freepint.com
www.google.com/alerts
www.google.com/analytics
http://scholar.google.co.uk
www.surveymonkey.com
www.wufoo.com

DOMAIN NAME REGISTRARS

www.123-reg.co.uk
www.just-the-name.co.uk
http://uk.godaddy.com

PUBLICITY AND PR

www.beatvexpert.com
www.dwpub.com/featuresexec
www.findatvexpert.com
www.sourcewire.com

RAISING FINANCE

www.angelsden.com
www.crowdcube.com
www.crowdfunder.co.uk

www.fundingcircle.com
www.gov.uk/bis
www.j4bgrants.co.uk
www.kickstarter.com
https://kriticalmass.com
http://microventures.com
http://mumsmeanbusiness.com
www.princes-trust.org.uk
www.seedrs.com
www.seedups.com
www.seiswindow.org.uk
www.startuploans.co.uk
www.ukbusinessangelsassociation.org.uk
www.virginstartup.org

EXPORT

www.gov.uk/passport-to-export-service

MANUFACTURING

www.mymas.org

INTELLECTUAL PROPERTY

www.ipo.gov.uk
www.itma.org.uk
www.own-it.org

MENTORS AND SUPPORT

www.aspirewomen.co.uk
www.bl.uk/bipc
www.getmentoring.org
www.mentorsme.co.uk
www.rootsandwings.biz

WELL-BEING: LOOKING AFTER YOU

www.authentichappiness.sas.upenn.edu/testcenter
www.flourishchallenge.com

www.flourishhandbook.com
www.headfixers.co.uk
www.lizearlewellbeing.com

DEAL SITES

www.huddlebuy.co.uk
www.retailchampion.co.uk

SOCIAL MEDIA TOOLS

https://bufferapp.com
https://hootsuite.com
www.socialoomph.com
www.tweetadder.com
www.tweetdeck.com
www.woobox.com

WEBSITE CREATION TOOLS

http://webstore.amazon.com
https://cacoo.com
www.create.net
www.e-junkie.com
www.google.com/analytics
www.google.com/websiteoptimizer
www.istockphoto.com
www.joomla.org
www.moonfruit.com
http://pages.ebay.com/storefronts/building.html
www.wix.com
wordpress.com
wordpress.org

CUSTOMER COMMUNICATION

www.audioboom.com
www.aweber.com
www.mailchimp.com
https://soundcloud.com
www.surveymonkey.com

GETTING ORGANISED

www.dropbox.com

https://evernote.com

www.google.com/drive

WEBSITES OF WOMEN WHO FEATURE IN THIS BOOK

Alex Polizzi: www.millersbakery.co.uk

Baukjen de Swaan Arons: www.baukjen.com, www.isabellaoliver.com

Bev James: www.BevJames.com

Caroline Castigliano: www.carolinecastigliano.co.uk

Chloe Macintosh: www.made.com

Chrissie Rucker: www.thewhitecompany.com

Dessi Bell: www.zaggora.com

Fiona Clark: www.inspiredmums.co.uk, http://inspiredmums.co.uk/services/mumpreneur-coaching

Gail Rebuck: www.randomhouse.co.uk

Jacqueline Gold: www.annsummers.com, www.jacquelinegold.com

Jennifer Irvine: www.purepackage.com, www.balancebox.com

Justine Roberts and Carrie Longton: www.mumsnet.com

Katy Hymas: www.mumlin.com, www.cherrypiepr.co.uk

Lisa Barber: www.rootsandwings.biz

Liz Earle: http://uk.lizearle.com, www.lizearlewellbeing.com, http://livetwice.org

Liz Jackson: www.greatgunsmarketing.co.uk

Lucy Jewson: www.welovefrugi.com

Lynne Franks: www.lynnefranks.co.uk, www.seednetwork.co.uk, www.bloomretreats.com

Myleene Klass: www.myleeneklass.com, www.mothercare.com, www.littlewoods.com

Sam Roddick: www.coco-de-mer.com

Shelley Barrett: www.modelcocosmetics.com

Thea Green: www.nailsinc.com

Thomasina Miers: www.wahaca.co.uk, www.thomasinamiers.com

Wendy Shand: www.totstotravel.co.uk

ACKNOWLEDGEMENTS

I'd like to thank Susanna Abbott and the team at Vermilion, including Louise Francis, Sarah Bennie, Di Riley and Caroline Butler, for believing in my book and supporting my vision for wanting to empower and inspire other mums in business.

Thank you to my wonderful co-writer Cheryl Rickman who helped bring so much positive and practical information to life, and the amazing entrepreneurs who gave me their precious time, personal stories and business advice to make this a truly inspired read.

A big thanks also to Sarah Smith my wonderful head of PR and marketing for her enthusiasm in helping me every step of the way to create this book.

I am indebted to the team at ico Design for their creative design; my mother who has been an incredible inspiration in my life; and Stephen Margolis, Nicholas, Lara and Scarlett for smiling, encouraging and believing in me (and to my loyal dogs Hamilton, Bono and Sabre for keeping me company during those late-night writing sessions).

A special thanks to Gail Rebuck for believing in my first book.

From the heart, I am truly thankful to everyone in my personal and business life who has given me the time of day, lent me their ear and thrown me a lifeline so that I could prove myself in business – you've made me the person I am today.

INDEX

Mumpreneur Sponsor

INTRODUCING HOME BUSINESS INSURANCE FROM DIRECT LINE

Starting a business from home is a big decision so it's important to have the right insurance in place to protect your investment, your livelihood and your customers from day one.

Home business owners face the same liabilities as businesses run out of shops or offices so your home insurance alone may not be enough to cover you.

Specialist Home Business Insurance from Direct Line for Business provides peace of mind for potential liabilities you could have to customers. It covers you for loss of stock or equipment and also loss of earnings following an insured event that means you can't run your business from home.

To find out more visit **www.directlineforbusiness.co.uk**